Where Is Theology Going?

Where Is Theology Going?

Issues and Perspectives on the Future of Theology

Millard J. Erickson

Baker Books

A Division of Baker Book House Co
Grand Rapids, Michigan 49516

Published by Baker Books
a division of Baker Book House Company
P.O. Box 6287, Grand Rapids, MI 49516-6287

Printed in the United States of America

Library of Congress Cataloging-in-Publication Data

Erickson, Millard J.
    Where is theology going? / issues and perspectives on the future of theology / Millard J. Erickson.
      p. cm.
    Includes bibliographical references.
    ISBN 0-8010-3224-5
    1. Theology—20th century. 2. Theology—Forecasting. 3. Evangelicalism—Forecasting. I. Title
BT28.E73   1994
230′.09′049—dc20
                              94-13404

Contents

Preface

I have worked on book manuscripts that were more difficult to write, but I have never authored one that was more difficult to mail. Given the very nature of the subject, one can never complete the study, so the temptation has been to continue working on this manuscript indefinitely. Indeed, while reading the paper at breakfast on the very morning that I was to print out the final copy, I found a news item that contributed to the manuscript. I said to my wife, "This goes in!"

All prognostication is, it seems to me, a mixture of what one thinks will happen, what one hopes will happen, and what one fears will happen. There are predictions in this book which I sincerely hope prove false. There are others which I eagerly desire to see come to pass. Venturing into such an area is surely risky. It will be interesting to see to what extent the speculations herein do come to reality. In many cases the reader will find statements like "If A, then X; but if B, then Y." It will be up to the reader to decide whether A or B is the more likely occurrence. Further, as the final chapter suggests, to at least some measure we can influence whether A or B is what occurs. If this book encourages some Christians to think seriously about the future of theology and to contribute to that future, my effort will have been worthwhile.

The choice of topics has been somewhat arbitrary. There might well have been chapters on the doctrine of the church (a topic that could have given rise to a fascinating discussion) and the doctrine of the last things. To some extent, elements in my treatment of the other doctrines touch on these matters. My intention was to be suggestive or illustratory, not exhaustive.

The stimulus for this piece of work came when Associated Canadian Theological Seminaries asked me to teach a course on the future directions of theology. I am indebted to the administration and faculty of those schools for encouraging me to think and read on this subject. The material developed for that course was tried out in several settings. I want to express my appreciation to the students in my class at Associated Canadian Theological Seminaries, Surrey, British Columbia, in the summer of 1991; in a similar course at Bethel Theological Seminary in the fall quarter of 1991; and in a doctor of ministry course at Trinity Evangelical Divinity School in January 1993. Chapters 1, 3, 4, and 11 were delivered as the Day-Higginbotham Lectures at Southwestern Baptist Theological Seminary, Fort Worth, Texas, on February 7–9, 1990; and chapters 1 and 5–8 constituted the Paschal Memorial Lectures at Baptist Missionary Association Theological Seminary, Jacksonville, Texas, on October 9–11, 1990. The interaction with the persons present on those occasions also was helpful.

I especially wish to recognize and commend the forward-looking leadership of Russell Dilday, former president of Southwestern Baptist Theological Seminary. It was on his campus that I first made my suggestion regarding research professorships. At a luncheon the following day he remarked, "We have such a position here." Neither he nor I anticipated that almost exactly two years later he would call me regarding such an appointment to his faculty. It is this type of vision and commitment to the endeavor of theological research that is needed in the years to come.

While we do not know the exact circumstances of the future, we know that our Lord asks for our faithful service in whatever comes, and promises his presence and help to the very end of time.

1

How Can We Tell
Where Theology Is Going?

From as far back as we can inquire, humans have attempted to know and predict the future. Numerous explanations could doubtless be given. One is the sense of the insecurity or the contingency of life, and of being helpless to influence much that affects us. Another is simply the native curiosity found among many humans. For us who hold a biblical faith in the God who not only was and is but also will be, who told Moses that he was the God of Abraham, Isaac, and Jacob, and also that this is his name for all generations (Exod. 3:15), there is a sense of challenge and excitement in exploring what God is doing and will be doing in the future.

But why is the future of theology important to us? Is not theology obscure enough in itself without compounding the difficulty by also looking at the future, which is an inherently perplexing topic? Is this not to deal with difficulty to the second power?

The Areas Affected by Theology

To begin with, it should be noted that theology is valuable. I will not attempt to develop that theme at great length, because I have done that elsewhere and because I assume a certain amount of conviction on the part of most of those who are reading this book. I do want to make just a couple of brief observations on the subject, however.

First, our theological beliefs affect the nature of our relationship with the Lord. Jesus certainly indicated that when, after inquiring of his disciples what people said of him, he also asked who the disciples thought him to be; only after receiving the desired answer did he commit to them the authority to be his representatives on earth, carrying out the work of his kingdom (Matt. 16:13–19). Similarly, Paul responded to the man who asked what one must do to be saved, "Believe in the Lord Jesus, and you will be saved" (Acts 16:31). He wrote later that "if you confess with your mouth, 'Jesus is Lord,' and believe in your heart that God raised him from the dead, you will be saved" (Rom. 10:9). Not merely belief in some undefined conception of this Jesus, but some very definite doctrines about him, constituted the type of faith that was required. This is borne out in 1 John, where the writer insists upon correct understanding and belief regarding Christ, especially his full humanity, but his deity as well (4:2; 5:5). It is not only correct belief which determines the relationship, however, since Jesus said, "Why do you call me, 'Lord, Lord,' and do not do what I say?" (Luke 6:46). Obedience, then, is essential, but obedience to the Lord as he truly is, not the product of our theological imagination.

Second, not only our relationship to the Lord, but our ministry will be affected by the nature of our theological beliefs. Obviously, our ministry will be affected by our doctrine of the church, which actually specifies what ministry is, who does it, and how. It will also be affected, however, by specific items of belief. If we believe that God is basically a loving God, and that his love is of the sentimental type that would not want to bring any unpleasantness to anyone, then we will minister in one way. We will minister in a different way if we see him as a sort of celestial police officer seeking opportunities to issue citations to all who transgress his rules.[1] Under such ministries particular types of congregations tend to develop, especially if ministers remain with a congregation for a long period of time. If we believe that people who have been born again are eternally safe in their salvation regardless of what they do, our ministry will differ from what it would be if we believed that one may at any time lose salvation through an act of sin, disbelief, or indifference.

The Benefits of Studying the Future of Theology

Anticipating the Nature of Future Ministry

But what is the specific importance for us of attempting to determine where theology is going? There are several benefits. For example, being able to anticipate the future of theology will also allow us to anticipate the nature of ministry in the years ahead. Because theology affects the nature of ministry, in terms of both the needs of the people to whom we are to minister and what we bring to ministry, the future of theology will have an impact upon the future of the ministry. We will therefore be able to project to some degree what ministry will be like and to prepare for it.

Maximizing the Opportunities for Ministry

Anticipating the future directions of theology will enable us to utilize the opportunities for ministry to the maximum. Knowing what will be the case will enable us to prepare and thus to minister from the very start of a new situation. When a new situation arises, there ordinarily is a period of assessment. The time invested in that process will be reduced to the extent that we have anticipated the situation. With every new circumstance there are persons who are quick to react, and others who are slower. Many factors account for the distinction between these

1. For an interesting set of illustrations of these tendencies, see J. B. Phillips, *Your God Is Too Small* (New York: Macmillan, 1969), pp. 15–59.

two groups. One is the speed with which they estimate a situation and then develop a course of action for dealing with it. Anticipating what will come will enable us to be at the very forefront of the action, to be the trendsetters in ministry.

I taught for some years in a Christian liberal arts college. A key word then was "relevance," a term which one rarely hears these days. To say that something was "relevant" or "irrelevant" was virtually an emotive reaction, something like "hurrah" or "ugh." A corollary of relevance was contemporaneity. If something was not contemporary, it could not possibly be relevant, at least not to modern people. I remember one young woman student who on returning after vacation complained about her home church, "They're so irrelevant. They're ministering to the people who lived fifty years ago." So when one of my teaching colleagues announced a new course that he planned to teach, I asked him, "Will it be contemporary, Chuck?" "Contemporary?" he responded. "It will be better than that. It will be predictive!" Those who know what the future is going to bring will have a ministry characterized by freshness, for they will be there, prepared and waiting, when the rest of the world arrives in the future. In anticipating the future there will be varying degrees of success, of course. Some will be much slower to recognize the new situation or will not see the pertinence of a contemporary ministry. But the risks of being unprepared for the future are much greater than any risks we might encounter in trying to anticipate it.

Preparing for Unfavorable Developments

Anticipating the future turns of theology will enable us not only to capitalize upon the opportunities presented by the positive developments, but also to react to and defend against the threats presented by unfavorable developments. If, for example, any of us had anticipated the arrival of the so-called New Age movement, we could have designed our teaching and preaching to prevent the inroads of that American adaptation of Eastern religion into Christianity. "Forewarned is forearmed." A danger here is that in some cases we may actually contribute to the rise of heresy by an excessive response that gives support to an opposite extreme. For example, legalism is a serious problem that needs to be attacked when it is a threat. But some persons, because of their past experiences, may react against legalism at a time when the real problem is antinomianism, and thus unknowingly contribute to that threat.

Dealing with the Future More Rationally

Understanding the future direction of theology will enable us to deal with it more rationally. Surprises have a way of elevating our emotions.

We experience fear if we disapprove of changes which occur, and elation if we approve. Emotion is an important dimension of life, and specifically of the Christian life. But too much emotion, whether fear or elation, can make it difficult to plan and execute the ministry to which we are called. Imagine a busload of persons riding on a mountain road. They may be filled with ecstasy at the beauty of the scenery, or with anxiety because of the dangerous turns. Perhaps at times they cheer, when a particularly difficult turn has been successfully negotiated. These emotions are appropriate, and the good ones are certainly desirable. But there must be some limitation upon the driver's emotion. If he becomes too absorbed with the beautiful view, too enraptured, the quality of his driving may be affected, with possible unfortunate results for all on the bus. If he has traveled the road before, or has at least been told where to expect a particularly beautiful scene or an especially hazardous turn, he can be prepared, and thus the potential rise in emotion can be smoothed to an appropriate and manageable level, where it helps rather than hinders his work. Now we are not merely passengers on the bus; we are drivers, engaged in ministry; and anticipation of what is to come will enable us to minister the more effectively.

Preventing Overreaction

Anticipating problems that may arise as theology develops will help protect us against overreacting and falling into the opposite error. Many of the heresies in church history have been simply an undue emphasis on one particular aspect of the truth. Frequently the reaction has been an overemphasis on the neglected aspects, which in turn has led to the opposite error. One can see this quite clearly, for example, by studying the christological controversies of the first five centuries of the church, and especially the period from 431 to 451. A more measured response will often be possible if one is able to anticipate the problem. Indeed, that will frequently help us develop a response rather than an overreaction.

Shaping Developments in Theology

Being able to anticipate the developments in theology will often help us to shape or affect those developments. We are called upon, as part of our commission from the Lord of the church, to be not merely spectators, but participants in what the church does. This includes its theology. If our calling is church architecture, we are called upon not simply to emulate what other architects are designing, but to take the lead in church design, producing edifices that enable the church to carry out its mission effectively and efficiently, while maintaining beauty and witnessing visually to the gospel as we understand it. Similarly, we are called upon not simply to follow the trends of theology, attempting to react to and correct what others are doing, but to exert influence upon what theology is and will be.

There is an old saying that people can be classified in terms of how they relate to change. Some cause things to happen, some watch things happen, and some ask, "What happened?" We should be among those who cause things to happen, and particularly, in view of the topic of this book, within the realm of theology.

The Complexity of the Theological Environment

In seeking to evaluate what is occurring and will occur in theology, we need to recognize the complexity of the environment within which we are working. By that I do not mean simply that there are many factors bearing upon us as we function within our environment. Rather, I am referring to the fact that the church lives and functions within a series of environments, each part of a larger whole. It is as if these various environments were nested within one another, so to speak. A large computer hard drive may contain literally thousands of files. To scan the directory of all the files could prove so time-consuming that one is encouraged to organize the files in a hierarchical series of folders. Each group of files is enclosed within a folder with other files of a similar general nature, and that folder is in turn enclosed with others in yet a more inclusive folder, and so forth. The milieu within which we function is something like that.

We do our theological work within a particular denominational framework, and the various developments taking place within that context will affect our work. Beyond that, our denomination is part of a larger theological tradition, such as conservative or liberal, evangelical or sacramental, Calvinist or Arminian. Making this even more complicated is that on a specific issue parts of our denomination may identify with one tradition and other parts with another. Furthermore, we are part of a larger religious environment, that of Christianity, as contrasted with Hinduism or Islam, for example.

In addition to the denominational framework, we do our theological work within a particular geographical environment, such as North America, and within a subdivision of that environment, namely, the United States of America, and even a geographical section of that nation. The religious influences operating upon us within our own denomination are themselves within the sphere of influence of the intellectual, social, and political milieu of Western and, more precisely, English-speaking North American culture, which in turn is affected by developments throughout the entire world. What happens on that macro level is felt on the micro level.

Think of the movement of a cog on a gear within a piece of machinery. The movement of that cog is relative to the movement of the gear, which happens to be a planetary gear, rotating on its axis while revolving around the edge of another gear, so that the cog in question moves in an epicyclic fashion. The movement of this gear mechanism causes the device of which it is a part to move on a track, and the track oscillates on each of two axes which are perpendicular to one another and to the track. The structure within which this movement is taking place is a spaceship in orbit around the earth, which in turn is in orbit around the sun.

Now the point of this perhaps excessively involved illustration is to suggest the complexity of the movements and influences bearing upon the church and the theologian in doing theology. We are influenced by factors rather far removed from our immediate position, and the farther removed they are, the more likely we are to be unaware of them. Note, then, that if the point at which we are presently located is moving or changing, for us make no changes relative to that point does not mean that we are not undergoing any change. It may mean that a great deal of activity is necessary if our position relative to some remote reference point is to remain the same. One may drive one's automobile onto a ferry or, as I once did in Austria, onto a railroad car, shut off the engine, set the parking brake, and if it is permitted, remain in one's seat, not changing one's position within the car or the ferry. Nonetheless, one's position relative to the shore will change if the ferry is functioning properly. That, after all, is why one boarded the ferry in the first place. Although the considerations we are introducing here might be construed as creating a sense of complete relativism, that is not the point we are trying to make. What we are attempting to do is to make us sensitive to the large number of factors that must be taken into account if we are to predict the future of theology with any degree of accuracy.

Theological Prognostication

Parallels in Other Fields

Before turning directly to the subject of theological forecasting, we might note parallels in two areas of endeavor which regularly attempt to predict the future: weather and the stock market. Weather reports are frequently given on television by meteorologists, who are probably the only ones who fully understand what they are saying, with the exception of other meteorologists watching the program. They try to explain what might happen the next day in terms of high and low pressure areas, warm fronts, cold fronts, stationary fronts, polar air masses, and so on. In my part of the country we amateurs who watch the weather forecast are especially attuned to predictions of "Alberta clippers," which always bring cold temperatures, and which we then send on down to Texas. If one of these cold air masses should collide with a warm, moist air mass coming up from the Gulf of Mexico, then especially unstable weather may result. What is most interesting is to listen to the weather report after the previous day's forecast has gone seriously awry. The explanations of why the weather turned out to be different from what was anticipated remind one of the complexity of the factors governing weather. In theory, a meteorologist who had complete knowledge of all factors affecting the weather could predict perfectly the weather for tomorrow, and perhaps for all eternity.

The stock market is similarly difficult to predict. Recently I read a book which discusses some forty different criteria by which people attempt to predict the movement of stock prices. Some of these prove to be relatively good predictors of stock prices, and hence are labeled leading indicators; other of these criteria turn out to be trailing indicators. Since every sale requires both a buyer and a seller, it appears that at any given moment half of the people are wrong in their judgment. What really affects the movement of stock prices, of course, is human opinion about whether they will go up or down. When more people feel that the market is going down rather than up, or have stronger feelings to that effect than do those who think it is going up, there will be more prospective sellers than buyers, and the market will indeed go down. Yet the contrarian theory of investing says that when there is deep pessimism a major bottom is likely in sight, and when there is buoyant confidence in the market a top will soon be achieved. So in the final analysis, successful investing may be less a matter of economics than of psychology or perhaps, to be more accurate, sociology.

General Principles

We now come to the discussion of how we read the future. We will begin with four general principles for prognostication and then flesh out the methodology somewhat more concretely. Note that we cannot lay out a precise process akin to the scientific methodology found in some other fields. We might wish for a step-by-step instruction sheet. A candidate for a professorship in the area of preaching once seriously proposed that he wanted to write an elementary manual of sermon preparation which would begin, "Step One: Open your Bible." Unfortunately, no such manual exists for theological prognostication, and none is likely to exist in the foreseeable future. We are just beginning to feel our way, and the best we can hope for is to sketch out some tentative proposals. The endeavor of forecasting theology will remain a mixture of art and science for some time to come. But on to the general principles:

1. We need to formulate a theory of the pattern of theological movement. In a sense, philosophers of history conduct a similar investigation when they ask not what forces produce historical change, but what the pattern of development is. Do we hold that theology moves in a cyclical pattern, an evolutionary pattern, a dialectical fashion, a straight-line advancement toward a predetermined goal, or what? This is a historical or an empirical concern, attempting to assess past developments on the assumption that the future will follow a similar pattern. We are reminded, for example, of the Elliott Wave theory in stock market forecasting.

2. We need to develop a theory of theological change. What causes a theology to be held? What factors bear upon it? What influences cause changes in the theology of an individual, or of a group of persons? Are these influences purely theological (e.g., exegesis of Scripture), or do historical and sociological factors, for example, also have a bearing?

3. We need to identify the leading indicators of theological change. To some extent this will be a function of principle (2). If we hold that changes in A effect changes in B (where B is theological doctrines actually held), then one way to anticipate changes in B is to observe changes in A and attempt to surmise what parallel changes in B will occur.

4. We need to develop a theology of theological change. By that I mean that the theology we hold should be brought to bear upon this endeavor of theological prognostication. The doctrines which will bear most directly upon this endeavor are those which relate the activity of God to history, namely, the doctrine of providence, the doctrine of the Holy Spirit, and the doctrine of the last things.

1. The Pattern of Theological Development

It is my observation that theological development tends to follow a pendular or oscillating course. This holds true with respect to the development of the general structure of theology as well as specific doctrinal areas. In other words, a trend continues until it reaches a position sufficiently extreme that a reaction develops against it. I believe this observation can be supported by an examination of the history of Christian thought. For example, Luther's reaction against the Roman Catholic Church was in large part theological in nature, involving a rejection of what he perceived as a doctrine of salvation by works. Over against this he articulated his doctrine of justification by faith. Luther's belief came increasingly to be understood as correct doctrine, and theology then developed in such a way as to give birth to two children: Protestant scholasticism and, in part, rationalism. In the nineteenth century various reactions took place. Pietism reintroduced the emphasis upon the living experience of Jesus Christ as over against merely correct doctrinal belief about him. Friedrich Schleiermacher went even further with a virtually pantheistic emphasis upon human feeling. Søren Kierkegaard, rejecting the rationalism found in his day especially in Hegelianism, emphasized instead subjective appropriation of the truth. By the time Karl Barth became a pastor in the twentieth century, however, Schleiermacher's subjective emphasis had led to an understanding of God without the dimension of divine transcendence—he was largely dissolved into human individuals and societal movements. Barth introduced a conception of divine transcendence so extreme that God was virtually cut off from involvement in the cultural history of the world. Rudolf Bultmann, blending this conception with certain existentialist tendencies deriving from Kierkegaard, split history into objective *Historie* and subjective *Geschichte.* Then Wolfhart Pannenberg strongly reacted with his view that history *is* revelation. Brief and oversimplified though this sketch has been, a more detailed examination would sustain our thesis.

We can now propound this principle in more definite fashion: a trend in theology, once firmly established, will tend to continue to grow until a significant theological leader or group deems it extreme and begins a reaction in the opposite direction. The reaction will continue along its course until it in turn provokes an opposite reaction. Each trend will continue and become magnified until it at some point leads to a reversal. The difficulty is that we cannot predict exactly at what point the reversal will come. Theology is like the stock market in this respect. Everyone knows that every bull market will end at some point and a bear market will begin. The problem is that we do not know how high a bull market will climb or how low a bear market will fall. Similarly, as theological trends develop, we know that sooner or later a reaction is coming, but we do not know exactly when.

Not knowing when does not mean that the principle is of no help to us, however. Far from it. For when a trend has been in place for some time, or seems to be reaching an extreme, or when factors are in place which make people less receptive to the trend, we should be alert to the likelihood of a reversal. This is not unlike the stock market, for when the dividend rate for the Standard and Poor's 500 drops below 3 percent of the stock price, we are wise to be aware that historically the chances of a further rise in the average are considerably less than the chances of a decline.

One reason for the cyclical pattern in many areas of culture appears to be that the generation that has gone through a particular experience with its problems is supplanted by a generation that has not had that particular experience. Failing to learn from history, the younger generation is often attracted to what seems to be new, but which may actually be a revisitation of an earlier situation. For example, in the realm of economics there is a cyclical pattern of depressions approximately every sixty years. One of the explanations offered is that by the time sixty years have elapsed, most of the people who experienced the previous depression are gone. The public observes that the stock market has gone up for as long as anyone can remember, so caution is abandoned. The consequent excesses bring on the next crash.[2] I have observed similar ecclesiastical phenomena. When one denomination came up with a new system of financial support, an older pastor observed, "We have a lot of young pastors who have never experienced the problem to which the old system was the solution." The only surprise with the new system was how short a time (about six months) it took to discover the problem.

We can expect that periods of expansion and reaction will probably be shorter in the future than they have been. Over the years the life cycles of theologies have been growing shorter. We may need to begin preparing ourselves for an overstatement and a reaction very soon after the establishment of a new trend.

Another point to bear in mind is that we may at times find ourselves in a strange situation if we believe and act on the principle we have been examining. For as a particular aspect of a doctrine receives increasing emphasis, we will be among those criticizing this one-sidedness and emphasizing the opposite. But as the reaction takes place, we will be aware of the danger of overreaction, and will at some point insist on retention of the original emphasis. Our insistence upon moderation will appear to some people to be a case of defending the status quo, and they may accuse us of betraying the revolution which we may have helped found.

2. Factors Bearing on Theological Changes

a. Among the several influences on theology are broad intellectual and cultural factors. We might wish that our doctrines were formed solely by sound exegesis of our primary sources (which for evangelicals is the Bible), but history suggests otherwise. This means that what may seem an obscure or esoteric or arcane conception may ultimately have

---

2. James D. Davidson, *The Plague of the Black Debt: How to Survive the Coming Depression* (Baltimore: Strategic Investment, 1993), pp. 47–48.

a profound effect upon doctrine, even at the level of popular belief. For eventually such notions may trickle down to the level of popular culture. As Francis Schaeffer pointed out, Georg Hegel's idea of the dialectic may have seemed strangely impractical when first propounded, but it has had a profound effect politically through its adaptation within Marxism and has affected and continues to affect theology.[3] Process metaphysics, existentialism, and views of revolutionary political action have likewise had their impact upon theology, as have the civil rights movement and the feminist movement.

Liberal theologians have been quicker to incorporate general cultural conceptions into their theology than have conservatives. In part this is because change and novelty are more naturally part of liberalism than of conservatism. In part it is because the classical motifs endorsed by conservatives have more staying power than do new ideas. Sooner or later, however, conservatism does feel the effect of general cultural influences, although it may be much diminished and greatly modified. Roger Lundin has noted the tendency of evangelicalism first to condemn, then to tolerate, and finally to adopt, in a modified form, many of the newer beliefs and patterns in lifestyle. After a summer seminar on deconstruction, he expressed the apprehension that, sooner or later, deconstruction, radical though it is, would also have an impact upon evangelical theology.[4] Ironically, conservatives may find themselves adopting an idea when it is fading from general culture, and may thus find themselves strangely out of phase with society. Thus we find some conservatives loudly proclaiming their Christian liberty to engage in formerly taboo practices such as smoking and drinking at a time when both are considered to have negative effects upon health, and organizations such as Mothers Against Drunk Driving (MADD) have gained national attention.

b. Global developments will influence theology in some fashion. There was a time when theology was insulated from other kinds of developments. A prime factor here was geographic. Theology tended to be done by persons working in Europe and in North America, which sent missionaries to other parts of the world and thus set the standards for theology. The theologians themselves tended not to have contact with the religions and cultures of other parts of the world. That is not the case today, however. Our global community has much more intellectual cross-fertilization. This, of course, is not necessarily bad, for it helps preserve us from the provincialism which sometimes read Western culture back into the biblical revelation. Today, by contrast, developments

---

3. Francis Schaeffer, *The God Who Is There* (Chicago: Inter-Varsity, 1968), p. 20.
4. Roger Lundin, "Deconstructive Therapy," *Reformed Journal* 36.1 (Jan. 1986): 15–16.

elsewhere are a major factor to be reckoned with; and with the improved means of communication, their effects will be quicker. An alert Christian will ask, for example, how the recent and continuing radical political changes in Eastern Europe will affect theology.

c. Eventually, popular Christian life and practice will also affect doctrinal position. We may prefer the paradigm in which doctrine is applied to practice, and that is often the case. This is not a unidirectional influence, however. We are faced here with what in other settings is termed a "feedback loop": practice also impacts belief. We are not as rational as we sometimes think we are; experience frequently influences belief.

d. There are certain perennial problems that by their very nature do not (and perhaps cannot) receive final and definitive treatment. Predestination, for example, will come in for recurrent attention. We can expect that as new environments arise, new approaches to such problems will also be propounded. Frequently these new approaches will be restated versions of an earlier position, but with a different expression.

e. Finally, some problems may never have been adequately treated in the past. We can anticipate that they will sooner or later find their way onto the agenda of theological discussion. James Orr (1844–1913) believed that he could predict the dominant topics of theological discussion in the twentieth century.[5] As theology moves onward, the agenda moves down to smaller details. We can expect those details which have not been previously treated, and which by virtue of the climate of the times have come to prominence, to receive attention. For example, in my judgment Baptists have never adequately treated the topic of the salvation of infants. We can expect that it will be dealt with sometime in the near future.

3. Leading Indicators of Theological Change

a. Among the leading indicators of theological change are popular piety and practice. For example, for some time before the major shift in doctrinal belief among Roman Catholics following Vatican II, there were indications that many American Catholics were not following the church's official position on birth control. If in practice they were rejecting the absolute authority of the church, it was just a matter of time before they rejected it on the doctrinal level as well.

Protestants may find clues to the future in somewhat different places. One indication of what people believe, or what they will believe, is what they sing in worship. This is partly because a great deal

5. James Orr, *The Progress of Dogma* (London: Hodder and Stoughton, 1901; Grand Rapids: Eerdmans, 1952).

of our lay theology is inculcated through the hymnal rather than from the pulpit. Take, for example, our ideas about the body of the ascended Christ. I am not certain exactly what it is like. I do not know whether it has scars. I have some doubts, for that matter, whether any of us will in the resurrection have bodies with scars or amputations or the like, or whether such is even an appropriate consideration relative to what Paul termed "spiritual body" (1 Cor. 15:44). I do know, however, that it is difficult even to suggest such an idea to a person who for years has sung, "I shall know Him, I shall know Him, And redeemed by His side I shall stand; I shall know Him, I shall know Him by the print of the nails in His hand." The blessed truth that we shall one day be redeemed and glorified in the presence of our Lord has become experientially welded to a concept which may have been introduced primarily for the sake of rhyme or rhythm.

There is another aspect to this. People will choose to sing a certain song because it expresses what they feel and believe. Thus one can get an indication of the popular theology of today and of the future by noting the doctrinal affirmations and implications of what Christians are singing. Later we shall discover some of the contours of today's theology by examining some popular chorus books.

b. Similarly, we may obtain a reading of general culture by looking at its popular expressions. Thus its music, movies, books (although less significant than before because of the decline of reading), television programs, and even advertisements tell us what the secular world thinks. Preachers who want to know what society in general thinks and feels, and what, accordingly, the church to some extent will soon think and feel, should guardedly and critically expose themselves to these phenomena. While books like *The Greening of America, Future Shock, Megatrends,* and *The Closing of the American Mind* discuss general trends, the popular material illustrates them.

c. Examining the views of young people will also give us helpful clues to the future direction of theology. In theory, their views are shaped by what their pastors teach them, and if they go to seminary, by what their professors teach them, but this is not entirely the case. Those who do go to seminary will eventually become the pastors, and somewhat later the seminary professors; and their views will become the views of the church. On this subject James Davison Hunter's *Evangelicalism: The Coming Generation* is very helpful although quite disturbing.[6] In addition, a discussion with campus pastors and youth ministers

---

6. James Davison Hunter, *Evangelicalism: The Coming Generation* (Chicago: University of Chicago Press, 1987).

in local churches might be extremely helpful in determining where theology will go.

d. Diachronic studies of shifts or trends are especially helpful. For our present views may be less significant than the relationship of those views to our views at some earlier point. Political pollsters find such data especially helpful just before an election, when there is insufficient time to determine last-minute changes.

The general direction of present views will be helpful in anticipating where theology will be in the future, but their force and the rate of shift may be even more significant. A rapid shift may indicate that one of the reactions of which we spoke earlier is in the beginning stages and thus can be expected to continue and grow. A slower rate of change, on the other hand, may indicate that the trend is near its crest, and that a reaction can be expected to set in sometime fairly soon.

e. We have spoken primarily of lay or popular opinions. We do not wish, however, to overlook or even to minimize the role of those who teach theology professionally. It might be a very helpful endeavor indeed to survey the views of those who teach theology and related subjects in seminaries and Christian colleges. This might best be done in two parts: (1) a survey as to how the present views of those who have been teaching for more than five years compare with their views at some earlier point; (2) a survey of those who have retired from teaching in the past five years and of those who have just begun teaching. Analysis of the change in views revealed in the first part of the survey and comparison of the views of recent retirees with those of their replacements may indicate the changes in theology to which the next generation will be exposed.

4. The Theology of Theological Change

Our final principle is that the theology we hold should be brought to bear on theological prognostication. It may be helpful here for me to summarize my own convictions. I believe both in the total depravity of humans and in the reality and intensive activity of Satan. I understand from the Bible that there is a continued tendency to stray from God's truth, just as the people of Israel did repeatedly in the Old Testament. This will be especially the case just before the return of the Lord (Matt. 24:10–12). At the same time my understanding of the providence of God is that he persists in accomplishing his will in the world, and raises up new individuals and groups to carry it out. He will bring his church back to faith in him; and revival, including a return to biblical truth, will occur, sometimes in the most unlikely of fashions.

The Methodology of Theological Forecasting

Content Analysis

One of the ways of attempting forecasts is content analysis. This involves selecting certain periodicals and doing an analysis of their contents over a period of time. One simply measures the column inches of print devoted to each of several relevant subjects. John Naisbitt used this method in *Megatrends*.[7] He assumed that topics that have made the news over a given period of time will continue as trends in the future. Ironically, without explicitly calling attention to the fact, Naisbitt and Patricia Aburdene seem to have abandoned this method in their later publication *Megatrends 2000*.[8]

Content analysis may be utilized in religious or theological forecasting as well. This may be done either directly or indirectly. Direct use of the method involves examination and analysis of the content of religious periodicals. An example is David Hesselgrave's *Today's Choices for Tomorrow's Mission*.[9] To get at religious trends, he traced the content in three missions journals. This approach is especially useful in comparing periods that are a few years apart. The indirect approach involves analysis of how secular trends, such as those tracked by Naisbitt, will affect religious trends. An example here is C. Richard Wells's "Ministry Megatrends."[10]

Direct Opinion Survey

Another approach is direct opinion survey. Here people are asked for their convictions on a number of subjects. The results may simply be reported without any attempt to predict future directions. Examples are the work of the Barna organization and the Gallup polls. Comparison of a number of such surveys over a period of time may detect trends that can be assumed to continue.

Generational Analysis

A variation of direct opinion survey might be called generational analysis. Here an effort is made to discern differences of view between different age groups, with the assumption that as the population ages, the views currently held by the younger persons will tend to become

7. John Naisbitt, *Megatrends: Ten New Directions Transforming Our Lives* (New York: Warner, 1982).
8. Consider, for example, their contention that the federal budget deficit is not nearly as serious as the media have made it out to be—John Naisbitt and Patricia Aburdene, *Megatrends 2000: Ten New Directions for the 1990's* (New York: Avon, 1991), pp. 17–18.
9. David J. Hesselgrave, *Today's Choices for Tomorrow's Mission: An Evangelical Perspective on Trends and Issues in Missions* (Grand Rapids: Zondervan, 1988).
10. C. Richard Wells, "Ministry Megatrends," *Vocatio* 3.1 (1991): 4–5.

dominant. The factor which cannot be directly assessed is the degree to which the position of the younger generation, as they become older, will become more like that of the generation before them. In other words, is the position of the younger generation different simply because they are younger, or is the younger generation really different from preceding generations? To be of maximum usefulness, such surveys should also compare the views of each age group with the views of a comparable group from an earlier time and with the overall views of the general population.

An example is the work of James Davison Hunter, who surveyed students in evangelical colleges and seminaries. Although the categories utilized do not correspond in every case, his comparisons with earlier surveys give valuable indications of trends. The Barna reports, with their demographic breakdowns and intention to do similar testing at a later date, have similar potential. The survey work reported each January in *The Chronicle of Higher Education* is also of this type.

Expert Insight

Another approach focuses on expert insight. This method, used by Howard Snyder in *Foresight: 10 Major Trends That Will Dramatically Affect the Future of Christians and the Church*, involves surveying experts in the field under consideration and asking their opinions regarding the strength and staying power of certain trends.[11] After an initial survey, Snyder isolated the most frequent responses and used them as the basis for a second survey. The assumption in using this type of methodology is that experts in a field are in the best position to identify the major trends.

Leader Conviction Surveys

Still another method is leader conviction surveys. Here those who are perceived as leaders in an area are asked, not for their opinions of what will be the case, as in the preceding method, but for their own convictions on these matters. The assumption here is that the views of leaders will eventually be the views of those whom they lead. Surveys of teachers in theological institutions and of clergy are especially helpful if posed in terms of how their views have changed, or how the views of new faculty compare with the views of those whom they have replaced. An example of this method is the clergy survey included in the *Christianity Today*–Gallup poll of 1979.

---

11. Howard A. Snyder with Daniel V. Runyon, *Foresight: 10 Major Trends That Will Dramatically Affect the Future of Christians and the Church* (Nashville: Thomas Nelson, 1986).

Factor Analysis

This volume utilizes a number of the methods that we have been discussing. One other technique, not always seen in other studies, has also
been a major component. Factor analysis is an attempt to identify the
various trends and events which may influence the future direction of
theology, to calculate what their effect will be, and then to assess their
combined influence. This is similar to vector analysis in physics. An
example in the political realm would be analysis of the collapse of communism in Eastern Europe, including the dissolution of the Soviet
Union. Much of this analysis will have to be of indirect effects, in particular of how this political event will change the life of the church, and
how those changes will then be reflected in theology. One source of help
in factor analysis is to identify the effects of analogical situations in earlier times. The limitations of this technique include the difficulty of
determining (1) precisely what has resulted or will result from the situation, and (2) the degree of analogy between the earlier and the present
situations. While not relating directly to theology, much of *Megatrends
2000* seems to utilize factor analysis.

Use of Paradigm Cases

Finally, there is a type of analysis which, instead of using statistical
surveys, seeks to identify trends by isolating significant developments
so widely recognized that they need little documentation. While this
method of analysis may seem to work from specialized anecdotal material, actual paradigm cases are usually utilized. These cases represent
such a broad segment of the particular population being considered that
they yield information of great generalizability. An example of this type
of endeavor is found in David Wells's *No Place for Truth*.[12] He traces the
history of Wenham, Massachusetts, the small town in which he lives. In
so doing, he illustrates the trends which have changed America and, to
some extent, the world since the nineteenth century, and which are still
at work.

We have taken a brief look at the benefits, general principles, and
methodology of theological prognostication. With this introductory
background we can now examine various trends operating today and the
effects they will have on the future of theology.

---

12. David F. Wells, *No Place for Truth, or Whatever Happened to Evangelical Theology?* (Grand Rapids: Eerdmans, 1993), pp. 17–52.

2

Cultural and Religious Trends

Societal Changes
    Breakdown in Military Alignment
    The Shift of Power from Military to Economic
    The Ascent of Developing Nations
    Geographical Shifts of Population
    Rurbanization
    The Shift to an Information-based Society
    Decentralization
    The Rising Role of Women
    Emphasis on the Individual
    The Growth of Relativism
    Demographics
Religious Trends
    Secularism
    Growing Religiosity
    Divergence over Worship
    Individualism
    Christian Colleges in Crisis
    Changes in Preparation for the Ministry
    Declining Financial Support

Before we can forecast what theology will be like in the future, we need to look at some of the general trends taking place within society both in the United States and worldwide. We must also examine some religious (as contrasted with distinctly theological) trends.

Societal Changes

Breakdown in Military Alignment

Among the most obvious changes in our world is the breakdown of the classic military alignment. For more than a generation, the world has been structured politically in terms of the two superpowers, the United States and the Soviet Union, together with their respective allies in Western and Eastern Europe and elsewhere. The unaligned nations of the Third World were constantly being tugged by the two superpowers to align with them. Much of life was understood in light of this confrontation. National resources were to a large extent committed to defense or to winning the Cold War. The doctrine of sin on anything beyond the individual level became, for some Christians, conditioned by the idea of communism. Good and evil sometimes became confused with capitalism and communism. Eschatologically, some Christians thought in terms of a nuclear holocaust which would bring the earth to an end. On the other side, religious freedom, including freedom to evangelize and engage in missions, was often restricted by communist governments, which were officially atheistic. In many cases communism appeared to take on some of the characteristics of religion, requiring a high level of devotion, replacing faith in God's providence with trust in the dialectic, and substituting the classless society for the hope of heaven.

Today, however, all this has changed. All the states of Eastern Europe have in varying degrees given up their communist regimes and adopted democratic governments. Great economic adjustments are being made. Those countries, once so self-sufficient, are now pleading for economic aid from the West. Great hardships are being experienced by the people as the shift is made from a controlled and subsidized economy to a free market economy. At the same time freedom of religion and of proselytization has been restored in most cases. Indeed, evangelical Christians from the West are teaching religion courses in the very department at the State University of Moscow where the required atheism course was taught.

These changes have affected many dimensions of life. Peoples who were once regarded as enemies are now neighbors to be helped. Accordingly, it is possible to redeploy some of the former defense budget to other purposes. And a great opportunity is presented for evangelism in places where the gospel has not gone in many years. In general this development will tend to favor a more conservative view of Christianity. On the other hand, the conservative eschatology which saw the ideological forces as destined to a great final conflict has been undermined.

The Shift of Power from Military to Economic

Along with the political restructuring, the major basis of power has shifted from military to economic. During the years of the Cold War it was common to think of the fundamental struggle in the world as being between the two military superpowers. Presumably the country that possessed the greatest military hardware would be the dominant force in the world. With the end of that struggle, however, we are seeing that economic forces are what make the difference. The Japanese economy has leaped forward in recent years, as has the German. International trade surpluses, full employment, investment in other countries, and low rates of inflation are the new hallmarks of strength. Economically powerful countries are in a position to dictate to less powerful nations, in much the same fashion that militarily powerful countries once could.

This whole situation is of course in a state of flux. Thus nations like South Korea and Singapore may soon present Japan with just the same sort of challenge that Japan has posed for the United States and other Western nations. Consequently, economic cooperation and alliances will increasingly take on the significance which military organizations once had. As the role of NATO diminishes, the role of the European Economic Community will increase. Similar economic alliances are arising in the Pacific rim and in North America. They are the wave of the future.

The Ascent of Developing Nations

Correlated with the new emphasis on economic power is a shift of impetus and interest to the developing nations, which have tended to be subservient, but will increasingly become partners with the developed nations. With the breakdown of the major alignments we will see more political power flowing to the developing nations. Countries such as South Korea and Malaysia are showing special prominence economically. With the emphasis upon globalization, Third World cultures will no longer be considered odd, as some Westerners have regarded them in the past, but as valid alternatives.

We have already seen the effects of this shift in economic and political matters. We must also, however, reckon with the fact that the intellectual forces of non-Western cultures will begin to shape the thinking even of Westerners. This is seen to some extent in the growth of ideologies with an Eastern basis, such as the New Age movement.

Geographical Shifts of Population

In the United States there is and will continue to be a shift of population, industry, and thus of political power, from the North and East to the South and West.[1] This trend was slowed somewhat as a result of difficulties in the oil industry. It will continue to slow because of the prospect of earthquakes together with increasing anxiety about living in large metropolitan areas such as Los Angeles, especially in the wake of the riots in April 1992. The general trend will continue, however, and at some point will again accelerate. Among the contributing factors is that labor and tax regulations in the South provide business with a favorable environment.

The effects of the geographical shift are not easy to calculate. In general the movement southward is into a culturally and politically more conservative area. It remains to be seen, however, whether the new arrivals or the area itself will be more changed. There are some indications that when people move from cities to suburbs, they tend to take on the values of the population that they are joining, but it may be that a latent possession of those values is a factor influencing the move. The move to the West, however, especially to the extent that it stems from the Midwest, is a move into a more secular setting.

Rurbanization

Another population shift is what Russell Chandler calls "rurbanization."[2] This is the movement of urban centers outward, so that what were rural areas are gradually being transformed into parts of large metropolitan areas. This phenomenon can be detected in various places. In California it has been stimulated by the high cost of urban real estate, so that some people commute to work in San Francisco from areas of the San Joaquin Valley as much as two hundred miles away. The result has been a sharp increase in housing prices in those formerly rural communities as well.

I grew up on a 106-acre farm located forty-five miles north of the heart of Minneapolis. Today there are three dwellings on that land, and the dirt road in front of the farm has become 397th Avenue N.E. House numbers on east-west roads in the county are determined by their position relative to University Avenue, which eventually runs through the University of Minnesota and ends at the state capitol. The county seat, ten miles to the south of our farm, is now within the metropolitan telephone area, and the auto dealers carry large stocks of vehicles. That town is now suburban, yet many people are still rural in their mentality, although that is changing. As this type of shift continues throughout the

1. John Naisbitt, *Megatrends: Ten New Directions Transforming Our Lives* (New York: Warner, 1982), pp. 207–29.
2. Russell Chandler, *Racing Toward 2001: The Forces Shaping America's Religious Future* (Grand Rapids: Zondervan, 1992), pp. 20–23.

country, we can expect that more and more people will take on the thinking patterns, including the theological beliefs, of urban dwellers.[3]

The Shift to an Information-based Society

The shift from an industrial to an information-based society is significant. With the explosion of knowledge, possession of information is increasingly more important than physical skills. Computers and robots are doing jobs which were formerly performed by human beings. One reason for the declining strength of the labor union movement is that less and less of the work being done in our society is of the type done by traditional union members.

As a result, influence and advantage will increasingly go to those who are able to deal with the techniques and technology of the information society. Recently I heard a commentator say that the problem with American young people is not that they are illiterate, but that they are innumerate. Whereas only about 7 percent of high school students in the United States take four years of mathematics, in Japan the figure is virtually 100 percent. In an information-based society, where computers are supreme, it is not difficult to see with whom the advantage will lie.

One of the general effects of the knowledge explosion is an increasing tendency toward objectivity and rationality. The call for hard information, truth, facts, will de-emphasize subjective or intuitive approaches. This situation will, however, as John Naisbitt has pointed out, necessitate an increase in high touch to counter the stresses that accompany the high-tech dimension of life.[4]

Another effect of the knowledge explosion is an increasing rapidity of change. As a theologian I have wondered why the life spans of theologies are diminishing. I now realize that part of the explanation is the much quicker dissemination of information and new ideas.

Decentralization

Another far-reaching trend is the move away from centralization. This shows itself in a number of ways, including the shift away from centralized political government. One of the planks that Ronald Reagan campaigned upon was smaller or less government. In a very real sense, however, he did not create the trend so much as reflect and capitalize upon it.

The move toward decentralization shows itself in corporate circles as well. Control is less concentrated in the central office than previously, with more initiatives being allowed to local branches. Similarly,

3. Ibid., p. 305.
4. Naisbitt, *Megatrends*, pp. 39–53.

denominationalism, with its concept of a strong central authority, is sharply declining. Each individual church is likely to be just that—individual—and independent. This means that there is more concentration upon making decisions and carrying out actions at the local level. A correlate idea is that funds should be kept as close to home as possible, so that they are spent where they can be overseen and where decisions can be made.

Part of this whole phenomenon is the demise of the old pyramidal structure. Power used to be concentrated at the top of an organization, in the chief executive officer, and flowed from there to those beneath. This has changed, however, so that although the pyramids may formally still be in place, functionally the situation is far different. In their place we find participatory decision-making and networking. Naisbitt gives three reasons for this change: the death of traditional structures; the din of information overload; and the past failure of hierarchies. The change accelerates as baby boomers, whose dominant style is networking, move into management. Another factor is the rising overall educational level. College-educated workers with managerial abilities and tendencies outnumber the available management positions. They find an outlet for their managerial skills in being able to govern, at least in part, their own situations. In addition, the information explosion has meant that teams of workers have in many cases had to take the place of individuals, since all the needed information is seldom possessed by one individual. All of this means that those organizations, including churches, which have tended to concentrate decision-making authority in a single office or a few persons at the top will either have to make some adjustments in their mode of operation or they will find the going very difficult indeed. The mood of the times does not favor that type of structure.

There is also a geographical decentralization that is seen in the form of regionalism. This is the tendency to identify more closely with one's part of the country and of the world than with other areas. These regional distinctions are more important than are the characteristics which one has in common with persons in other parts of the country. For some time regionalism has been most apparent in the South. For example, although the South has tended until recently to elect Democrats to Congress, those Democrats have voted more consistently with Republicans than with Northern Democrats, feeling that they have more in common with the former than with the latter. Regionalism is also quite prominent in the West, where anything non-Western is labeled as being from "back East." Such feelings have implications for the church, where there may be more of a sense of commonality with local churches of a different denomination than with nonlocal churches of the same denomination.

The Rising Role of Women

One of the most conspicuous and most significant trends today is the rising role of women in society, and especially in positions of leadership. Only a generation ago women expected to take subservient jobs and, rather than pursuing a career, to marry and spend their primary efforts as homemakers. Higher education, especially as preparation for a profession other than teaching or nursing, was not an option. Since men were the primary source of financial support for their families, they would go into the more significant occupations, some of which, such as medicine, law, and engineering, were not seen as appropriate lines of work for women. In my high school graduating class, almost none of the women went on to college, even though two of them were among the top three students in the class.

The situation has changed radically in our time. The number of medical degrees awarded to women went from less than 7 percent of the total in 1966 to 32.3 percent in 1987; an even more dramatic increase took place with law degrees, where the rate went from 3.5 percent in 1966 to 40 percent in 1987.[5] The number of women earning business administration degrees nearly tripled between 1975 and 1987, and the number receiving engineering degrees increased thirteenfold in the same period of time. In business, women today hold some 39.3 percent of the 14.2 million executive, administrative, and management positions. In finance they have reached the halfway mark: more than half of all officers, managers, and professionals in the nation's largest commercial banks are women. And female enrolment in seminaries has changed from tokenism in each class (generally in Christian education programs) to anywhere from 20 to more than 50 percent today.

Women are also making major inroads into politics. Golda Meir in Israel and Margaret Thatcher in the United Kingdom were pioneers. The situation in the United States has slowly changed so that a woman was the vice presidential candidate of the Democratic party in 1984, and in 1992 a large number of women candidates ran for national office. Even in Japan, where the very word *wife* means "inside the house," a woman has come to head the major opposition party.

The authors of *Megatrends 2000* suggest that one of the reasons for the increasing presence of women in places of influence is the change

---

5. John Naisbitt and Patricia Aburdene, *Megatrends 2000: Ten New Directions for the 1990's* (New York: Avon, 1991), p. 238.

in thinking regarding leadership. They say, "To be a leader in business today, it is no longer an advantage to have been socialized as a male."[6] They believe that women may even hold a slight advantage since it is not necessary for them to unlearn the old authoritarian behavior.

It is apparent that the status of women has changed and is continuing to change in American society and throughout the world. Laws regarding sexual harassment and salary discrimination have made clear that there are to be no double standards in the workplace or anywhere else. The trend to actual, not merely formal, equality for women is very real.

Emphasis on the Individual

We also need to note the shift toward the individual. This is expressed both in the sense of individual rights and autonomy, and in the sense of individual responsibility. The former is implied in the shift away from a centralized, hierarchical governmental structure. The latter can be seen in the changing attitudes toward traditional forms of welfare. The workfare program in the state of Wisconsin, for example, appears to be a successful experiment.

America has from the beginning had a strong emphasis upon individualism. This is what made possible the settlement of the frontier. It was, however, an individualism limited by a strong sense of religious commitment and the well-being of the community. Unfortunately, as Robert Bellah contends in his book *Habits of the Heart*, the commitment and responsibility associated with this individualism have declined. These dimensions have been replaced by new ideals. One of these new ideals is "utilitarian individualism," or the "pursuit of one's own material interest."[7] Another is what he terms "expressive individualism," or the "freedom to express oneself, against all constraints and conventions."[8] So pervasive is this tendency that Richard Wells believes it deserves to be called "the Megafact."[9] There is an emphasis upon one's right to do and say whatever one wishes, but there is no concomitant willingness to accept responsibility for one's actions. Thus gay groups continue to demand increased government expenditures for AIDS research (although it already receives as much as does the research upon all forms of cancer), but they do not emphasize equally the necessity of taking responsibility for their own behavior, a step which would make them considerably less vulnerable to the disease.

---

6. Ibid., p. 239.
7. Robert N. Bellah et al., *Habits of the Heart: Individualism and Commitment in American Life* (Berkeley: University of California Press, 1985), p. 33.
8. Ibid., p. 34.
9. C. Richard Wells, "Ministry Megatrends," *Vocatio* 3.1 (1991): 4–5.

There are some indications, however, that the emphasis on individual responsibility is beginning to reappear. It can be seen in the reformation of welfare systems. Ronald Reagan in the United States and Margaret Thatcher in Great Britain did much to shrink the welfare system. There is growing support for the idea of workfare, where able-bodied persons on welfare are expected to perform needed services, often in the public-works domain, in return for the government assistance which they receive. This is one of many indications that society expects individuals to accept responsibility for themselves rather than relying upon government to provide for them. This trend will favor those ideologies which have traditionally emphasized individual responsibility.

The Growth of Relativism

Accompanying the spurt in individualism is a growing relativism. While this social trend is too pervasive and varied to be discussed fully, we might note some of its manifestations, for example, a breakdown in acceptance of the sense of contradiction. Both the premodern and the modern periods held, as part of their faith, that if a statement was true, its contradictory could not also be true, at least not at the same time and in the same respect. This conviction is breaking down in the postmodern period. In deconstructive postmodernism the referent of words is not external, independent objects, but other words; and the old criteria of internal consistency and coherence not only are not highly valued, but are believed to be inapplicable.[10] This breakdown in logic and the accompanying rise in relativism are beginning to appear most strongly in the "baby buster" generation (i.e., the post-baby-boom generation), where inconsistency is no problem, but they are also to be found in other generations as well.[11]

In part, the rise in relativism is a function of the increase in individualism as applied to epistemology. For truth as measured by one person's experience may be quite different from truth as measured by another person's experience. When the Barna survey proposed the statement, "Nothing can be known for certain except the things you experience in your own life," 30 percent of the general public agreed strongly and another 30 percent agreed moderately. Baby busters had the highest percentage of agreement, followed by senior citizens, the preboomers, and finally the baby boomers, although the last two groups were quite close. Agreement was inversely proportional to education,

10. See David R. Griffin, "Introduction: Varieties of Postmodern Theology," in *Varieties of Postmodern Theology*, ed. David R. Griffin (Albany: State University of New York Press, 1989), pp. 3–4.

11. Leith Anderson, *Dying for Change* (Minneapolis: Bethany, 1990), pp. 107–8.

income, and level of job. Thus this type of relativism was not a function of intellectual achievement, but of subjectivism in epistemology.[12]

In an earlier polling the Barna organization had found what they considered to be indications of a strong relativism. Those polled were asked to give their reaction to the statement "There is no such thing as absolute truth; different people can define truth in conflicting ways and still be correct." Of the general sample, 28 percent agreed strongly, 39 percent agreed somewhat, 13 percent disagreed somewhat, 16 percent disagreed strongly, and 5 percent said they did not know. There was an inverse relationship between agreement and age: at one end of the spectrum 72 percent of the baby busters agreed and 26 percent disagreed; at the other end 56 percent of the senior citizens agreed and 32 percent disagreed. Even 52 percent of those who said they were born again agreed, as did 53 percent of those in evangelical denominations.[13]

Barna, interpreting the responses quite literally, registers considerable alarm.[14] Actually, it may be that the high level of agreement with the statement at least partially reflects humility rather than relativism. In other words, it may indicate a sense that our understanding of the truth is incomplete and only partial; that is, "we have absolute truth, but we do not understand it absolutely." Nor does Barna's conclusion really take into account the "civility" of which James Davison Hunter writes,[15] the unwillingness to say that others are wrong. Either of these interpretations, unlike Barna, places more emphasis upon the second part of the statement ("different people can define truth in conflicting ways and still be correct") than upon the first ("there is no such thing as absolute truth"). Nonetheless, the responses to the statement do give some indication of an increasing relativism.

Demographics

Finally, we must take brief note of the demographic phenomena which characterize our day, and the ways in which they differ from earlier periods. Most noteworthy are the baby boomers. This generation, born between approximately 1946 and 1964, constitutes an unusually large segment of the population. They are currently in the age bracket which traditionally has provided the bulk of the leadership, funds, and

12. George Barna, *The Barna Report 1992–93: America Renews Its Search for God* (Ventura, Calif.: Regal, 1992), p. 252.

13. George Barna, *The Barna Report: What Americans Believe* (Ventura, Calif.: Regal, 1991), pp. 84–85.

14. Ibid., p. 83.

15. James Davison Hunter, *Evangelicalism: The Coming Generation* (Chicago: University of Chicago Press, 1987), p. 47.

service to the church. In the past it was customary for that generation to learn and adopt the values and beliefs of the preceding generation. There is some indication that this pattern has been disrupted in our day, however, and that because of the sheer number of baby boomers, their values have usurped the dominant place in society.[16]

Another major development is the bulge of senior citizens, who constitute the most rapidly growing segment of the American population.[17] This is a result partly of demographics, since a large number of babies were born in the years preceding 1930, and partly of improvements in health care. Senior citizens have considerable power. They are concerned about and involved in politics to a greater extent than are other age groups. Their retired status affords them time to give to politics. They also have considerable organizational skills derived from their life experiences. Although they may not always get the sort of publicity that the baby boomers receive, their influence is indicated by the extreme reluctance of politicians to make any changes in the social security program.

Yet senior citizens feel a certain amount of alienation and frustration. They are the generation that had to suffer deprivation because of the Great Depression. They had to work hard, to practice self-discipline. Many of them cared for their aged parents and also put their children through college. They sometimes found themselves supporting three generations simultaneously. That is why a few years ago *Changing Times* magazine called them "the Pooped Generation." Moreover, they feel shortchanged by the shift in values. Whereas they had to practice self-denial and deferral of gratification, the generation that followed them has sought self-indulgence and immediate gratification. One seventy-year-old lay church leader put it this way: "When we were young, we were told to respect our elders, which meant that at meals they went first, and we followed. Now, however, at potlucks and buffets the children rush in first and we take what is left."

Ironically, the baby boomer generation also feel that they are being shortchanged. For example, it is their social security taxes which are paying for the benefits of today's senior citizens. Whereas the current retirees will receive considerably more than they paid into the system, the younger workers will probably never recover all of their payments. Another factor is the national debt, which mushroomed during the 1980s. This will place a load of interest charges upon the backs of those

16. Howard A. Snyder with Daniel V. Runyon, *Foresight: 10 Major Trends That Will Dramatically Affect the Future of Christians and the Church* (Nashville: Thomas Nelson, 1986), pp. 142–43.
17. Chandler, *Racing Toward 2001*, pp. 36–39.

who pay taxes in the future. Obviously the potential for conflict, political and otherwise, between these groups is great.

Religious Trends

We now turn to some major religious trends in our society. Some of them follow rather obviously from the secular trends described above, and some stem from uniquely religious influences. Not surprisingly, then, a few are in competition with each other.

Secularism

One major trend is the growing secularism, which entails several factors. It is primarily an emphasis upon the spatial and temporal, the here and now. It is pursuit of material objects as the highest values of life. It is belief that truth, rather than being revealed from some transcendent realm, is discovered by humans through examination of the observable universe. It is reliance upon science and technology, which respectively study and harness this observable universe, as the means to accomplishing our goals. It is conviction of the self-sufficiency of the human race to solve its own problems.

Secularism, which in many ways dates to the Enlightenment, has been accelerating in our day. Among the causes is the rising level of education, which has led even young evangelicals in the direction of secularism.[18] The immense practical success of modern technology has also contributed to the growth of secularism.

Growing Religiosity

A seeming paradox, in light of the preceding point, is the growing religiosity within American society. In part the two elements in this paradox may involve different segments of the population; or some people may have a split mentality, so to speak, functioning on two different levels or with two completely separate compartments of their minds. What is happening in America is part of a worldwide growth of religious interest. Particularly in Eastern Europe religious belief is growing, according to a study sponsored by the International Social Survey Program and authored by Andrew Greeley.[19]

This increased religiosity is, however, in some cases a matter of interest in rather unconventional, nontraditional, or unorthodox religion. I

18. Hunter, *Evangelicalism*, p. 171, cites five major post-1950s studies which support the belief that education secularizes.

19. "Study Suggests World Is Experiencing Religious Revival," *Minneapolis Star Tribune*, 18 May 1993, p. 2A.

have in mind here, for example, the rise of the New Age movement and various elements from Eastern religions, including Yoga, meditation, and the human potential movement.[20] This trend, while in keeping with an increased interest in "spirituality," is opposed to organized religion.

Conservative Christianity is also prospering and will continue to do so at least for the foreseeable future, especially in its fundamentalist and charismatic varieties. While mainline churches have continued in perpetual decline, conservative groups have far outstripped them in every area that gives evidence of growth. This is not something new, for it goes back at least fifty years, but the divergence of these two segments of Christianity is becoming ever more conspicuous.[21]

Divergence over Worship

Anyone alert to what is going on in evangelical American churches is aware of the shift toward a more informal, experience-centered style of religion. Celebration is replacing meditation, praise choruses are supplanting hymns, worship teams have succeeded robed choirs, organs are sitting unused in favor of guitars, hymnals are replaced by words projected on a screen or inserted in the worship folder, casual attire is worn instead of Sunday-go-to-meeting clothes. One church leader, observing that a change-oriented congregation had just installed an organ costing over one million dollars in its new sanctuary, commented, "Think how many guitars that would have bought." This youth-oriented trend is gaining momentum.

Less obvious and much smaller in size is an opposite movement. An increasing number of persons, especially college students, are turning to denominations emphasizing tradition, historical connection, and liturgy. I have in mind the movement of people like Robert Webber and Walter Dunnett into the Episcopal and Anglican churches.[22] An even more radical step is the movement of evangelicals into the Eastern Orthodox Church. Peter Gillquist, a major leader in this movement, has described the journey of two thousand evangelical Protestants toward Eastern Orthodoxy.[23] One issue of his magazine *Again* featured the testimonies of recent evangelical converts to Eastern Orthodoxy.[24] Among

20. Naisbitt and Aburdene, *Megatrends 2000*, p. 298.
21. Ibid., pp. 298–301; Dean M. Kelley, *Why Conservative Churches Are Growing: A Study in Sociology of Religion* (New York: Harper and Row, 1972).
22. Robert E. Webber, *Evangelicals on the Canterbury Trail: Why Evangelicals Are Attracted to the Liturgical Church* (Waco: Word, 1985); Willmar Thorkelson, "Christian Colleges Settle with Ousted Professors," *Christianity Today* 37.2 (Feb. 8, 1993): 61.
23. Peter E. Gillquist, *Becoming Orthodox: A Journey to the Ancient Christian Faith* (Brentwood, Tenn.: Wolgemuth and Hyatt, 1989).
24. "Why Are Protestant Schools Producing Orthodox Clergy?" *Again* 14.3 (Sept. 1991).

the more conspicuous is Franky Schaeffer, son of the late Francis Schaeffer.[25] A few, such as Thomas Howard, have even been attracted to Roman Catholicism.

This movement is small, but it is real and of potentially great influence because it includes young people who could be the leaders of the evangelical movement in the years ahead. Unless mainstream evangelicalism finds ways to meet the needs of young people desiring some tie with the historic faith and with more-formal worship, more of them will leave for denominations that offer real alternatives to popular experience-centered worship.

Individualism

We have already seen that individualism is a growing feature of society in general. There are also a number of evidences of religious individualism. One is the tendency simply not to join religious organizations or to make definite commitments to them. This is apparent in the fact that baby boomers are not joiners. Another evidence is their giving patterns. They will respond to an appeal that involves a single gift, a brief commitment, a specific project or task which interests them. What they will not ordinarily do is take on long-term commitments or assume ongoing support of an organization or individual.

One result of the baby boomers' individualism is the decline of denominationalism. There was a time when persons who were Baptists or Presbyterians signed on with that group for life. When they moved to a different area, they sought out a congregation of the same denomination and united with it. That one church was the center of their religious activities. The one exception to this pattern was involvement with the ministry of interdenominational or nondenominational groups. This phenomenon was perhaps the beginning of the breakdown of denominational loyalty as such.

Today's baby boomers do not necessarily stick with the denomination in which they grew up. They select whatever group seems to meet the needs which they feel. Further, they do not restrict themselves to any one group at a time. They may involve themselves in the programs of a half dozen congregations and religious organizations.[26] Their giving reflects this dispersed approach to religion.

One feature that has emerged from this trend is the megachurch. While the individualism driving the megachurch is not always recognized as such, it is usually present. The megachurch is a relatively

25. For his testimony see *Again* 14.4 (Dec. 1991): 13–14.
26. Anderson, *Dying for Change*, p. 96.

recent phenomenon that adds a special dimension to the large congregation, which has of course been with us for some time. For the megachurch is in a sense its own denomination. Its programs are the locus of interest and energy, not those of the denomination. The megachurch is, then, the other side of the decline in denominationalism.

The megachurch feels that it can best prepare persons for its ministry. This is in part a reflection of the idea that the ministry of each megachurch is unique, so that only persons specifically prepared for it can serve effectively there. We have here an implicit rejection of the "one size fits all" approach typified by the denominational seminary. Beyond that, however, are both the feeling that the megachurch can train its staff better than can anyone else, and the wish to have full control of what is done. I do not think we will see megachurches forming associations to train their staffs together. Anyone who has attempted to get megachurches to share such an endeavor knows what I mean.

Independence also characterizes the mission programs. Rather than working through established denominational programs, megachurches pick and choose where they will send their mission volunteers, or even establish their own mission programs, which are usually short-term. Similarly, megachurches frequently develop their own educational curricula and camping programs.

Nor does the megachurch work through established denominational channels in church planting. It is not unusual to see a megachurch plant a daughter church in a rapidly growing suburb where there already is another church of the same denomination, for it is not the denomination but the local church that is the point of identity. Such churches develop networks of their own satellite congregations, which sometimes bear distinctive names to identify the connection. Thus a sort of minidenomination is established, as it were. This is nothing new, of course. Many a Christian college and mission organization began with the ambition and endeavor of a dynamic senior pastor of a large and growing congregation. What is different is the increase of this trend.

There will be definite effects upon the total work of the kingdom of God; for example, a supply-side evangelism, as it were. Worthy projects and needy communities will not necessarily be cared for. There will not necessarily be a benevolence approach to ministry. Inner-city churches and other congregations without extensive resources will languish, for resources from outside may not be forthcoming. Smaller congregations, unable to compete with the extensive programs of megachurches, may dwindle and disappear. In a sort of ecclesiastical Darwinism, the megachurches will survive and grow larger. One megachurch pastor, when asked about this, indicated that he did not care if smaller congregations died. He intended for his church to grow at the expense of other congregations which, in his opinion, were not getting the job done. Rural churches in particular appeared to him to be an anachronism.

In the past, part of the motivation for cooperation between congregations, which usually took the form of denominations, but sometimes more loosely organized associations, was stewardship of the resources of the kingdom of God. There was efficiency in pooling resources and functions, which meant that finances went further. The megachurch phenomenon claims to be doing the same thing, by in effect submerging the functions of many smaller churches into one large operation. In practice, however, this is not necessarily the case. In fact, even some of what the larger churches used to do cooperatively, such as theological education, missions, and camping programs, is being replicated in many places rather than one. In the long run, either the quality of these many individual endeavors will diminish, or the resources available will not reach as far.

Christian Colleges in Crisis

The typical Christian college will fall on difficult times and will move toward general liberal arts education rather than church-related or Christian higher education. Among the factors contributing to this trend is an ambiguity or uncertainty regarding the purpose of the Christian college. Traditionally, the church regarded its colleges as means of extending its own ministry. Its young people went off to those schools to receive a Christian higher education. In addition to continuing the Christian education program provided by the local church, the Christian college prepared the student for life in the broader sense, including a vocation. It was expected that the Christian college would provide higher education from a Christian perspective, so that faith would be reinforced rather than undermined.

There is a growing body of evidence, however, that Christian colleges do not really meet this expectation. The research done by Hunter confirms that, in general, additional education tends to have a liberalizing effect upon believers. Ironically, his survey of nine evangelical Christian colleges indicates that in situations of supposed "high insularity" there is a greater tendency to depart from traditional evangelical beliefs and lifestyle than is the case in institutions of "low insularity," that is, in avowedly secular institutions.[27] He comments, "The setting of the Evangelical college, we can infer, does allow for a relaxation of 'cogni-

27. Hunter, *Evangelicalism*, pp. 171–78.

tive defenses.' Yet it is in the safety of this setting that the erosive effects of education can take place. In this case, the threat is not external and visible but internal and, by and large, unperceived."[28] Hunter finds the threat in large part in the views and attitudes of many of the faculty, especially those in the social sciences and humanities: "There is then, among many faculty, a sense that true and vital Christianity depends upon a debunking of many of the traditions of conservative Protestantism."[29]

Hunter's research confirms what many conservative Christian parents have found. After sacrificing to send their young people to expensive private Christian colleges, they find that the schools have the very opposite effect from what they desired. The sense of disappointment and anger is real. The experience is not greatly unlike that which a former neighbor of mine felt when he was still working to pay for the expensive wedding of his daughter, who was already divorced. For many evangelicals Christian higher education is out of reach financially. One Christian couple put it this way, "Why should we give to a school that our sons and daughters can't afford, so that kids from an affluent suburb and another denomination can have a good time on a nice campus?"

Reaction to the problems we have outlined is taking several forms. For some middle-class families the choice is a relatively secular private school where for approximately the same cost an academically superior education can be obtained. For others the choice is a secular public institution where the student can be involved in Inter-Varsity Christian Fellowship or Campus Crusade for Christ. In a time of declining financial resources, the church is asking whether the Christian liberal arts college is a good investment. There is little difference in the content of physics, engineering, or even business as taught in a Christian college and in a state university. Furthermore, if sociology and literature are taught no differently except for some affective matters, is there value in studying them in a more (supposedly) insulated environment? Indeed, teachers at Christian colleges who are reacting against their fundamentalist backgrounds are frequently less objective and fair than many of their counterparts in secular institutions. Hunter's book has made relatively little impact at the popular or lay level, perhaps because schools of the type in his survey have managed to mute its discussion. I anticipate, however, that the church will increasingly ask itself whether its goals might not be more effectively accomplished by supporting a strong student-ministry program on secular campuses. As a result,

28. Ibid., p. 177.
29. Ibid., p. 176.

Christian colleges will turn to a broader clientele, as has been the case with other church-related schools in the past.[30]

There is one other dimension to this issue. Traditionally, Christian colleges existed in part to provide preparation for the ministry. Indeed, the earliest colleges in the United States were begun for this purpose. Later, they served to provide preseminary preparation for future ministers. One of the problems seminaries are encountering now is their students' high level of indebtedness. Many come to seminary already encumbered with educational indebtedness, and in some cases a similar indebtedness by the spouse. It may become increasingly necessary for preseminarians to do their undergraduate work in public institutions to keep the cost at a minimum. This, coupled with the factors described above, will mean that Christian liberal arts colleges will less and less be the schools of choice for seminary-bound students.

Changes in Preparation for the Ministry

There will also be changes in the way one prepares for the ministry. A century or more ago the prospective minister "read theology" with an established pastor, in much the same way the prospective doctor "read medicine." This was a form of apprenticeship with a strong cognitive basis. Then the theological seminaries arose as a more efficient means of accomplishing the objective: the content was taught in courses at an academic institution, and practical experience was gained through a program of field education. This has been the standard practice for some time, with the educational requirements being progressively raised over the years.

There has always been criticism of this system: seminaries are ivory tower institutions far removed from the realities of life and ministry; they are so cognitively oriented that they exude spiritual sterility and aridity. Some critics even labeled seminaries cemeteries. More recently, the chorus has become louder and more concentrated. The megachurches, in particular, are contending that they can do a better job of preparing persons for ministry, at least for their ministry, than can the seminaries. Seminary education is seen as too long, too expensive, and too irrelevant.[31]

---

30. The quandary of the Christian college is illustrated by two articles in *Christianity Today* 37.14 (Nov. 22, 1993): Nathan Hatch's editorial "Our Shackled Scholars" (pp. 12–13) advocates greater freedom for the faculty of evangelical institutions to pursue answers to intellectual and ethical problems; Andrés Tapia, "Homosexuality Debate Strains Campus Harmony" (pp. 38–40), discusses the debate on Christian college campuses regarding the relationship between the homosexual lifestyle and Christian faith.

31. "Seminaries and/or Teaching Churches: A Report," *NAPCE Newsletter* (National Association of Professors of Christian Education, now known as North American Professors of Christian Education), summer 1991, p. 1.

There is, to be sure, some very valid basis for this complaint. Some faculty members have never served full-time pastorates, or have not had sufficient recent pastoral responsibility to be able to relate to the types of issues their students will encounter upon graduation. Their understanding of the role of a minister may overlook the fact that seminary professors constitute only a minute percentage of the total churchgoers in the nation, so that what they want in a sermon (which often resembles an academic lecture) is far removed from the needs of most Christians. Some professors do not even possess a standard seminary degree. They may be primarily academics rather than ministers. Their professional interests may be more like those of a university professor than of a local church pastor. As Bruce Shelley puts it, "The image of the pastor-theologian [with the emphasis on theologian!] is the ideal for most theological faculties."[32] Students who identify closely with such an instructor will often experience culture shock in their first pastorate. They may find that the picture of ministry which they bring to the local church tacitly assumes that the fax machine, telephone, radio, television, and even the automobile have not been invented.

On the other hand, the fallacy of the megachurch reaction will eventually become apparent. Without the strong theoretical basis for ministry which seminary supplies, ministers will be more like mechanics than like engineers. They will be able to minister in the church in which they received their training, but will have difficulty transferring that skill to other cultural situations, or even other parishes; they will not know how to construct new forms and patterns of ministry when those they have learned become obsolete.

Another shortcoming of the megachurch training is that those who are most successful at a given activity are not always the most adept at teaching others that skill. Many outstanding athletes have made very poor managers and coaches, while some of the most successful coaches had rather mediocre careers as players. One reason for this is to be found in the fact that some persons succeed because of unusual gifts which cannot be imparted to others (a basketball coach once quipped, "The one thing I can't coach is height"). In other cases persons who succeed have assimilated their skill to the point where they are no longer conscious of how they did so. Thus, some pastors have had little education, but succeed because of outstanding natural persuasive or communicational skills. There is already considerable anecdotal evidence of persons in ministry who have been unable to emulate the natural gifts of their pastoral mentor. These people will be dependent upon someone

32. Bruce L. Shelley, "The Seminaries' Identity Crisis," *Christianity Today* 37.6 (May 17, 1993): 42.

else to retrain them. At some point the shortcomings and inefficiency of professional training by the megachurch will become apparent, and something like seminaries will begin to reemerge. Indeed, seminaries and other Christian institutions of higher education have historically arisen out of local church programs.

We will also see some major changes in traditional theological education. Seminaries are now facing enrolment problems stemming from the same demographic facts that colleges faced a few years ago. In an attempt to maintain and even increase enrolments, they are starting satellite operations on a large scale. If they were to go to extremes, every seminary would be operating an extension in the backyard of every other seminary. This assumes that theological students who could not come to the main campus of a given seminary would prefer to study at a local extension rather than at the main campus of another institution located in their vicinity. This assumption, however, overlooks the lack of institutional loyalty of baby boomers. Just as baby boomers will choose a church that has more appealing services over a church of the "brand" which they formerly patronized, so the baby boomers who attend seminary will not necessarily prefer a local extension of their brand over a local full-service main campus of a different brand. Eventually, unless the number of seminary students increases, an assumption which is tenuous at best,[33] the competition will simply mean that the same number of students are being educated at greater cost.

At that point some seminaries will be forced to close, just as a considerable number of colleges have closed. Others will merge into a single institution with multiple campuses. Thus, instead of Chandler Seminary in Bridgetown, Pennsylvania, with an extension in Centerville, Missouri, and Wilson Seminary in Centerville, Missouri, with an extension in Bridgetown, Pennsylvania, there will simply be Chandler-Wilson Seminary, with an east campus in Bridgetown and a west campus in Centerville. Schools able to form such unions will survive.

Two other types of seminaries will survive. One is the school that has a substantial endowment, so that it is not heavily dependent upon new gifts and high tuition. The other is the school that is able to attract large gifts from churches, foundations, and individuals for its current operation. Such schools have entrepreneurial presidents, who see their major role as presenting the task of the school winsomely to potential donors.[34]

33. See Millard J. Erickson, "Is a Shortage of Clergy Coming?" in idem, *The Evangelical Mind and Heart* (Grand Rapids: Baker, 1993), pp. 175–89.

34. David Allan Hubbard, "The Twenty-first Century Seminary," *Christianity Today* 37.6 (May 17, 1993): 45–46. Hubbard says, "Seminaries need affluent people to step up

These types of schools will be able to maintain student enrolments at reasonable levels. For one major factor in the crisis in theological education is the cost of tuition.[35] Some denominational seminaries have continued to provide virtually free education, and recently some other schools have adopted a similar policy for persons from their denomination. It will not take long for students to realize that instead of paying $7,000–8,000 per year they can obtain a basically similar education for $2,000 or less by a simple move of a few hundred miles. Schools with low tuitions will prosper at such a time as this.

Declining Financial Support

In a closely related trend, we will see a decline in financial support for various types of ministries, beginning with those beyond the local church. It has been estimated recently that 80 percent of all the funds for missions comes from persons fifty-five years of age and older. James Engel and Jerry Jones have concluded that only 10–15 percent of Christian baby boomers have a high interest in spreading the gospel overseas through conventional missions.[36] Over three-fourths of Christian baby boomers disagreed with the statement that the need for missionaries today is greater overseas than in the United States, and 95 percent said that it is just as important to be a missionary in downtown Chicago as it is to go overseas.[37]

Although only anecdotal at present, there are indications of large ministries in financial difficulty. One such ministry reports in its weekly newsletter that the number of worshipers on the previous Sunday was fourteen thousand, while the number of givers was twenty-six hundred, a figure which does not vary greatly from week to week. A congregation which gears its ministry largely to young people, and to people recovering from preaching that fixated on guilt and duty, meets in a large public school. Though approximately five thousand persons attend each weekend, not only can the congregation not afford to erect a building, but it is having difficulty making payments on the undeveloped land on which it plans to build. One Canadian congregation

and lay large gifts on the table to subsidize student aid and to subsidize programs" (p. 46). It is unlikely, however, that such persons will come forward without aggressive approaches to them by the schools. Yet the list of requirements for Hubbard's successor as president of Fuller Theological Seminary did not even include direct fund-raising as a primary responsibility.

35. Ibid., p. 46.

36. James F. Engel and Jerry D. Jones, *Baby Boomers and the Future of World Missions* (Orange, Calif.: Management Development Associates, 1989), p. 27.

37. Ibid., p. 20.

reported that on one Sunday it had both the largest attendance in its history and the smallest offering in the five years that it had been keeping weekly financial records. Another congregation, with a strong ministry for "seekers" (i.e., unbelievers), is approaching two thousand in weekly attendance, but is in imminent danger of foreclosure. They have, for the past five years, paid only the interest on the mortgage.

What is happening is that persons who were brought up to give substantially and even to tithe are retiring and dying. In some cases they are also being alienated by congregations which so strongly emphasize youth and contemporary worship that the older persons feel they are unimportant. In their place are baby boomers who do not possess the institutional loyalty and the commitment to financial giving that the earlier generation displayed. They have sometimes been attracted to a church by an emphasis on what they will receive rather than on what they will give. One young elder, in appealing to his congregation for money to support the current fund, said, "I am a baby boomer, and we baby boomers do not like the 'M' word. If we hear the 'M' word, we will go somewhere else where we do not hear the 'M' word. I am here to tell you, however, that we have to talk about the 'M' word."

It might be helpful to keep in view the current shift in focus from seeing the church as ministry to seeing the church as business. The church is engaged in marketing, in patterning its program to the needs and desires of the constituency it perceives. If, however, the church is going to approach its work as a business, it will need to give more attention to its accounts receivable and payable, or it will be in serious difficulty.

All of this suggests that we may see not merely the decline, but the crash of some large and significant ministries. This will be preceded by a reduction in giving to organizations outside the local parish, which are traditionally referred to as missions. Thus, what occurred in mainline missionary programs will also happen to evangelical missions. Should the reduction in spending for missions prove insufficient to solve the financial crisis, we will see churches trying to provide programs to meet the needs of people unable, unwilling, or unchallenged to support them. One of the major tests facing the church will be to find ways to induce baby boomers and baby busters to give financially as the preceding generation has done.[38]

We should also note that there will probably be a shift in the leadership of the Christian church. The pastors of today's megachurches speak as if their congregations will always be the most prominent. Any reader

---

38. James F. Engel, *Averting the Financial Crisis in Christian Organizations: Insights from a Decade of Donor Research* (Wheaton, Ill.: Management Development Associates, 1983), pp. 51–52.

who has been active in church circles for a generation, however, will know that the churches and the pastors that dominated the religious news of a generation ago are much less well known today. There is every reason to believe that the present front runners will also have difficulty maintaining their freshness, relevance, and success.

3

The Role of Nontheological Disciplines

In our opening chapter we observed that theology does not do its work in a vacuum. Theology develops within several environments, including denominational, geographical, and broadly cultural. We need to inquire at this point a bit more about its relationship to some other disciplines. We should, of course, to be most accurate in our theological prognostication, attempt to predict the developments which will take place within those disciplines as well in the years and decades ahead. To do so would exceed, however, both the competence of the author and our space constraints. We will, therefore, limit our discussion of what seem to be the future developments in the disciplines relating to theology.

In defense of this decision, I offer what may sound like a rather snide justification, but which I think is correct. It is that theology frequently is not completely current in its use of philosophy, psychology, and other "sciences." Consequently, the views that theology responds to ten years from now may not be the philosophy, for example, which is new at that point but, rather, the philosophy which is new today. The reason is that it takes time for new ideas to be accepted in any field, and those outside the field will respond to them later than will those within it. In that sense theology, as an outsider, is not necessarily out of date in the psychology or anthropology which it adopts and utilizes; it simply is not among the avant-garde. Generally, a given cultural movement reaches theology only after it has surfaced in philosophy, art, music, and other areas. One exception occurred when Wolfhart Pannenberg and his circle began linking historical reasoning and faith in opposition to the dual-history view of Rudolf Bultmann.[1] Here was a case where a theologian or a school of theology seemed to be initiating the turn away from the prevailing culture. Unfortunately, this lead does not seem to have been extensively followed either by other theologians or by scholars in other disciplines.

A Megatrend: Subjectivism

Postmodernism

One aspect of contemporary secular culture deserves special treatment, because it may well represent a paradigm shift. It is a clue to a change in the whole culture to which we are relating as we articulate our theology. In a sense Christianity, and specifically Christian theology, is or should be a counterculture. What we are seeing today, however, is the rise of another counterculture, which may itself eventually become the dominant culture. We must be aware that we might find ourselves developing our theology in relationship to a culture which already has been displaced.

The movement being referred to here is what is oftentimes called postmodernism. We are all familiar with the modern period, which dates largely from the Enlightenment, and especially from Immanuel Kant and Georg Hegel. Though the modern and the premodern period contrasted, they did have a number of beliefs in common. Both believed that reality had a rational character and that it could be understood by discovering this pattern of rationality. Further, both believed that there was some structure to history, some force or cause which produced the occurrences which collectively constituted history.

There were, of course, vast differences between the premodern and modern approaches. For premodernism there were transcendent factors.

---

1. *Revelation as History*, ed. Wolfhart Pannenberg (New York: Macmillan, 1968).

Christian theology had its God, who was the Creator, sustainer, and director of all. Ancient philosophy placed the extramundane elsewhere. Plato, for example, spoke of forms that gave reality and existence to particulars, which were shadows cast by the forms under the illumination of the form or idea of the Good. These forms or ideas were the cause of what occurred within the world.

In the modern world there was still an expectation of rationality, but this rationality was within the observable world rather than being somehow transcendent to it. Thus both the character of things and the cause of what happens within the world were understood in terms of fixed laws of nature. This rational pattern had to be discovered and utilized if what was to happen in creation was to be predicted and controlled. This was the way of natural science, especially in the days of Newtonian physics. In the case of dialectical materialism, the philosophy of communism, although the direction of movement was dialectical or dialogical rather than logistic or linear, it was the inherent patterns and tendencies of matter that caused what occurred. In all of these systems there were certain assumptions: the orderliness of reality, the rationality of human nature, and a connection between what happens and certain causal forces.

In both premodernism and modernism, and especially in the latter, one could arrive at the truth through a rational process in which logical rules applied. Thus, if A was true, it necessarily was the case that not-A was false. Argumentation and debate were desirable. The offering of superior reasons for one's view and of criticisms of opposing views was the means to arriving at the truth. There was a belief in objectivity, or at least in intersubjectivity of the truth.

The postmodern period represents an abandonment of this basically optimistic outlook. Instead of reflecting reality, thought is believed to create it. Instead of there being a pattern of history which thought is to discover, there is a creative role for reason. William Dean has summarized the major tenets of what he terms the new historicists:[2]

1. *A rejection of foundationalism.* The new historicists deny the idea that there are some kinds of foundations beyond history, such as a transcendent God. They share this view with the modernists or the older historicists. They do not believe that it is desirable or even possible to return to a medieval or premodern understanding of reality and specifically of history.

2. William Dean, *History Making History: The New Historicism in American Religious Thought* (Albany: State University of New York Press, 1988), pp. 6–7.

2. *A rejection of realism.* The new historicists deny the existence of any realities independent of human experience. There are no objective universals for humans to discover and understand.
3. *A rejection of the idea of universal psychological factors.* The new historicists deny the idea that certain subjective characteristics are inherent in all persons. This contradicts such widely different views as those of Immanuel Kant and Sigmund Freud.
4. *A radical pluralism.* This is understandable since there are no universals beyond the particulars of history to which to appeal. Although there are generalizations from experience, they should not be thought of as anything more than that. They are mere abstractions, attempts to describe the particulars of the world as one experiences it, but not actual objects that exist in their own right.
5. *Pragmatism.* Since there are no absolute or objective factors, verification in some absolute sense is not possible. Rather, pragmatism is the order of the day. With the elimination of realism, there obviously cannot be a correspondence theory of truth. That is to say, the truth is not a quality of ideas that accurately reflect that to which they refer; rather, the truth is whatever leads to the most satisfactory consequences.
6. *Interpretive imagination.* Almost as a corollary of the preceding tenets, there is what Dean calls "interpretive imagination." Instead of simply discovering or abstracting ideas from something within or beyond history, the individual imagination creates its own ideas to make sense of history. These ideas are a genuine contribution to history rather than something extracted from it.[3]

This mood, for that is what it really is, or postmodernism, is probably best epitomized by the French movement known as deconstruction. Associated especially with the name of Jacques Derridá, who was influenced by Martin Heidegger, deconstruction represents a negation of much of what was found within the modern period. Existentialism, with its strong antirationalism and its emphasis upon will, had anticipated deconstructive postmodernism. Here truth was not primarily a function of correct ideas, but of inward subjectivity. The antirationalism led either to a despair, an abandonment of hope, or to a subjective leap which not only denied the rational but embraced its contradictory. Georg Hegel's thought, with his characteristic emphasis upon the nonpermanence of events and qualities, which in the dialectic are swal-

3. Ibid., p. 7.

lowed up, together with their antitheses, into syntheses, also contributed to postmodernism.

Of earlier approximations to this mood theologically, the closest in many ways was the Death of God theology, which flourished very briefly in the mid-1960s. One of its proponents, Thomas J. J. Altizer, is still active, and is quite closely identified with deconstructive theology. According to Altizer's earlier writing, such as *The Gospel of Christian Atheism*, truth is not discovered or tested by rational, logical processes. It is found in a virtually mystical experience, an immediate intuitive grasp of reality. Thus, when on one occasion Altizer was asked to give a basis for his belief that the primordial god became completely immanent, he replied, "Moby Dick." In Altizer's view, Herman Melville's depiction of the great white whale's going down into the water for the final time is a profound portrayal of the process of God's becoming fully immanent within the world and the human race. But this is an answer which one can neither defend nor criticize rationally. It is simply a type of vision, and one either has the vision or does not.

Broader Manifestations of Irrationalism

We need to be aware that in such an environment rational arguments will no longer be the means by which discussions are concluded. Most of us have grown up thinking that being caught in a logical contradiction was a conclusive argument against what one was advocating. In the type of atmosphere we are describing here, however, if we say, "You are contradicting what you said earlier," the reply may simply be, "So what!" There may be laws of logic, but there is no way to enforce them. People cannot be punished for logical fallacies.

And yet people cannot get away completely from logic. For although they may not have to think logically, they do have to live (unless they choose suicide). And at that level difficulty will emerge. For there are practical or pragmatic difficulties which occur when one violates logic. When, for example, one attempts to communicate with others, or to persuade others of one's view, one assumes some sort of objectivity, some realm into which both parties can enter in order to communicate. Here the violation of logic brings serious pragmatic difficulties.

I have a T-shirt which I purchased at an annual meeting of the American Philosophical Association. I sometimes wear it to class when I want to make a particular point about logic. I remove my coat and outer shirt, displaying this T-shirt. On the front are the words, "The sentence on the back of this shirt is false." On the back is the message, "The sentence on the front of this shirt is true." I ask my students whether they like my shirt, and then whether they believe in it. What does one do with statements like that? Or what would you think if I said to you, "The statement I am now uttering is false." Would you believe me or not? And how would you like to take a true-false examination in a course taught by an instructor who makes such statements?

What we are saying is that even people who refuse to accept logic on rational grounds may have to assume it, or else suffer significant consequences. They will be unable to communicate. One of my techniques when dealing with such people is to say, "You are absolutely correct; I disagree with you totally," and then wait silently to see what happens. Thus the practical problem with a position like deconstruction may be more telling than the logical.

There is a broader point that we are making here. To the extent that philosophical and other cultural movements which will become significant in the years ahead are of this subjective nature, theological evaluation may have to rely more upon pragmatic considerations, including practical inviability, than upon rational considerations, such as logical consistency and coherence. This is paralleled in other areas of society as well. In the last few years we have seen the collapse of a whole series of communist governments throughout Eastern Europe and even the dissolution of the Soviet Union. What brought about this virtual demise of communism was not some conclusive intellectual refutation of its philosophy, but its hopeless failure, economically and politically. And in a sense that is not surprising, because the appeal of communism has not been primarily intellectual, but practical. The idea of dividing wealth has a powerful appeal to those who have none. It was the discovery that communism created a new aristocracy and enabled them to engage in self-aggrandizement, while greatly curtailing the freedom and initiative of the masses and failing to raise their standard of living, that led to its rejection. It was not that communism was not a plausible explanation of reality, although I believe that is also the case, but that it simply did not work.

If, then, theology must make its case increasingly on pragmatic grounds in the days ahead, perhaps we also need to recognize that human nature, at least as we now find it constituted, is not as rational as we have thought it to be. Theologians have often thought of the image of God in humans as consisting in the reason. Perhaps such a conclusion is not surprising, since theologians are by nature among the more rational members of the human race. And that consideration helps to underscore the point we are making, namely, that one's assessment of matters is affected by the type of person one is and by one's situation in life.

In a sense this should not surprise us. For our theology tells us that we are all sinners, and one major aspect of sin is bias toward oneself.

This self-interest shows itself, for example, in the human tendency to be more easily convinced of those positions which have especially advantageous personal results. And insofar as we as Christians are less than fully sanctified, that is true of us as well.

A friend of mine who is an attorney and also teaches part-time at a law school tells me that law students have one persistent difficulty with the law. Again and again, when various statutes are being discussed, students will raise their hands and say, "But that isn't logical." While acknowledging the correctness of the comment, the instructor has to explain that the illogic makes no difference. Legislators do not vote to pass a particular piece of legislation because it follows rationally from some principles which they have accepted as authoritative, or because it is logically consistent with other existing statutes. They frequently vote on the basis of the lobbying that has gone on, which of course is intended to serve self-interests. And the response of a legislator to a given bit of lobbying may be greatly affected by how it affects the chances of being reelected. In addition, politics frequently operates upon the reciprocal principle "I'll do it for you, because you have done it for me," or "you do it for me, because I have done it for you." Such an approach lies very near the bottom of the scale of moral development as schematized in particular by Lawrence Kohlberg.[4]

These kinds of considerations affect far more segments of life than we may wish to acknowledge. Some years ago a noted dean wrote a book on seminary curricula. He discussed what he termed the aesthetic and the political factors in constructing a curriculum. The aesthetic factors are those which would ensure a good, functional curriculum for the benefit of the students. The political factors, on the other hand, are those which are necessary in order to get a curriculum adopted. Whose courses will be required and whose will be elective, and whether one's favorite course will be required or elective, are highly personal considerations for the faculty. Here personal preferences and even job security may overrule what might otherwise be recognized as the best choice.

Influential in helping to shatter the image of humans as essentially rational beings was Sigmund Freud. He argued that our behavior and, for that matter, our beliefs are not arrived at primarily through rational thought that carefully weighs and evaluates the evidence, options, and consequences. Rather, powerful unconscious forces bear upon our beliefs, decisions, and actions.[5] Whether we agree with his emphasis on

4. See Lawrence Kohlberg, *The Psychology of Moral Development: The Nature and Validity of Moral Stages* (San Francisco: Harper and Row, 1984).

5. Sigmund Freud, "The Anatomy of the Mental Personality," in idem, *New Introductory Lectures on Psychoanalysis* (New York: W. W. Norton, 1933), pp. 82–112.

the role of sexual energy and aggression, his general point is increasingly being recognized as valid. Much more of our activity than we might want to admit is motivated by such considerations as our need for approval, acceptance, and reassurance.

Specific Disciplines

Philosophy

Logic and Linguistic Analysis

When we look at the specific disciplines that will influence theology, we can anticipate a growing role for philosophy in at least two areas—logic and metaphysics. One of the traditional roles of philosophy has been to provide a medium for the expression and conveyance of the theological message. Within the past two centuries this task has been fulfilled by absolute idealism, personal idealism, existentialism, process philosophy, as well as traditional Thomism. At times philosophy has even presented not only the form or vehicle, but the content or the substance of the message itself. This has been particularly true in those periods when the authority of the Bible was not held in especially high esteem. Then the church, needing a message, turned elsewhere for it. I do not think this is likely to happen in the near future—at least the church will not turn to any very formal or organized sense of philosophy. There are, however, several ways in which philosophy is likely to take on a significant role in the years ahead.

One major role which I believe philosophy will have will be in helping to clarify and purify the methods of exegesis. I hope my friends who practice the exegetical art will forgive me if I engage for a bit in analysis and evaluation of their discipline. I hope they will see me as a friend and not an opponent if I point out what seem to me to be some difficulties. If I inflict any wounds in the process, my intention is that they be like the wounds that a surgeon lovingly inflicts to bring healing and strength, rather than like those which an assailant maliciously inflicts to bring suffering and hurt. It is my hope that the exegetes who read my comments have themselves already become aware of the need for some of the ministrations which I am here seeking to introduce.

It is approximately two centuries now since scholars began to apply to the Bible the various techniques of analysis and evaluation which were coming to be used in the study of literature and history. Under the term *biblical criticism* we have seen a wide variety of techniques and procedures, including literary criticism, historical criticism, higher criticism, lower criticism, textual criticism, source criticism, form criticism, tradition criticism, comparative-religion criticism, and numerous others. One variety of critical study has risen to prominence only to be superseded by another type. Within a given type of critical methodology differing schools have competed with one another. Some Christians have seen the contributions of these critical methodologies as extremely helpful in enabling us to determine the meaning of the Bible, while others have seen the entire endeavor as destructive of true faith. The use of symbolic abbreviations and reference to the methodologies as "tools," thus conveying a sense of concreteness and solidity, have frequently given an air of scientific precision to the process. This is no place for a full-scale assessment of the contributions and accomplishments of critical biblical study, which seem to me to be rather considerable. We know a great deal more about the Bible because of these techniques than we would without them. Yet a lack of precision in certain areas seems to place current biblical criticism in a state of considerable confusion, at times approximating what could better be termed chaos.

There is a lack of precision regarding what constitutes proof when one is working with several different possible interpretations of a passage. Frequently the procedure followed is of offering considerations which seem to support one particular theory; this is occasionally accompanied by pointing out considerations which constitute problems for competitive interpretations. But what constitutes establishment of one of these theories as over against the others? Here it seems to me there is often a lack of clarity at best. The difficulty, of course, is not unique to biblical studies. Attorneys attempting to argue their case in court face somewhat the same problem.

Part of the difficulty seems to stem from lack of real understanding of inductive logic. A large number of cases are required to establish probability. If in one hundred cases where A would entail B, we find one hundred cases of B, then it is reasonably safe to assume that we have A. There are two significant problems, however. First, it is possible that C would also entail B, and that C may then be as likely as is A. We must find some other grounds for choosing between them. Second, whenever we have a limited number of cases, perhaps only three or even two, we are working with a much lower degree of probability. Unfortunately, not only do exegetes often work with just a few such cases when they interpret a given passage, but they ordinarily do not attempt to spell out just how many and what these cases are. It would be extremely helpful if exegetes could engage in dialogue and reach agreement on this subject, so that there would be some way to evaluate the various competitive views.

61

Another important insight from inductive logic is that the method of disagreement (a situation where two given variables are both absent) is much more powerful than is the method of agreement (where each of these variables is always accompanied by the other), which we have been especially appealing to here. Thus, if X is accompanied by Y in ten out of ten cases, and then we have a case where X is absent and Y is also absent, we have a powerful argument that X is in some sense the "cause" of Y (with all the difficulties which accompany the use of that word). This is especially true if W and Z are present in all eleven cases. For with the eleventh case we have proof that neither W nor Z nor a combination thereof is the cause of Y.

What we are suggesting here is that if the confusion attaching to exegetical methodology is to be cleared up, there really needs to be some agreement among exegetes as to what constitutes the verification of an interpretation, and with regard to a specific passage, what would establish one interpretation over another. The present state of affairs will probably not go on indefinitely. We may well see two diverging developments. On the one hand, we may see a growing dissatisfaction with all attempts at objective exegesis, and an adoption of some sort of subjective or intuitive approach to understanding a biblical passage. The beginnings of deconstructive exegesis are samples. On the other hand, logicians may make increasing contributions to the discipline, resulting in criticism of the criticism and thus a more truly scientific approach. I suspect that what we will find is the coexistence of these two approaches as competitive schools of thought.

Besides the lack of precision regarding exegetical proof, there is a lack of clarity regarding the presuppositions of the methodology; in fact, there is in some cases a seeming ignorance that such things as presuppositions are even factors. Rudolf Bultmann was explicitly conscious of his presuppositions (at least some of the more significant ones) and openly avowed them. This is true with respect to both his existentialism—his belief that the message of the New Testament is largely to be understood through existential categories—and his naturalism, expressed in the idea that reality is a closed continuum within which certain things can and other things cannot occur.[6] There does not seem to be a similar degree of insight and candor, however, in the work of one of the leading American Bultmannians of the last generation, Norman Perrin. Not acknowledging his presuppositions, he repeatedly seems to put his arguments in the "Have you stopped beating your wife yet?" form. The

6. See Rudolf Bultmann, "The New Testament and Mythology," in Rudolf Bultmann et al., *Kerygma and Myth: A Theological Debate*, ed. Hans Werner Bartsch (New York: Harper and Row, 1961), pp. 1–16.

conclusion is virtually assured by the issues included or excluded from consideration.[7]

We will not give an extensive treatment here to the role of presuppositions, because we will soon address that general issue when we talk about presuppositions in theological (as distinguished from exegetical) methodology. My anticipation is that, as in the matter of exegetical proof, we will eventually begin to see philosophy making a major contribution by helping exegetes see that their differences are in part a function of differing presuppositions. Philosophy will help them to recognize presuppositions both in their own exegesis and in that of others, and to evaluate or vindicate one presupposition (or set of presuppositions) over against another.

This contribution of philosophy should have a salutary effect upon exegesis and thus indirectly upon theology. It will help to reduce pseudoarguments like the one in William James's story of the two men who were arguing about whether a man circling a tree went around a squirrel on the trunk of the tree. They could make no progress, because by "go around" one disputant meant to circle the squirrel directly, that is, with no object intervening between the man and the squirrel at any time, in which case, of course, the man never "went around" the squirrel; while the other disputant meant simply that the man would first be to the north, then to the west, then to the south, and then to the east of the squirrel, in which case the man did "go around" the squirrel.[8] Philosophy both defines terms and isolates assumptions.

Philosophical analysis also calls attention to the failure to draw parallels between the methodology used in biblical studies and that used in other disciplines. In theory, if the discipline of biblical studies utilizes the same method as do various secular disciplines, then it should be possible to cross-check the method in some of these other fields.

One rather well known example is given by C. S. Lewis. A reviewer of a collection of Lewis's essays has singled out a particular essay as the only one in which the author obviously had no real interest. In actuality, the very reverse was the case. Lewis observes that biblical critics are doing much the same type of analysis of the writings of the biblical authors, and then he makes a most telling comment: "The biblical critics, whatever reconstructions they devise, can never be crudely proved

---

7. See, e.g., Norman Perrin, *Rediscovering the Teaching of Jesus* (New York: Harper and Row, 1976); idem, *The Resurrection According to Matthew, Mark, and Luke* (Philadelphia: Fortress, 1977).

8. William James, "What Pragmatism Means," in idem, *Pragmatism* (New York: Meridian, 1955), pp. 41–62.

wrong. St. Mark is dead.["]9 If biblical study uses the objective methodology employed in other disciplines, then it should be possible to submit that methodology to a test.

When I taught a course on the theology of C. S. Lewis, we read his comments about biblical criticism very early on. I then proposed to the students that we perform an experiment. At the beginning of the course they had been asked to write a two-page essay summarizing their understanding of Lewis's thought. Each student was to keep a journal that would be periodically updated with new insights. Each journal would eventually be developed into some sort of overview incorporating the different understandings from the different periods. We would then submit three or four of the final reports to a New Testament professor who was a rabid advocate of form criticism, and ask him to apply his methodology—classifying, stratifying, and evaluating—to what had been written. The students were enthusiastic about the idea. The professor in question dismissed the idea flatly, even though it gave him an opportunity to demonstrate the utility of his method. Only when critical methodology is submitted to such scrutiny will we be able to speak even in modest tones of what is now sometimes referred to as "the assured results of critical scholarship."

An autobiographical note may shed some additional light upon this subject. In my biblical studies in seminary I really was not exposed in any depth to critical methodology. After seminary I completed a master's degree in philosophy, and my doctoral program in theology included a minor in philosophy as well. In a course on Plato at the University of Chicago and a course on Aristotle at Northwestern University, we were introduced to the form-critical approach to their thought. Neither of the instructors gave much credence to such an approach, rejecting it on logical grounds. This was my immediate background when my doctoral program finally came to an in-depth study of biblical criticism. I still smile when I hear a professor of biblical studies who has not gone through such rigors as I experienced in my philosophy courses dismiss as precritical or uncritical those who do not follow the form-critical methodology.

A final analytical contribution of philosophy will be the isolation and identification of the presuppositions in various theologies. We spoke earlier about this role with respect to exegesis. We also want to note it in the broader matter of constructing a theology.

A fair amount of theological discussion seems to proceed on the assumption that there is a set of facts with which all theologies are to

---

9. C. S. Lewis, "Modern Theology and Biblical Criticism," in idem, *Christian Reflections*, ed. Walter Hooper (Grand Rapids: Eerdmans, 1967), p. 161.

deal, and that the difference between them is the inclusiveness and seriousness with which they treat these facts. It is assumed that there is a common starting point or perspective for all theologies. But if this is the case, why are there such radically different conclusions? I recall a philosophy class in which a student raised the question whether the variety of views did not suggest that truth is subjective. The instructor's response was that the last analytical comment one can make before drawing so radical a conclusion is that the different parties might be talking about different things. I would suggest another possibility, namely, that the different parties are looking at the same things from different perspectives. That is to say, different assumptions or presuppositions may separate us. We do not all start from the same point.

One of the tasks which I believe philosophy will help perform in the coming years is the identification of presuppositions. Some of them may be philosophical, some theological; some may be methodological, others substantive. Recognizing presuppositions is an analytical function, and here philosophical skills will make a major contribution. In evaluating evidence we must ask, "What would this evidence look like if I approached it from this perspective rather than that?" We must, so to speak, think our way into the ideological skin of Eastern persons, learning to look upon life and the world the way they do, and then ask whether the system that follows from their set of presuppositions makes better sense of reality than does the system that follows from our own presuppositions. As we come to realize the need for true dialogue rather than merely haranguing at one another from set positions, such analysis will be seen as essential.

Metaphysics

I believe there will also be increasing attention to metaphysical issues in the years ahead. During the first two-thirds to three-fourths of the twentieth century, there was a strong aversion to metaphysics in theology. This aversion came from several sources. One was the antimetaphysical mood created by logical positivism, and to a lesser degree by later varieties of analytical philosophy. It was an age in which normative judgments were restricted to issues pertaining to the proper use of language, which itself was restricted, at least in the later developments, to ordinary language, or the way people actually used language, rather than some ideal language or specified language of given roles. Here ethics became metaethics rather than normative ethics, and metaphysics became metametaphysics. The other major philosophical objection to metaphysics came from pragmatism and allied philosophies, which held that some of the ultimate questions are unanswerable and that it really does not matter that they are, for there is no practical difference between the proffered answers. Theological objection came from Karl Barth, who insisted upon the autonomy of theology, refusing to allow it to be assimilated to any other discipline, including philosophy. Theology did not need to meet the canons of any nonrevealed discipline, nor could any of its content be derived from natural discovery by human beings.

In recent years, however, philosophers have realized that ultimate questions about the nature of reality have to be dealt with; so they have begun modest attempts to deal with specific problems, and even to offer some generalized characterizations of reality. One school of thought, process philosophy, offers a full-scale metaphysics, although of a quite different sort from what is traditionally espoused in the West.

I believe that theologians will be more active in the realm of metaphysics in the next few years. This will be occasioned by two factors. One is the presence of process theology. This is a thoroughly metaphysical theology, and responding to it will require a metaphysical treatment. The other is the growing awareness that many of the issues that theology deals with assume a metaphysics. We can no longer afford to have these matters decided by mere assumption. Theologians will seek to develop some limited areas metaphysically; eventually they will also develop larger-scale metaphysical systems.

Cultural Anthropology

Like philosophy, cultural anthropology will make increasing contributions to theology. Today one of the strong emphases in theological education is globalization, and that emphasis will increase. In addition, the growing diversity of American culture and the shrinking of our world, which means increased contact with persons of other cultures, will force us into an awareness that some of our theological thinking may be at least in part a reflection of our nationality, race, social class, age, or gender. In discussing Baptist polity, including local church autonomy and the priesthood of the believer, a Japanese pastor once said to an American professor, "Your view of Baptist polity is derived more from the Bill of Rights than it is from the New Testament." Whether he was correct is not of concern here. What is worth observing is that we have a tendency to read our political ideas, whether American, Japanese, Hungarian, Brazilian, or whatever, into our understanding of the Bible. The insights derived from practical experiences like the one just described and from the formal discipline of cultural anthropology will enrich our theological understanding by helping us see that there are other ways to view matters.

Two recent experiences have especially helped confirm this truth to me. In a chapel service a woman professor from another school spoke on

David and Bathsheba. She developed the biblical account from the perspective of Bathsheba, giving the woman's point of view. Many of us males in the audience saw truths in that passage that we had never seen before, not because they were not there, but because the limitation of our male outlook had prevented us from noticing them. Similarly, a pastor and professor from Argentina who lectured at the same institution gave us some insights which those of us who had spent our entire lives in the northern half of the Western Hemisphere had not seen before. Some of what he said was at points quite critical of United States policy, and was not appreciated by every person present. He did us an immeasurable service, however, by calling our attention to another way of viewing the world.

Eventually the seminary where the two events I have just described occurred made the decision to create a new faculty position, director of multicultural affairs, to be staffed by a minority person as part of an expanding emphasis upon a more diverse community. It is widely assumed that the major effect of this position will be on the minority students, but I suspect there will be an even greater contribution to the Anglos on the faculty and in the student body. I hope that the outlook of the director of multicultural affairs in tandem with an increase in the number of minority students will make the rest of the community more aware of their provincialism.

From what we have been saying one might draw a relativistic conclusion, namely, that how we view life and the world is totally dependent upon who and what we are, and that the truth is therefore different for different people. This need not follow, however. To say that there are different ways of seeing things is not to say that they are all equally true; rather, it is to say that we may have seen only part of the truth. Problems arise when we absolutize our own view. What male scholars see in the biblical story of David and Bathsheba may well be true, but it is not the whole of the truth.

There is, of course, the danger that the application of anthropology will lead to some sort of absolute relativism which denies the existence of objective truth. That will, of course, place the participants in intercultural dialogue in the sort of practical difficulty we described earlier (pp. 57–58). But an intense effort to apply cultural anthropology properly will assure that we obtain the truth and as much of the truth as possible.

Psychology

I believe we will also see an increase in the role of psychology, followed by a reaction. Initially, the recent introduction of psychology into the church came more in terms of finding ways of applying the content of the Christian message than of defining that content. There were, for example, people who believed that God is all-powerful and watches providentially over the world, but who could not bring this truth to bear upon their own emotions and attitudes. They were anxious and distraught about the future. There were others who fully believed in the gracious atoning work of Jesus Christ, but nonetheless were ridden with guilt because their belief in forgiveness did not connect with their actual feelings. Pastoral counseling in those days often consisted of trying to find biblical passages which applied to the situation and sharing them with the counselee. The realization that humans are not fully rational and that personal problems are not to be dealt with on a purely cognitive basis did not come easily. Conservative Christian groups were among the slowest to adopt the insights of psychology into how the human personality functions. When seminaries first began to search for persons trained in psychology to teach pastoral counseling, the process was often a long and difficult one. Very few had been trained in both theology and psychology.

That situation has changed rapidly and radically. Now many evangelical seminarians are preparing themselves with study in psychology and cognate fields. For a time in the early 1970s, more seminary students were interested in careers in counseling than in pastoring a local church. The Theological Schools Inventory of matriculating students showed a significant recent shift in motivation from evangelism to a ministry of helping and healing. The popularity of books on the application of psychology to the Christian life further attests this trend. The Christian counseling movement is a large and rapidly growing development.[10]

Somewhere in the process a change in the role of psychology has taken place. Rather than simply being a means for applying the Christian message, psychology has in some circles taken on the role of contributing at least in part to the content of that message. This can be seen in two shifts of orientation. First is a shift from a theocentric to an anthropocentric focus. A manifestation is the emphasis on self-esteem. In some circles talk about sin, guilt, unworthiness is considered negative and demeaning, destructive of self-esteem. Building up the goodness, worth, and value of the individual is commended instead. "I'm O.K., you're O.K.," becomes virtually "I'm O.K., I'm O.K."

Christian theology, when true to its biblical roots, has always been concerned with the self-worth of the individual. It recognizes the unfor-

---

10. Tim Stafford, "The Therapeutic Revolution," *Christianity Today* 37.6 (May 17, 1993): 24–32. Compare a simultaneous article in a secular newsmagazine—Erica E. Goode with Betsy Wagner, "Does Psychotherapy Work?" *U.S. News and World Report*, 24 May 1993, pp. 56–65.

tunate effects which a poor self-image has on a person's life and on one's relationships with others, even with God. The basis for the sense of value and importance and dignity has been theological, however, rather than psychological. The great truth that every human being is made in the image and likeness of God, and thus is different from all other creatures, is an enormous source of self-worth. In addition, the Christian doctrines of incarnation and atonement, which say that God so highly valued each human that he was willing to come to earth himself in the person of Jesus of Nazareth and die to provide redemption from sin for every one who will believe on him, also place an enormous value upon each human. That each individual is important to God is Jesus' emphasis in the parable of the lost sheep (Luke 15:3–7) and his teaching that God watches over each of us with a concern greater than that which he has for sparrows (Matt. 10:29–31). He has entrusted each of us with the work of his kingdom and the privilege of being his ambassadors and representatives (e.g., Matt. 28:18–20). Now the value of an assessment, the significance of a compliment, depends upon the stature and the knowledge of the person making the assessment. To know how God, the sovereign Creator and Lord of the entire universe, regards us is a great source of self-worth. We have an infinite value conveyed upon us by God himself. We are precious to him.

By contrast the psychological basis for pursuing self-worth is the goodness and greatness of the human being. Note that this approach also represents a shift from indirect to direct means of satisfying human need. One of the principles which underlay much of Jesus' teaching was that satisfaction does not come from seeking it directly, but as a by-product of doing God's will. So, for example, he said, "For whoever wants to save his life will lose it, but whoever loses his life for me and for the gospel will save it" (Mark 8:35). He said to those who were worried about food, clothing, and other material provisions, "Seek first his kingdom and his righteousness, and all these things shall be yours as well" (Matt. 6:33 RSV). Inasmuch as this is a principle of Jesus' teaching and of the structure of the kingdom, attempts to obtain self-esteem will ultimately fail. They will, indeed, be self-defeating.

The second shift of orientation to which psychology has contributed is a diminished concern for other persons. For many the new emphasis upon wholeness is also a shift to concern for one's own needs. In a sense the psychology that we are referring to here is evidence of a generation gap. Much has been written about the baby boomers and their effect upon organized religion and the life of the church. One phenomenon that has been observed is that they are not joiners; they do not commit themselves to organizations. They are not interested in the church as a worshiping community with a mission to fulfil. Rather, they are looking for a place where their needs will be fulfilled. This is what humanistic or naturalistic psychology emphasizes. It is certainly not indifferent to the societal dimensions of human experience, but it does emphasize the individual self to the relative neglect of concern for others. Paul, on the other hand, using Jesus as an example, pleaded with believers not to concern themselves only with their own needs, but also with the needs of others (Phil. 2:1–5). This is appropriate, since Jesus himself taught his disciples that a man has no greater love than to lay down his life for his friends (John 15:13).

I anticipate that we will continue to see the growth of a psychology based on humanism and centered on the individual. This will be true not only of the more liberal churches, where psychological and emotional wholeness has taken the place of a gospel of personal regeneration, but also of the more evangelical churches. At some point, however, there will be a reaction akin to Karl Barth's early in the twentieth century.

The subjective, human-centered theology that began with Friedrich Schleiermacher had kept developing through the nineteenth century. The increasing anthropocentrism reached the point where, as Ludwig Feuerbach correctly pointed out, God was regarded as simply man's projection of himself.[11] Man had, in other words, created God in his own image. Then in August 1914 ninety-four German intellectuals signed a statement endorsing the war policy of Kaiser Wilhelm. Several of Barth's theology professors were among the signatories. About that time Ernst Troeltsch shifted from the faculty of theology to the faculty of philosophy. Barth saw Troeltsch's abandonment of theology as the logical outcome of the anthropocentrism of liberal theology. The intellectuals' endorsement of the war and Troeltsch's action were to Barth indications of the utter impoverishment of the theological tradition in which he had been raised.[12] His reaction strongly emphasized the transcendence of God, the uniqueness of Jesus Christ, and the sinfulness of human beings. Barth insisted that theology is an autonomous science not answerable to the canons of other disciplines, and that revelation is separate from culture in general. While his reaction may have been excessive, it did reverse the positive, optimistic anthropocentrism of the time.

I anticipate that we will see a similar reversal. There will be a shorter wait this time, for the cycles of church life and theology are becoming shorter and shorter. It may come upon us in the next ten years or so.

An overreaction could of course occur. It is possible that all types of psychology will be discarded, and we will turn to a purely biblical the-

11. Ludwig Feuerbach, *The Essence of Christianity* (New York: Harper, 1957).
12. Karl Barth, *God, Grace and Gospel* (Edinburgh: Oliver and Boyd, 1959), pp. 57–58.

ology which makes the Bible speak even to matters which it does not address. That would be a great loss, quite frankly, costing us the benefits that come from the insights of a properly based psychology. What I hope will occur instead is that a more biblically based and theologically sound psychology will be retained. It is notable that some rather secular sources (e.g., Karl Menninger's *Whatever Became of Sin?*) have made a few hints along this line. The insights into human nature provided by psychology ought to be developed in the light of biblically based presuppositions, such as the nature of human goodness and of sin and the place of self-esteem. I believe, however, that it will be necessary for the trend toward a more secular psychology to go further in the shaping of theology before the reaction occurs.

Other Behavioral Sciences

The final area to be examined briefly is the tendency to incorporate other behavioral sciences into the life of the church, sometimes to the virtual exclusion of the work of the Holy Spirit. We see this tendency, for example, in the area of marketing. At one point in the past the church was loath to utilize any scientific techniques in carrying out its work. Gradually, however, the church has become aware that as a social institution it is affected by some of the same dynamics as are the other institutions within society. Thus today marketing research is utilized to determine the best location for a new church, the name, the style of architecture, the logo, slogan, and other distinctive features. This has been a needed corrective to the somewhat prophetic approach sometimes utilized in the past, where someone (often a leader with strong personal charisma) reputedly received a message from the Lord telling the group what to do. Ideally, the new techniques should supplement the usual ways of determining the Lord's will, including prayer, Bible study, and meditation. In practice, there has been an increasing tendency to regard the scientific surveys as virtual replacements for the more direct and extraordinary guidance of the Holy Spirit.

One area in which the growing influence of the behavioral sciences is apparent is that of calling into special service. We have seen a gradual trend, documented by the Theological Schools Inventory, away from special leading ("God told me he wanted me in the ministry") and toward general leading ("I seem to have abilities and interests which match those of successful ministers"). Much pain has undoubtedly been avoided by counseling issuing from behavioral testing. Similarly, pastors and congregations alike have benefited from studies in the field of conflict management. So we must not depreciate the value of the social sciences. But we also need to be wary of the tendency which my doctoral mentor described with tongue in cheek, "For two thousand years we had to depend upon the Holy Spirit to determine who was called into the ministry; now that we have the Minnesota Multiphasic Personality Inventory, we don't need the Holy Spirit anymore."

A similar trend is also at work in the area of missions. David Hesselgrave devotes an entire chapter of his book *Today's Choices for Tomorrow's Mission* to what he terms the "science orientation." He indicates that there are three sources of missiology: revelation (in the Scriptures), research (in the social sciences), and reflection (upon the missionary experience). The tendency, he observes, has been increasingly toward informing missiology from the social sciences. Comparison of articles and book reviews in the *Evangelical Missions Quarterly* and the *International Review of Missions* suggests that this tendency has been more marked among evangelical than among conciliar missiologists.[13]

I suspect that we will see a continued dependence upon the social sciences to the gradual exclusion of more direct ways of God's working; this dependence may at times even contradict the clear teaching of the Scriptures themselves. Then, at some point, we will see a reaction in the form of an insistence that God is able to work outside of the processes that can be plotted by scientific means.

13. David Hesselgrave, *Today's Choices for Tomorrow's Mission: An Evangelical Perspective on Trends and Issues in Missions* (Grand Rapids: Zondervan, 1988), pp. 139–42 and appendix 2.

4

General Trends in Theology

Having discussed cultural and religious trends as well as the role of nontheological disciplines, we now need to look briefly at some of the major general trends in the field of theology. These are developments which will affect the very framework and each of the specific parts of theology.

Loss of the Antithesis

One development which has been occurring for some time will in all likelihood continue and become even more accentuated. It is the breakdown of the sense of antithesis between what might be called the sacred and the secular or profane. Throughout the history of Christianity there has been contrast, even a sense of opposition, between what was most important to Christians and the way of the world. This contrast has taken many different forms and borne many different labels.

The Traditional View

In the very earliest period of Christianity, that is, in New Testament times, the sense of opposition was strong. In John's Gospel we find the imagery of darkness and light. These are obviously two opposed principles engaged in virtual combat with one another. Jesus expressed the antithesis in several ways. He said that we cannot serve two masters, God and money. We will inevitably love one and hate the other. He contrasted himself, the Son of the heavenly Father, with those Jews whose father was the devil (not Abraham, as they claimed). When he spoke to Nicodemus about being born again, he contrasted that which, being born of the flesh, is therefore flesh and that which is born of the Spirit and therefore is spirit. Paul expressed the opposition through the negative imagery of the world, the positive principle being less clearly labeled. In John's Epistles and the Apocalypse there is a contrast between Christ and the antichrist. Throughout all of the Bible the struggle between God and Satan is prominent.

In the Book of Acts the contrast frequently takes concrete form. People are faced with the question of whether to obey God or humans, with the clear implication being that it is either/or rather than both/and. The correct choice is also clear. Although government is not necessarily inherently evil, it is other than God, and is to be rejected whenever it takes or stipulates a course of action other than what he wants his people to follow.

The concept of antithesis was developed in a number of ways during the course of church history as well. In Augustine's thought, for example, there were the two cities, that of God and that of this world.[1] Each had its own ways and was opposed to the other. Because Augustine lived after Constantine had virtually made Christianity the official religion of the empire, one might think that the antithesis between the two would have collapsed, but this was not the case. Martin Luther expressed the contrast as being between the two kingdoms.[2] In many cases the antithesis was thought of as largely political in nature. On the one hand were the believers, a small minority lacking in political and

---

1. Augustine *The City of God* 11–22.
2. E.g., Martin Luther, "Temporal Authority: To What Extent It Should Be Obeyed," in vol. 55 of *Luther's Works*, ed. Jaroslav Pelikan and Helmut T. Lehmann (Philadelphia: Muhlenberg, 1962), p. 88.

other types of power; on the other hand was the state or society in some other form. Among the more radical elements of the Reformation, the Anabaptists, for example, the antithesis often seemed to take the form of church versus state.[3]

The belief in antithesis had a number of theological ramifications. One was the sense of the otherness of God. God was separate from the creation, which was precisely what the word denotes. The creation had not always existed, nor had it come into being through an emanation or outflow from the divine nature. God had willed it to be, and had brought it into existence without the use of preexisting materials. It thus was other than God, both in identity and also in nature. Even in the case of those members of the creation that God made most like himself, the angels, which are pure spirit, and humans, who are made in his own image and likeness, there is a similarity, but not an identity of essence or nature. If one were to diagram the scale of being, with God at the top and the lowest type of inanimate matter at the bottom, there would be several places where a horizontal line should be drawn to separate types of beings which are fundamentally different. The boldest line would be drawn between God and humans, for that is the major gap qualitatively. This metaphysical otherness means that however much we might be favored by God with his grace, and however we might grow in obedience to and imitation of him, we never will cross that line separating divine from human. We will always be human beings; we will never become God.

There is another implication of the otherness of God. Idolatry is strictly forbidden. The second command, "You shall not make any idol," is in a sense a subpoint of the first command, "You shall have no other gods besides me." For to make from created material any likeness of God is to run the danger that the likeness will become not merely an aid to the worship of God, but an object of worship in itself. And this God strictly prohibits.

God's otherness also means that although the created world serves as a revelation of him, it is an incomplete and imperfect revelation, for it is an impress, as it were, in a fundamentally different medium. The revelation in creation is necessarily incomplete when compared to the revelation in the person of Jesus Christ, the incarnate Son of God, who thus revealed what God is by nature.

Akin to the distinction in revelations is the distinction of what were later to be called nature and supernature. In addition to this created universe, which is governed by immanent laws (believed to have been

3. William R. Estep, *The Anabaptist Story* (Nashville: Broadman, 1963), pp. 175–96.

implanted by the Creator), there is a realm outside and "above" it. This realm, the locus of God, is not governed by the laws affecting nature. What happens within the created or natural realm can, however, be affected from without, that is, by the supernatural realm. There are occurrences within nature which cannot be accounted for by any known forces or laws within nature and which in a sense appear to contradict those laws. These events, generally referred to as miracles, represent the action of God within this natural realm, introducing his power in ways that would not otherwise occur. They cannot be reduced to nor explained as merely natural factors.

The dualism is not only metaphysical, but also ethical. In the traditional view of the antithesis this created world is understood as sinful, or as having somehow fallen from the pattern God intended for it. Political institutions are regarded as suspect, because they are the manifestations of the will and working of fallen human beings, and thus project in larger fashion humankind's rebellion and willfulness as over against God. Human nature, in what is now its natural state, is not in continuity with God's moral will. It lacks the integrity with which the human race was created. It has been fractured by sin's effects. Consequently, the natural thinking of human beings is not necessarily in keeping with God's truth, and must be regarded with an element of suspicion. One's own rationality is also so affected that what seems reasonable is not necessarily true, and is to be rejected when it conflicts with God's revealed truth.

Further, the ethical antithesis means that there is a need for a supernatural transformation of human nature. Salvation is not something that comes naturally, through simply following to the best of our ability the divine precepts, or carrying out to the fullest degree the dictates of our higher nature. Not only are we likely to judge incorrectly what is right and what is wrong, but we are not naturally inclined to do that which is right. Indeed, Jesus' clear statement to Nicodemus, "You must be born again" (John 3:3), and his strong contrast between that which is of the flesh and that which is of the Spirit, indicate the need for supernatural transformation. Thus the idea that salvation involves regeneration is a very vital corollary of the fundamental antithesis. Even where regeneration is believed to involve the use of a natural substance such as the water of baptism, that substance is not thought to be the actual source of the regenerative power, but only a means employed by God.

Finally, ethical antithesis carries implications for the understanding of sanctification. To a large extent the natural conduct, the institutions, and the values of the human race are thought to be corrupted. So withdrawal or separation from the world is part of the paradigm of sanctification and Christian living. This has taken widely differing forms:

Roman Catholic monks have withdrawn from the ordinary circles of society to preserve themselves holy to God; some conservative Christians abstain from the use of certain substances (alcohol, tobacco) and avoid certain places (theaters, pool halls). This is a rigid interpretation of James's call to keep oneself from being polluted by the world, which is part of his definition of true religion (James 1:27).

Now perhaps we should pause for a few moments to observe how the traditional view works out in practice. I will give illustrations from my own experience in high school and college. I suspect readers with a conservative background and upbringing may be able to identify with some of the things that I describe.

As a young person I was taught that worldliness included certain practices which were clearly wrong. Not only theft, lying, and premarital sex, but smoking, drinking, and attendance at motion pictures were taboo. We also believed that there were systems of thought opposed to the things of God. A considerable amount of learning stemmed from atheistic premises, and could be expected to conflict with the divinely revealed doctrines and practices taught in the Bible, in which case the secular learning was wrong. Higher education was not wrong; it was very highly prized in our circles. But anyone who attended a secular institution had to be on guard against teachings which were anti-Christian and could threaten one's religious faith. Erroneous beliefs were inevitable in this world because the minds of human beings in rebellion against God were blinded by sin. No matter how intellectual they might be, they were not truly rational, because their intellects were distorted by the fall.

We were to be careful in our affiliations also. We should not be unequally yoked with unbelievers, a principle which was usually interpreted to mean two things: we were not to enter into business partnerships with non-Christians, nor to marry anyone who was not a true believer. Human emotions being what they are, this usually meant that it was safest not even to date non-Christians. We followed this pattern quite carefully. We avoided the taboo practices and the persons who engaged in them. Our high-school student body could be neatly sorted into the Christians, the non-Christians, and a group who lived clean lives but were not part of an evangelical church (they were frequently Lutherans in that Scandinavian county). We did not date the non-Christians, even though some were better-looking and more interesting than the Christians.

At the University of Minnesota, where I had transferred from a small Christian college, I was a philosophy major, with minors in psychology and sociology. These were the disciplines with the greatest potential for conflict with the biblical teachings on which I had based my theology. I enrolled expecting to have my conservative faith challenged, and I was not disappointed. On the very first day of my abnormal-psychology course, the instructor recited one of the old clichés: "If you think you have a soul, hang it on one of those hooks along the wall; we don't believe in such things here." And in a philosophy class entitled "From Puritanism to Pragmatism" the instructor posed in full seriousness the old conundrum of whether God can create a rock so large that he cannot lift it. Logical positivism was the orthodoxy of that philosophy department, and the psychology faculty were, without exception, behaviorists. I found frequent challenges to my beliefs, but I was prepared because I had expected that what I would hear would not be the whole truth. I supplemented my reading with healthy doses of apologetics, attended Inter-Varsity Christian Fellowship regularly, and kept active in church. I worked very hard at attempting to integrate, really integrate, what I was learning in psychology classes and what the Bible teaches about human nature.

The Nineteenth-Century Assimilation of Sacred and Secular

With the nineteenth century came an increasing trend toward eliminating the antithesis between sacred and secular. One of the major forces in this development was Georg Hegel's dialectic. Instead of the Aristotelian square of opposition in logic, Hegel stressed the merging or blending of thesis and antithesis into a synthesis, which gathered up elements of both into a higher unity. There also was a breakdown of the idea that certain historical events were unique. Jesus of Nazareth, for example, was not thought of as the unique incarnation of God in humanity, but as an illustration of an ongoing and repeated process. The singular significance of other such events was diminished, and the separateness of any special history was dissolved into the entire stream of history. Everything, historical and otherwise, was absorbed into a great system.[4]

Voices of Protest

The one nineteenth-century voice protesting the assimilation of sacred and secular was Søren Kierkegaard. He insisted emphatically upon antithesis. Either/or, he asserted, is the road to heaven; both/and is the way to hell. Unlike Hegel's system, in which all antitheses are ultimately synthesized, religious truth is in Kierkegaard's scheme distin-

---

4. Georg W. F. Hegel, *Lectures on the Philosophy of Religion*, 3 vols. (New York: Humanities, 1962), vol. 3, p. 2.

guished by paradox; and subjective passion of commitment, not objective correctness, is the goal and the sign of truth.[5] Kierkegaard did not make a major impact upon the stream of Christian thought in the nineteenth century. His primary influence was to come later, in the twentieth century. Nineteenth-century theology developed further along universalistic, naturalistic lines. This was true even of those philosophies that were classified as idealisms, but were not supernaturalistic.

It was Karl Barth who spoke most emphatically against the elimination of antithesis. He did so by insisting that the methodology of theology was not to be simply the application of some universal methodology found in many disciplines. Theology must have its own methodology appropriate to its objects of study. Further, it does not have to answer to universal canons of rationality imposed from without. Theology is scientific, in the broad sense of that term, but it is autonomous.[6]

Barth also reintroduced the antithesis by redefining revelation. To be sure, Barth joined the nineteenth century in applying the methods of literary and historical criticism to the Bible, just like any other book. But he broke with the mood of his age by refusing to identify revelation with the Bible's content, or with factual or representational information of any kind. Revelation comes through and in connection with the words of the Bible, but it is not identified with those words as such. Since revelation is distinguished from the literature which criticism studies, criticism does not really work on revelation.

Barth separated God from the world in several ways. The extreme transcendence of God means that there is no continuity between him and the human, as liberalism had thought.[7] We cannot really capture him with our language.[8] He cannot be known through natural means or by our powers of reason. Natural theology is an impossibility.[9] God is totally free. He is not subject to nor governed by any of the laws which control the world. He is therefore not predictable in his actions, nor is he subject to our desires and whims.

Barth also reintroduced the antithesis by making religious concepts and categories unique. For example, sin had been treated as an ethical concept, as wrong actions which violated socially defined standards of

5. Søren Kierkegaard, *Concluding Unscientific Postscript* (Princeton, N.J.: Princeton University Press, 1941).

6. Karl Barth, *Church Dogmatics*, 2d ed. (Edinburgh: T. and T. Clark, 1975), vol. 1, part 1, §2.

7. Karl Barth, *The Humanity of God* (Richmond: John Knox, 1960), pp. 42–43.

8. Karl Barth, *The Word of God and the Word of Man* (New York: Harper, 1957), pp. 198–217.

9. Karl Barth, "No!" in Emil Brunner and Karl Barth, *Natural Theology* (London: Geoffrey Bles, 1946).

correct behavior. Instead, Barth treated sin as a religious category, actions against God.[10]

One might say that Barth reintroduced the antithesis that had characterized the orthodoxy of an earlier period, but his version of the concepts was somewhat different. For example, having redefined revelation, he also viewed the relationship between the Bible and revelation not as simple or univocal, but as dialectical. This was, indeed, a *neo*-orthodoxy. It was the introduction of a neo-antithesis, as it were.

A New Integration of Sacred and Secular

In time, Barth's sharp antitheses, which some judged to be overreactions to the liberal theology and idealistic philosophy of the nineteenth century, began to soften. This can be documented by reading through the successive volumes of the *Church Dogmatics*, or more quickly and easily by reading his essay *The Humanity of God*. Also softening the antithesis was the fact that those events which had given plausibility to his "theology of crisis," as some termed it—the two world wars, the Holocaust, and economic depression—were beginning to fade not only from people's consciousness, but even from their memories. A more integrationist type of theology began to develop.

This shift from the antithesis is signaled in several different ways. It is seen in the growing study of religion, including Christianity, by various sciences. The Society for the Scientific Study of Religion is an example. So is the accelerating trend for dissertations in such fields as psychology and sociology to investigate religion. Further, the absorption of large bodies of material from the behavioral sciences into Christian preaching and practice is more reminiscent of nineteenth-century liberalism than of Barthianism.

This shift toward integration of the sacred and secular is evident across all segments of the theological spectrum, but is probably less apparent on the left or liberal edge, where there already was considerable approximation. It is on the right or conservative edge, where the contrast was sharpest, that the shift is most clearly seen. A number of recent studies have documented this shift among evangelicals. Some of the earlier work in this area, which was done by Richard Quebedeaux, was rather anecdotal in nature. At times, in fact, his books read almost like a gossip column. Although not especially scientific in methodology, his writings did make contact with reality. His first book, *The Young Evangelicals* (1974), described with some admiration the changes both

10. Thomas F. Torrance, *Karl Barth: An Introduction to His Early Theology, 1910–1931* (Naperville, Ill.: Allenson, 1962), pp. 65–67.

in belief and practice that some of the younger evangelicals, as contrasted with older or establishment evangelicals, were making. The sequel, *The Worldly Evangelicals* (1978), was somewhat more reserved, at times concerned. He acknowledges that he is no longer as optimistic or uncritical of the evangelical left as he once was. It is not that he considers Christianity to be either a liberal or a conservative matter, but that it is to be inherently radical, as Romans 12:1–2 indicates.[11] He sees evangelicalism as losing its radical nature, adopting and assimilating the general culture and its values.

What Quebedeaux had described in an admittedly unscientific fashion, James Davison Hunter treated from a more systematic perspective in his book *Evangelicalism: The Coming Generation*. Although his selection of groups to include in the sampling may be questioned, and the theological analysis of the issues and responses may be inadequate at times, there is considerable value in his work, which represents a survey of students at nine evangelical liberal arts colleges and seven evangelical seminaries. He is careful to point out that the book should not be understood primarily as attempting to predict the future, since attitudes are changed following college by such circumstances as marriage, parenthood, occupation, and place of residence. Nonetheless, his study contains considerable indication of a shift, especially in matters of lifestyle, but also on such issues as whether salvation is to be found exclusively in Jesus Christ. Hunter notes that the process of "tradition conforming to the cognitive and normative assumptions of the modern world view" has been found in the theological enterprise generally, and that, though relatively new to evangelicalism, the process is now clearly there as well.[12] One particularly pungent statement sums up well the tendency in the more conservative circles:

> In a word, the Protestant legacy of austerity and ascetic self-denial is virtually obsolete in the larger Evangelical culture and is nearly extinct for a large percentage of the coming generation of Evangelicals. The caricatures of Evangelicalism as the last bastion of the traditional norms of discipline and hard work for their own sake, self-sacrifice, and moral asceticism are largely inaccurate. Far from being untouched by the cultural trends of the post–World War II decades, *the coming generation of Evangelicals, in their own distinctive way, have come to participate fully in them.*[13]

11. Richard Quebedeaux, *The Worldly Evangelicals* (San Francisco: Harper and Row, 1978), p. xii.

12. James Davison Hunter, *Evangelicalism: The Coming Generation* (Chicago: University of Chicago Press, 1987), pp. 48–49.

13. Ibid., pp. 73–74.

We could probe into how this development in evangelicalism is affecting major areas of doctrine, but that would go beyond the scope of our present inquiry. We will, however, at the end of this chapter briefly note the implications for a number of doctrines.

The Coming Reversal

It seems likely that the assimilation of sacred and secular will continue for some time, and then a reversal will take place. The reversal may well be precipitated by some historical event which begins to demonstrate the practical untenability of the scheme we have been discussing. Just as the First World War pointed up the inadequacy of liberalism's assimilation of culture, and the Second World War put even further to rest the drive toward synthesis that was just beginning to reawaken, so some external event will probably once again have to make the flaws of assimilation apparent. It also seems that assimilation will continue until an extreme is reached. The time is not yet near, but it is certainly coming.

I anticipate that the spokesperson who will spark the return to an antithesis will be someone from the ranks of those who most emphatically promote assimilation. It will not be someone who has perennially opposed synthesis. It may even be someone who does not espouse the Christian faith per se. Just as it was not conservatives but a repentant liberal, Karl Barth, who in 1919 issued the manifesto of neoorthodoxy, so it will probably be someone satiated with the integration of sacred and secular who will most effectively reject it. We may not fully understand the reasons for this pattern, but it does seem to be present. Moreover, it explains why the reaction may well be an overreaction: the personal history may heighten the subjectivity, thus reducing the objectivity.

My expectation regarding who will lead the reversal does not imply that those who have for a long time spoken against the status quo will not play an important part in the revolution. Indeed, their faithful advocacy of a countercultural stance may be used in bringing about the change in the influential prophet. They will have to be content with the change, for the accolades (and abuse) will go to the one publicly perceived as having wrought the transformation.

One reason for expecting the reversal about which we have written is that we are beginning to approach the extreme of assimilation: a reaction must necessarily set in. Another reason is that some articulate voices are beginning to be heard, calling for such a change. They may well form the nucleus of the next movement, and their ideas may become dominant; but that is not likely to be accomplished by a gradual transition, since changes of this type inevitably entail trauma.

Anthropocentrism

We must now look at another major trend which cuts across the several areas of theology, another factor affecting the whole framework. It is the shift from a theocentric to an anthropocentric orientation. Historically, the Westminster Catechism had defined the end of man as being to glorify God and enjoy him forever. Generally the emphasis was placed upon the glorification of God. This was what was important, even if it was accomplished through the damnation of human beings, or at least some of them. The ultimate in dedication seemed to be willingness to sacrifice oneself for the sake of God. In the nineteenth century, however, the focus shifted from a God who existed in his own right and for his own sake to a god who existed for the sake of humans. There were several evidences of the erosion of the traditional position:

Humanity as the Measure of Truth

In the nineteenth century the understanding of truth came to center in the human. To put it another way, the human became increasingly the judge of what was true. Now in one sense, of course, this must always be the case. Even if we accept that God is the source of truth and the standard of truth, we as human beings have to determine what God is saying, or what is really a channel of revelation from God. This is the role of hermeneutics and biblical exposition. But nineteenth-century theology went beyond this. Decisions were made regarding what God could do. Miracles, including resurrection and the virgin birth, were purged from the revelation because of their conflict with the laws of nature or with the characteristics of the visible universe as humans perceived them. Note that we are not suggesting that the scientific study of nature was somehow inherently antitheistic. Rather, the shift lay in the assumption that humans could decide that the natural realm was all there was to reality, that there could not be intrusions that would contradict what usually occurred within it.

The Notion of God's Responsibility to Spare Humans from Evil

The shift toward anthropocentrism was revealed in other ways as well. One was a judgment, sometimes subtle, sometimes not, of what God had a responsibility to do. The problem of evil has always been a severe difficulty for Christian theology. In the nineteenth century, however, the problem intensified as humans expanded the list of what they thought they had a right to expect from life. In addition to freedom from pain, they now expected freedom from inconvenience and discomfort.

Beyond deliverance from starvation, they expected freedom from poverty. Willingness to endure inconvenience or to sacrifice or postpone gratification was not evident to any great degree.

It is interesting to note that many people today give God less authority in their lives and at the same time place greater responsibility upon him. With the diminishing sense of sin we view God as the explanation of our problems, as if he were under some obligation to make sure that everything works out well for the human race. For example, in the midst of a severe drought in the agricultural heartland of the United States, a reporter called to ask me what I as a theologian had to say about it. It was apparent that what he hoped to hear from me, and what apparently some of the other people whom he had contacted had suggested, was that the drought was a sign of divine judgment for the country's general failure to turn to Christ. I suggested that there were many possible factors, including the lack of ecological responsibility; careless treatment of the environment and unrestrained material consumption, even on the part of Christians, might be contributing to the buildup of the carbon-dioxide layer and the resultant greenhouse effect. This was not what he wanted to hear, so his article contained no statement reflecting what I had said. The general point I am making is that it is easier to blame God for sending judgment upon the world for the sins of someone else, than to accept blame for our own failure to take note of the way in which he has structured the creation, and to govern our behavior accordingly.

Narcissism

The so-called baby boomers are frequently referred to as the "me generation." In many cases they display a narcissism, a fixation upon self-gratification, which is more interested in the church for what they can receive to meet their own needs than as a place to serve and contribute to others and to the cause of Christ. Such persons have no strong sense of commitment. They are not joiners. They cannot be counted on to give, either of their finances or of their time and abilities. When their needs are not being met as they desire, they do not hesitate to move to another place where those needs can be better met.

This fixation on self is what I have sometimes called inverted theology. God has been put in the inferior position, the position of the servant; and the individual human holds the superior position, the position of the lord. The human decides what is good and right and true. It is the human's wishes that are to be respected and met.

One facet of this narcissism is the "entitlement ethic," which has replaced the work ethic. Far from merely wanting something, most people today feel that they deserve it. As Faith Popcorn states, "In a consumer culture—that is, a culture that offers choices beyond sur-vival basics—the motive has never been need, but want. Pushing that motivation beyond *want* to *deserve* is a recent, and powerful, cultural transformer."[14]

Lack of Concern for Divine Commands

In some ways, the shift toward anthropocentrism is most clearly reflected in the attitude toward divine commands. The short-range wel-fare or happiness of the individual is supreme. Any attempt to suggest a different course of action because God has commanded it is rejected as legalism, as hewing to the letter, as going by the book. Rather than seeing the law as an expression of God's desires and intentions, and upholding it as a means of showing respect and bringing satisfaction to him, the immediate need of the individual, which is sometimes quite trivial, is the concern. There is a lack of true personalism here, for the character of the law of God as an expression of his personal will is over-looked. In the language of Paul Tillich, from the perspective of auton-omy theonomy is misunderstood and interpreted as heteronomy, the imposition of something extraneous, impersonal, and harmful.

A Coming Reaction

I believe the tendency toward anthropocentrism will continue to build until it reaches an extreme. Then, however, a reaction will set in. Like Luther who pled for people to "let God be God," there will be those who recognize that a god who is not at the center of human life is not a god at all, or at least not a god worth having. They will plead for com-mitment, austerity, holiness, rather than self-gratification. They will see the meaning of life as coming, not from a desire to serve themselves and to have God serve them, but from serving him. I believe this develop-ment will come from an element of younger people. There is an ideal-ism there which has sometimes been expressed in the espousal of radi-cal political causes. Those causes are beginning to collapse or at least to erode and corrode on a worldwide basis. Although still in a minority among Christians, the seriousness and commitment of this group will begin to make a difference. By the same token, theology will return to a sense of the exalted status of God. He will not be seen merely as the one who answers prayers and satisfies human needs. There will be some-thing of what the Death of God theologians and Dietrich Bonhoeffer

14. Faith Popcorn, *The Popcorn Report: Faith Popcorn on the Future of Your Com-pany, Your World, Your Life* (New York: Doubleday, 1991), pp. 39–40.

called "religionless Christianity," although in a different sense from what they meant by the expression.

Effects of the General Trends in Theology

Suppose we pause now and note what effects anthropocentrism and loss of the antithesis will have in specific areas of theology. We will make only the merest of suggestions, which could and should be developed into full-fledged treatments of the future of each of these doctrines. For the moment these suggestions will have to suffice as indications of what might be the concomitant effects of the developments we have discussed. It should be apparent by now that I anticipate the continued development of some of the prominent trends I have sought to identify. They may continue for some time, possibly well into the twenty-first century, before the reversal begins.

Among the effects we can anticipate is a strong emphasis upon the immanence of God. Many will continue to see him as at work in institutions not identified with Christianity and in persons who are not necessarily Christian.

As anthropocentrism proceeds and increases, we can also expect God to become increasingly thought of as finite rather than infinite. This will result both from the sense that we are in control of our own destinies and from the sense that God has failed, and hence must be unable, to meet all our needs and desires.

In the area of Christology we can expect the uniqueness of Jesus to receive less emphasis. There will be a growing accent upon his humanity. And his unusual characteristics will come to be seen as very much like those of other outstanding human beings.

Humanity will be understood increasingly in natural categories and hence as having great affinity with the other members of creation. The value of the human race will not be seen as conferred from above, by a God who made us in his own image and likeness, but as coming from below, humans being the highest product of the evolutionary process.

Sin will increasingly be a social and human concept rather than a religious concept. It will be thought of less as violating God's law or falling short of his standard for us, and more as a matter of failure to live up to one's potential or *telos*. Guilt will increasingly be displaced by feelings of meaninglessness, estrangement, and emptiness.

Salvation will accordingly be thought of less as a supernatural or otherworldly matter, and more in terms of adjustment, self-understanding, and justice. The struggle to achieve wholeness will displace holiness. In the broad sense of the word, the mission of the church will be geared more to a social gospel than to a message of the need for personal regeneration and sanctification. Evangelism will lose ground to personal counseling and social action. Further, salvation will not be viewed as restricted to those within the church or those with a conscious and explicit faith and trust in Jesus Christ. Other world religions will be seen as leading to the same goal, and all persons of good will who are altruistic in their concern and actions will be thought of as brothers and sisters.

Eschatology will increasingly lose its futuristic or at least its other-worldly character. The present and earthly dimension of the kingdom of God will be emphasized more than the future and spiritual aspect. The emphasis that the kingdom will be introduced by the supernatural personal second coming of Christ will yield to the idea that it will be brought in by human endeavors.

We conclude with an observation on the practical level. Given the shifts in doctrinal emphasis that we have mentioned, preaching will be more horizontal than vertical. It will be geared to meeting human needs and comforting human hurts rather than to glorifying God and declaring his expectations of and promises to us.

5

The Doctrine of Scripture

It is particularly significant that we begin our examination of the future directions of theology by looking into the future of the doctrine of Scripture. On the surface this seems to be a doctrine where there is relatively little difficulty. A surprisingly large percentage of the general population have a high regard for the Bible's authority. We do note, however, a rather significant decline in what might be called biblical literalism. In the 1963 Gallup poll, 65 percent indicated agreement with the statement "The Bible is the actual Word of God, and is to be taken literally, word for word" (option A). By 1976, however, that figure had dropped to 38 percent. It then remained quite constant (37–39 percent) from 1976 to 1984.[1] By 1988, however, it had declined to 31 percent.[2] Another 24 percent believed that "the Bible is the inspired Word of God. It contains no errors, but some verses are to be taken symbolically rather than literally" (option B). Thus 55 percent, a majority of the population, basically accepted the full authority of the Bible. The highest affirmative response to these two options was among those 50 years of age and older—60 percent. That figure dropped to 51 percent among those in the 30–49 age bracket, but increased to 55 percent among those under 30 years. This may indicate among younger persons some resurgence of belief in biblical inerrancy. The limited inerrancy view—"The Bible is the inspired Word of God, but it may contain historical and scientific errors"—was selected more frequently (24 percent) by the 30–49-year-olds than by either the younger or older group.[3]

One point of interest and possible significance is the responses given by different racial and cultural groups. Whereas 29 percent of whites in the 1988 sample indicated adherence to the literal view (A), and 25 percent accepted inerrancy tempered by some symbolism (B), the figures for blacks were 45 percent and 23 percent respectively, and for Hispanics 40 percent and 20 percent.[4] Thus blacks and Hispanics have a more conservative view of Scripture than do whites. As the United States moves increasingly toward a situation in which minorities will constitute a majority, the overall view of the Bible may become more conservative. On the other hand, this biblical conservatism is inversely proportional to the amount of education and the level of income.[5] These data are confirmed by the Barna research.[6] This may mean that as minorities move up the educational and income scales, their natural conservatism will tend to be offset. Moreover, those churches and denominations which especially target upper-class and upper-middle-class whites will probably tend to move toward a less conservative view of Scripture. We can expect that they will move away from the theology taught in the Bible as well. This may not come through outright rejection of those doctrines, but through neglect of biblical teaching in favor of psychology or some similar interest.

1. *Religion in America. 50 Years: 1935–1985*, Gallup Report 236 (Princeton, N.J., May 1985), p. 48.
2. *Religion in America 1990* (Princeton, N.J.: Princeton Religion Research Center, 1990), p. 50.
3. Ibid.
4. Ibid.
5. Ibid.
6. George Barna, *The Barna Report 1992–93: America Renews Its Search for God* (Ventura, Calif.: Regal, 1992), p. 255.

The study of the doctrine of Scripture is important because it is in many ways fundamental to all the others. Changes in it can serve as an indicator and predictor of similar changes in other areas of doctrine. While changes in the doctrine of Scripture may not immediately result in changes in other areas, sooner or later such changes are inevitable. Conversely, changes in other doctrines do not usually affect doctrines other than themselves, with the possible exception of the doctrine of Scripture. For if something which seems to be clearly taught by Scripture is rejected, there will be a necessary change in the view of Scripture. This argument could be depicted as follows:

> If the Bible is the inspired Word of God, whatever it teaches is true.
> Something taught by the Bible is not true.
> Therefore, the Bible is not the inspired Word of God.

The conclusion of this argument—which takes the logical form of denying the consequent (*modus tollens*)—will indirectly affect other doctrines that rely on the Scripture.

We should note that in some cases influences which have a direct effect upon another doctrine force a rethinking of the basic doctrine of Scripture. A historical example is found in the science of geology. Because of certain developments in that area, some Christians came to believe that the earth was not, as they had thought, six thousand years old. They found it necessary either to adjust their understanding of the doctrine of Scripture, which they believed taught this view, or at least to alter their understanding of what Scripture really taught. A more contemporary instance is the tendency of popular psychology to emphasize the importance of a positive self-understanding and self-esteem. In some cases this conflicts with the biblical teaching regarding universal human depravity. Those who adopt the more positive view of human nature as part of their doctrine of humanity also find it necessary to modify their doctrinal understanding of the Scripture.

Some specific doctrines, of course, are so closely linked that a change in one inevitably changes the other. For example, the doctrine of the person of Christ is so intimately linked with the doctrine of salvation that a shift in the former produces a change in the latter. Note, however, that these correlations are on a very limited basis. There is not the global effect that one finds with the doctrine of Scripture. Because it affects all other areas of theology and is thus a leading indicator of theological change, there is special value in studying the doctrine of Scripture.

Tensions Relating to the Doctrine of Scripture

Exegetical Expertise and Lay Bible Study

We begin our examination of the doctrine of Scripture in itself by noting two developments which, if not contradictory, are at least sufficiently contrasting to cause us to wonder how they will interrelate in the years ahead. One is the growing movement in which laypersons, with the encouragement and approval of the clergy, are engaged in study of the Bible. Frequently with little sophisticated training in biblical interpretation, and with little scientific help other than a good translation, they are approaching the Bible either as individuals or in study groups. Their conclusions may be a common denominator of what the several translations available say, or the consensus of the persons in the group.

Preceding and paralleling the lay movement is the growth of the science of biblical exegesis and interpretation. The scientific study of the Bible has become a very technical and at times even esoteric endeavor. A major consideration here is that the preacher and the theologian, unlike the layperson, possess a knowledge of the original languages of the Bible. Increasingly, as the sciences of biblical criticism have continued to grow, exegetes have found meanings in the text which are in many ways quite different from what the average person would think the sense to be.

We have in the two parallel developments the potential for some tension. If the professional clergy seem to obtain from the Bible a message different from what the laity find therein, the church faces a dilemma. Here is a case where the doctrine of the church, and in particular its understanding of the relative roles and functions of the clergy and the laity, come into play. Inasmuch as the tension is likely to continue, it would be helpful to try to anticipate what is going to happen to these two distinct tendencies.

Objectivity and Subjectivity in Biblical Criticism

Biblical criticism has gone through several stages. Initially, it participated quite fully in the spirit of the modern age. Attention was focused upon objective concerns. Lower or textual criticism primarily tried to establish the original text. Higher or historical criticism sought to determine the actual events that gave rise to the narrative portions. Source criticism sought to isolate the actual written documents on which the final products which we now have are based. These endeavors all related to rather objective, existent materials. In addition, they claimed to utilize objective criteria which anyone should be able to understand

and apply (although a considerable amount of subjectivity was involved in their application).

Some of the succeeding stages and methods of biblical criticism were more subjective. Thus form criticism sought to identify, not the written documents or sources underlying the final products, but the preceding oral traditions passed on by the church. Oral tradition in itself is more subjective, in the sense of being fluid and thus more difficult to identify and to understand than is a written source. The criteria of authenticity utilized by form critics have also been rather subjective, as scholars like Morna Hooker have pointed out.[7] Redaction criticism, which focuses its attention on the theological interest and intent of the author rather than on the Christian community, also shows some subjective qualities. For frequently the interest and intent of the author are determined by examining what he has written, which in a circular pattern is then interpreted from the perspective of the author.

One of the problems of biblical criticism, even in its more objective phase, has been how to arrive at agreement about a given passage when several critics presumably utilizing the same method disagree. A comparison of several commentaries on the Pentateuch, all utilizing the documentary hypothesis, will reveal considerable agreement but also significant disagreement upon the exact extent of J, E, D, and P. This subjectivity has become even more pronounced in later criticism.

One endeavor in recent years to overcome this subjectivity is structuralism. Structural exegesis looks for the meaning of the text, not in something brought in from the writer's personal agenda, or from some transcendent source, namely God, but in certain universal human themes. Present in all literatures is a depth of structure stemming from the human soul. The meaning is objective, but its locus is not the particular text, but the universal character of humanity.[8]

Structuralism seems to have been the last endeavor to maintain an objective meaning for Scripture. The current alternative is what has come to be known as "reader-response criticism," which is actually part of the broader movement known as postmodernism. Here there is no search for objective meaning within the text, whether believed to have been put there consciously by the author, by God's inspiration of the author, or by some universal forces. Rather, meaning is something which the reader creates or brings to the meeting with the text. Thus the

7. Morna Hooker, "On Using the Wrong Tool," *Theology* 75 (1972): 570–81; idem, "Christology and Methodology," *New Testament Studies* 17 (July 1971): 480–87.

8. Carl E. Armerding, "Structuralism," in *New Dictionary of Theology*, ed. Sinclair B. Ferguson, David F. Wright, and J. I. Packer (Downers Grove, Ill.: Inter-Varsity, 1988), pp. 664–65.

words of the text do not rest upon some basic meaning beneath them, nor do they point to some basic meaning behind them. The meaning emerges from the individual's encounter with the words; it consists in what they signify to the reader.[9] The essential characteristic of this movement, then, which has precursors going all the way back to Søren Kierkegaard and Georg Hegel, is its strong element of subjectivity.

I anticipate that the trend toward subjectivity will continue. The fact that strongly subjectivistic views cannot readily be discussed or communicated will present problems to the professional theologian. For theologians, like scholars in all other disciplines, must be able to communicate if they are to convince others of the correctness and profundity of their insights. This is very difficult to do, however, if the locus of meaning is not in the text itself, but in the person interacting with it. Then even the symbols written by the postmodern theologian do not carry objective meaning. They tend to slide toward emotive or ejaculative endeavors, which is how the logical positivists characterized all propositions of the nonscientific and nonmathematical type.[10] At some point the theologians will of necessity either grow silent or move toward restoring some measure of objectivity.

It should be noted that there is a growing criticism of the methodology of biblical criticism. A feeling is gaining momentum that biblical criticism as it has usually been practiced is considerably less objective and precise, and consequently its conclusions are less reliable, than has often been claimed. I recall quite vividly a panel discussion at an annual meeting of the American Academy of Religion. One professor from a prestigious liberal university referred several times to the "assured results of biblical criticism," which he maintained disproved a number of the contentions that had been advanced by other members of the panel. Finally a woman theologian on the panel spoke up quite pointedly, saying, "You need to know that a growing number of us are not impressed with the utility of biblical criticism. We think 'the assured results of criticism' to be a gross exaggeration, and if you persist in your claim that all Christian theologians must rely upon your method, we will present you with the term *Christianity* as a gift. We will simply call what we believe 'biblical religion,' or something of that type." It was a forceful reminder that the pronouncements of biblical critics are not infallible. It appears that cracks in the method of biblical criticism of a

9. Edgar V. McKnight, *Postmodern Use of the Bible: The Emergence of Reader-oriented Criticism* (Nashville: Abingdon, 1988), p. 15.

10. Rudolf Carnap, "The Rejection of Metaphysics," in *Philosophy and Logical Syntax,* reprinted in *The Age of Analysis: Twentieth Century Philosophers*, ed. Morton G. White (New York: New American Library, 1955), pp. 219–21.

certain type are beginning to widen into fissures, and the result may be dramatic. Biblical scholars are becoming increasingly aware that they must overhaul their method and conclusions, defend them, or be prepared to move to an alternative.[11]

It is important to bear in mind that biblical criticism was historically the major factor in undercutting the orthodox view of the Bible. To the extent that the credibility of critical methodology continues to decline, we can probably expect to see some resurgence of the more conservative view of the Bible. It should be noted that generally a reversal on a theological issue is not simply a return to the view held earlier. It is a return toward that end of the spectrum, or that end of the pendular swing, but with some characteristic modifications. Thus neoorthodoxy, which reacted so strongly against the immanentism and anthropocentrism of liberalism, was not simply a return to orthodoxy, but a *neo*-orthodoxy which resembled the older orthodoxy in many respects, and indeed surpassed it in some, but also differed in some significant ways. On the broad theological scene we can expect at some point a more conservative view of Scripture and an atmosphere more congenial to the historic view of the Bible, but not merely a wholesale adoption of its traditional form.

Future Developments in Popular Understanding and Practice

Selectivity in the Utilization of Scripture

As we turn to consider future developments that relate to the doctrine of Scripture, we note once again the popular interest in study of the Bible. This phenomenon has been quite remarkable, and even appears in the Roman Catholic Church, where the laity had until recently not been strongly encouraged to study the Bible on their own. Within these Bible study movements, however, there is a growing tendency toward selectivity in the interpretation and application of the biblical message. Frequently the portion or interpretation of Scripture which is especially assimilated relates to a special need of the persons reading or hearing the Word. This will undoubtedly continue to be the case, and increasingly so as the effects of some contemporary evangelism and preaching spread. In certain conservative circles there is currently a strong emphasis on presenting the gospel message as the answer to people's needs. Consequently, Scripture is selectively utilized. Many

11. See, e.g., Peter Stuhlmacher, *Historical Criticism and Theological Interpretation of Scripture: Toward a Hermeneutics of Consent* (Philadelphia: Fortress, 1977); Gerhard Maier, *The End of the Historical-Critical Method* (St. Louis: Concordia, 1977).

people neglect those passages that do not speak directly to their needs. Among those passages are "If anyone would come after me, he must deny himself and take up his cross daily and follow me" (Luke 9:23), and "Bring the whole tithe into the storehouse" (Mal. 3:10). What seems to give validity to a biblical passage is that it speaks to one's need. This means that in actuality the basis of authority is not the content of the message, but the internal condition of the person hearing it. From being a criterion for the evaluation and application of the message, one's internal state has become its content.

The Displacement of the Bible with Personal Experience

The *Christianity Today*–Gallup poll of 1979 indicated that young people, instead of looking to the Bible, are looking for a direct speaking by the Holy Spirit.[12] Accordingly, we can expect an increase of interest in "revelations" rather than in revelation. This is one manifestation of a general movement, the earliest form of which in the twentieth century was ordinarily referred to as Pentecostalism. About 1960 this was followed by neo-Pentecostalism, the charismatic movement. Whereas Pentecostalism often drew its members from lower socioeconomic groups, and formed separate denominations which in H. Richard Niebuhr's classification were more like sects than churches, neo-Pentecostalism cut across all social groups and was found within major denominations, including the usually formal and unemotional Roman Catholics, Episcopalians, and Lutherans. Neo-Pentecostalism's exercise of the special gifts of the Holy Spirit was relatively restrained and orderly. The most recent variation in the general movement has termed itself the "third wave." It also is known as the "signs and wonders" movement or "power evangelism." In this group, whose leaders include John Wimber and Charles Kraft, there is relatively little emphasis upon glossolalia, but a great deal of emphasis upon miracles as modern manifestations of the power of God.

The third wave, just like the two preceding waves, tends toward anti-intellectualism. Kraft goes to great lengths to argue that the reason we do not see signs and wonders today as frequently as in biblical times is that our rationalistic Western worldview does not permit us even to conceive of miracles.[13] But the evidence offered for miracles today, by contrast, is experiential, the actual observance of such occurrences. Thus the belief in miracles is not based upon a rational hermeneutic accord-

12. Walter A. Elwell, "Belief and the Bible: A Crisis of Authority?" *Christianity Today* 24.6 (March 21, 1980): 20.
13. Charles Kraft, *Christianity with Power: Your Worldview and Your Experience of the Supernatural* (Ann Arbor: Servant, 1989), pp. 91–100.

ing to which such events are still to occur today. Nor is there any attempt on the part of the third wave to deal with the problem of other religions and even demonic groups which also claim to have valid miracles occurring in their midst. The argument, in other words, is less concerned with proving the exclusive truth of Christianity and whatever is unique to it, including the Bible, than with making the case that miracles actually do occur today.

As the third wave gains momentum, it will have several effects. First, it will offset whatever loss of faith in the literal truth of the Bible was based on rejection of miracles. If miracles can be shown to be occurring today, then there presumably is no reason for doubting their occurrence in biblical times and thus the full truthfulness of the Bible. On the other hand, primary authority will shift from the Bible to personal experience. The third effect will be that the uniqueness of the biblical teaching will not be established. If one accepts the authority of the Bible because the phenomena which it describes are occurring in our time, then one has opened the door to acknowledging something else as authoritative on similar grounds, and thus may have established more than one wished.

An additional factor in the third wave is the so-called word of knowledge.[14] This is a special communication from God. It is ordinarily not a matter of doctrine, but rather of insight in a specific situation. It often involves an understanding of the spiritual or physical condition of the person being dealt with. In light of this limited scope it seems more appropriate to think of (and refer to) this activity of the Holy Spirit as guidance rather than revelation. It is not difficult, however, to imagine an expansion in the range of this phenomenon. For instance, a special word from the Holy Spirit could be used in the interpretation of biblical passages. Examples are not uncommon in the earlier varieties of Pentecostalism (i.e., the first and second waves). The effect would be to displace somewhat the authority of the objective meaning of Scripture (as determined by the scientific methods of exegesis) with this subjective inner experience.

Decline in Bible Reading

In general, the emphasis upon personal experience can be expected to grow. Involvement with the present, with what one is currently experiencing, has led to a decline in interest in history. Yearning for intense experience, which is stronger than considerations of the consequences of one's actions, has led to abuse of controlled substances. In addition

14. Ibid., p. 2.

there is, especially in countries like the United States, a mania for video games which militates against reading. The immediate stimulation of a video game is much more appealing than reading, which is considered boring.

One may anticipate that with the general decline in reading will come a decline in reading of the Bible and in conscious adherence to the teaching of any written document. It may well be that the content of the Bible will continue to be treated as authoritative, but not necessarily because it is in the Bible. Rather, the content may be presented in some other form or through some other medium. Obviously it is imperative that the church find ways to convey and teach what the Bible says. When our children were young, we made long auto trips, generally one each summer. Like many families, we devised games to help pass the time. One favorite of our children was a Bible game called "Who am I?" It involved a series of cards, each of which had three clues to the identity of a particular Bible character. Soon the game had been played so often that each of our daughters knew the identity of each character from the very first clue. That required some innovation; it generally fell to Dad to create new clues for some other Bible characters. It was quite amazing how much Bible knowledge our children acquired through playing that game. The church will need to develop some similarly innovative techniques for conveying the content of the Bible. In so doing it is important to emphasize that the teaching is true because it is found in the Bible, not because the mode of presentation is attractive or impressive.

It should be borne in mind that the decline in attention to the Bible as a written document is a popular trend. In general, professional theologians, those who construct official theology, are much more oriented to printed material than are, say, junior high students. The broad cultural trend will have its impact, however, sometimes on a very unconscious basis, and may eventually affect even the level of professional theology.

The 1991 Barna report sheds some interesting light upon the practical outworking of belief in the authority of the Bible. Relatively little difference was found in the responses of various age groups to the statement "The Bible is the written word of God and is totally accurate in all it teaches." The number who strongly agreed declined only from 51 percent of those 65 and older to 46 percent of those in the 18–25 age bracket, but when the categories of those who strongly agreed and those who agreed are combined, the 18–25-year-olds actually scored 1 percent higher than did the senior citizens.[15] When we examine actual practice

15. George Barna, *The Barna Report: What Americans Believe* (Ventura, Calif.: Regal, 1991), pp. 292–94.

with respect to the Bible, however, significant differences begin to appear. When asked whether they had read the Bible within the preceding seven days, 61 percent of the senior citizens said yes. The percentage declined with each succeeding generation: 52 percent of those 55–64; 51 percent of those 45–54; 43 percent of the baby boomers (26–44); and only 32 percent of the "baby busters" (18–25). When asked whether they read the Bible every day, 31 percent of the senior citizens said yes; only 4 percent of the baby busters responded affirmatively.[16]

The Barna data from one year later suggest an accentuation of this trend. Belief in the authority and inerrancy of the Bible declines steadily from the older to the younger age groups. Thus 82 percent of the senior citizens agreed or strongly agreed with the statement "The Bible is the written word of God and is totally accurate in all that it teaches," but only 65 percent of those in the 18–25 age bracket did.[17] When we look at the practice of Bible reading, this trend is even more marked. Among those 65 years and older, 33 percent read the Bible every day during a typical week; 26 percent did not read it at all. Among those 18–25 the figures were 2 percent and 50 percent respectively.[18] One might argue that this largely reflects the leisure time available to senior citizens, but the progressive trend within the intermediate age groups argues otherwise.

Among other significant statistics is that Bible reading is notably higher among black Christians than among white Christians.[19] While the 1991 Barna data did not include figures for other minority groups, the 1992 data showed that Hispanics read the Bible less frequently than did whites. With the decline of dominance by whites within an increasingly multicultural Christianity, it may be that Bible reading will increase somewhat. Another trend seems to be pointing in the opposite direction, however. As education and income level increase, there is a notable decline both in belief in the authority of the Bible and in Bible reading. With the continued upward mobility of evangelicals socioeconomically, we may well see a decline of belief in and use of the Bible.

---

16. Ibid., pp. 286–88.

17. The sharp increase in the affirmative response of senior citizens (69 percent in 1991; 82 percent in 1992) may be in part due to a sampling error in the first survey. Steps were taken to ensure that the sample would be truly representative of the general population with respect to gender and geography, but not age. Although senior citizens constitute 15 percent of the adult population, they constituted only 9 percent of the survey sample, the remaining 6 percent being equally divided between baby boomers and baby busters. The following year the sampling error had been corrected.

18. Barna, *America Renews Its Search*, p. 292.

19. Barna, *What Americans Believe*, pp. 286, 288–89, 291; Barna, *America Renews Its Search*, p. 292.

One encouraging point should not be overlooked, however. The Gallup data for 1954 and 1982 show an increase in biblical knowledge. The number of persons who knew who delivered the Sermon on the Mount increased from 34 to 42 percent; those who could name all four Gospels increased from 35 to 46 percent; those who knew where Jesus was born went from 64 to 70 percent of the general population. On the other hand, the 1979 *Christianity Today*–Gallup poll included a multiple-choice question regarding what Jesus said to Nicodemus. Only 29 percent of the general public correctly selected "Ye must be born again"—9 percent chose "I will make you a fisher of men"; 14 percent, "Take up thy bed and walk"; 4 percent selected "Feed my sheep"; and 44 percent said they did not know.[20] This type of question was not asked in any of the later surveys we have been citing. Informal and anecdotal sources, such as teachers of introductory Bible courses in colleges and seminaries, suggest, however, that the picture is not totally positive.

The foregoing discussion indicates that Bible reading will decline in the years ahead. Accordingly, people will be less likely to treat the Bible as their authority in matters of faith and practice. On what alternative will they rely? While there are several possibilities, one of the most likely is personal experience. Another possibility is reliance upon the presentations at church services, whether preaching or some other means like drama, which is becoming increasingly popular. Those who plan and present drama have a heavy responsibility to make certain that its content is biblically based. The same is true of preaching. The trend may go in two directions. The relative ignorance of the Bible may persuade preachers to give strong emphasis to biblical content in their preaching. On the other hand, the lack of familiarity and possibly of interest on the part of their audience may influence preachers to include relatively little content. There are some indications, not yet documented scientifically, that the trend, especially in churches gearing their services toward younger people, is of the latter type. To the extent that people rely upon the presentation, whatever form it may take, it will come to be the functional authority. Eventually, dilution of belief in the authority of the Bible is inevitable.

Another alternative to the Bible as authority is the increasing reliance on narrative, both in preaching and in doing theology. There are various uses for narrative. The simplest is as a communication device.[21] Here we are talking simply about the use of illustratory material. The second role is hermeneutical. Here we have the idea that the narrative portions of

20. Elwell, "Belief and the Bible," p. 22.
21. Belden C. Lane, "Rabbinical Stories: A Primer on Theological Method," *Christian Century* 98.41 (Dec. 16, 1981): 1307.

Scripture are the key to its interpretation; in other words, they are the normative portions.[22] Finally, there is the heuristic or epistemological role.[23] This involves the idea that the content of the Christian faith is not limited to Scripture. The life stories of persons of faith add to the content. To the extent that this third use for narrative grows, as it seems to be doing, the unique authority of Scripture will be diluted.

The Increasing Influence of Third World Christianity

One major development of global proportions will have definite effect upon the doctrine of Scripture. For a long time Christianity has been a European (and in its Protestant variety a North and West European) phenomenon. Missions emanated from Europe, as did much of theology. The momentum evangelistically, however, has shifted to North America. This has tended to define the dominant paradigm of Christianity and thus, to the extent that theology is generated upward from life experience rather than downward from official theologians, the framework of theology as well.

More recently, however, the most active and most rapidly growing form of Christianity is to be found in the Third World. Vitality found in Latin America and in Africa outstrips anything in North America. Gradually the paradigm of Christian experience will come to be colored by this expansion. It will be quite some time before these regions begin to exert a strong influence upon theology, but that will also come. The reason for the delay is that theology, being a systematic endeavor, is a somewhat later development than evangelism. But when the time comes, the cultural characteristics of the Third World will influence theology.

A noteworthy characteristic of Third World cultures is a strong group consciousness, as contrasted with the considerable individualism of the West. This entails a greater tendency toward objectivism, toward that which is truth for all in the group, as contrasted with subjectivism, seeking that which is truth for oneself. The Third World also has a stronger emphasis upon tradition than we find in many Western cultures. Although this emphasis is frequently oriented toward oral tradition, it does point out the validity of that which has been handed down; and the transition to a written preservation of the oral tradition is not a major or difficult one. Also included in the Third World emphasis is an insistence upon exact adherence to the content of the tradition. Thus the ascent of the Third World should favor an increased trust in the authority of Scripture.

22. Darrell Jodock, "Story and Scripture," *Word and World* 1.2 (Spring 1981): 133.
23. George W. Stroup, *The Promise of Narrative Theology: Recovering the Gospel in the Church* (Atlanta: John Knox, 1981), pp. 200–201.

Tension with the Secular World

Meanwhile, in the Western world there is a continuing secularization which has an impact upon religious thinking. By secularization I mean the tendency to conceive of reality and to establish one's values in terms of the observable or the mundane, the worldly. By contrast many less sophisticated people conceive all of life in spiritual terms. In the Middle Ages, for example, angels and demons were thought to have a great deal of influence in the world. Certain cultures believe that illness is caused by evil powers. A person who is of a particularly spiritual orientation will value spiritual qualities more highly than material possessions or fame. The thinking and attitudes of such a person will be shaped by the sources of spiritual truth, such as the Bible and the church, rather than by contemporary societal factors, such as the popular media.

Earlier generations were inclined to view life through spiritual or biblical spectacles, as it were. Many people were very familiar with the King James Bible, and quotations therefrom often settled an issue in their minds. Today a number of sayings from the Bible (such as "the handwriting on the wall" and "the spirit is willing, but the flesh is weak") live on in popular culture. Many people, however, are unaware of the origin of these sayings and thus of their true meaning as well. A few groups, of course, have gone to great lengths to keep their thinking, attitudes, and values immune from any element of modernity. A notable example is the Amish, whose clothing, means of transportation, and societal practices set them apart. In a sense they have sought to avoid granting any legitimacy to modernity.

Unlike earlier generations and groups like the Amish, most Christians have to some extent attempted to live in both worlds, the present mundane realm and the future-oriented, heaven-focused spiritual realm. For them something of a tension arises. The question is where the boundary between the sacred and the secular falls. To put the question another way: How much of what one believes is to be established on the basis of the Bible, and how much on the basis of science, broadly understood? Or, to paraphrase Jesus, how much shall be rendered intellectually to Caesar, and how much to God?

One especially interesting phenomenon is the shift in the content of two leading evangelical periodicals, *Christianity Today* and *Leadership*. Founded in 1956 as an alternative voice to the *Christian Century, Christianity Today* has articulated and defended evangelical theology. In a comparative analysis of the 1959 and 1989 volumes, David Wells documents the sharp decline in biblical and theological content and the increase in religious news, stories of personal experiences, and advertising. He also points out that over an eight-year period less than 1 percent of the material in the articles in *Leadership* made any clear reference to biblical content, even when dealing with topics such as temptation and sexuality, on which the Bible has much to say.[24]

There has been a tendency to separate the Bible from scientific and historical matters. To many people, for example, evolution is not a theological issue, for they do not regard the Bible as saying anything bearing upon such matters. Certainly, few would try to establish an understanding of nuclear physics upon the basis of biblical teaching. Nor can the Bible be treated as a guide to surveying, or acoustics, or anything of that type.

Some areas are not so easily dealt with, however. These include psychology and ethics. For example, what guidelines should advertisers follow when they draw up their appeals to people to purchase a particular product; what place should be given to the Bible's pronouncements, and what place to the results of market research? In deciding the proper attitude toward practicing homosexuals, what emphasis should be placed upon the writings of biblical authors, and what emphasis upon the claims of certain psychologists? And should we conceive of ourselves and others on the basis of the inherent depravity of all humans which the Bible seems to maintain, or on the basis of the positive assessment of human personality which popular psychology proposes?

We noted in an earlier chapter (pp. 67–71) that popular psychology is becoming influential even in conservative Protestant circles, a trend that will likely continue. This does not mean that biblical teachings are being rejected because of a perceived opposition to psychological insights. Indeed, there is little talk of any significant tension between the two sources. Rather, what is happening is that psychological material is being found within the Bible. In some cases portions of Scripture which appear favorable to ideas emanating from psychology are being emphasized at the expense of other biblical themes. In other cases biblical passages are being interpreted on the basis of data imported from psychology. This is a highly refined form of eisegesis, generally unintentional. The impact of such developments is to diminish the authority of the Bible.

Some people have managed to live with two different worlds, keeping their religious outlook and their scientific perspectives in sharp isolation from each other, keeping them sealed in "logic-tight compartments," as the expression goes. Increasingly, however, there is a tendency for Christians to adopt the beliefs, attitudes, and practices of the

---

24. David F. Wells, *No Place for Truth, or Whatever Happened to Evangelical Theology?* (Grand Rapids: Eerdmans, 1993), pp. 113–14, 207–11.

world. Even spiritual beliefs and theological doctrines are being shaped, sometimes indirectly and even unconsciously, by secular sources.

The Rise of Competitors to the Bible

We must also note the rise of competitors challenging the Bible's claim to supremacy as a source of belief and practice. We have already mentioned popular psychology. Traditionally, philosophy dealt with many of the same topics as did theology, and thus was understood as being either its helper ("handmaid" was the term the medieval thinkers employed) or its competitor. In the middle of the twentieth century, however, the discipline of philosophy moved away from a normative to a descriptive role. Instead of attempting to settle its traditional problems, philosophy attempted to refine the definitions of the terms involved in the discussion. In recent years, however, philosophy has begun to resume a more normative approach. Thus, once again, philosophy will in some circles take the place of theology and specifically of biblical revelation as the basis of belief.

To some extent, the rise of competitors is a result of a diminished appraisal of the Bible, which in turn is largely a result of biblical criticism. One of my graduate school professors observed that as belief in the the sufficiency of biblical authority declines, theologians tend increasingly to rest faith upon something additional to the Bible. Thus late-nineteenth- and early-twentieth-century liberalism made much of philosophy. Even Karl Barth, when he reinitiated his magnum opus in order to oppose any role for philosophy relative to theology, renamed the work *Church Dogmatics*, thus indicating reliance on the church. Wolfhart Pannenberg has shifted the emphasis from philosophy to history, which is inclusive of, but not exhausted by, the Bible as a revelatory source.

The role played by biblical criticism raises the question of its future direction. There is a considerable amount of confusion abroad in this area, and as we suggested a bit earlier in this chapter, we will probably see a growing bifurcation of views. On the one hand, there will be movement toward increasingly radical views, particularly toward a greater subjectivism. On the other hand, a significant number of conservative scholars who are firmly committed to the historical dependability of the Bible are also working with critical methods. To a considerable extent, the future of the doctrine of Scripture rests with those biblical scholars and theologians who succeed in integrating their methodology and their understanding of the nature of Scripture. One area where such integration is needed is what I call the problem of secondary naturalism, a reluctance to discuss the supernatural elements involved in the recording of the Bible. This is one of a number of issues that remain unresolved and will require considerable attention in the years ahead.

Unfinished Agenda

The Problem of Secondary Naturalism

A certain group of biblical scholars, the most prominent being Rudolf Bultmann, approached the Bible with a basically naturalistic worldview. They spoke of a "closed continuum," which meant that the events described within the Bible must be seen and interpreted in the light of natural or scientific law. So, for example, the resurrection of Jesus cannot be accepted as a literal occurrence or fact, since it is contradicted by what we know of the laws governing what happens to corpses. And, in regard to 2 Kings 6:6, axheads cannot float, since such an occurrence contradicts the law of gravity. Indeed, all miracles must be reinterpreted or rejected; what one does with them will depend on whether one is an existential demythologizer or a more liberal scholar.

Conservatives have consistently defended the reality of the miracles reported in Scripture. While some have not interpreted every account literally (for example, the story of Jonah's being swallowed by the large fish), there has been a strong conviction that the miracles taught by the Bible are entirely possible for the almighty God, and thus are historically true. There has been, in other words, a thoroughgoing supernaturalism with respect to the interpretation of the events reported in the Scriptures.

On a different level, however, conservatives have some unfinished business. They must reconcile their supernaturalistic philosophy with their understanding and explanation of the process by which the Scriptures came to be written. For there is the danger that, while they would not hesitate to explain certain biblical events in supernaturalistic terms, they will explain the existence of the Bible itself only in terms that are fundamentally naturalistic.

What we are saying is that some biblical commentators, when explaining why an author wrote what he did, restrict their discussion to natural factors. For example, they may say that Matthew wrote what he did because his audience, given their background, needed a particular message, or because he was motivated to make a specific point. In other words, the *Sitz im Leben* of the early church or of the Gospel writer himself may account for what is written. The implication seems to be that past experience and environment are sufficient explanations for what appears in the Bible.

Here it must be acknowledged that even some very conservative biblical scholars proceed in a fashion which seems to assume that a naturalistic explanation is sufficient. There is little if any reference to the Holy Spirit's work of direct revelation and inspiration. While the commentator would not hesitate to explain a particular historical incident as a miracle, there is not a similar willingness to explain the recording of that incident on a similarly supernatural basis. But if one of the Gospel writers reports something which is not found in any of the other Gospel accounts, and thus presumably not in any recognized tradition, why is there not serious consideration of the possibility that God through his Holy Spirit might have revealed to the Scripture writer something that he would not have otherwise known, and then inspired him to record it? Is this hesitancy on the part of the commentator not a form of secondary naturalism, or perhaps an epistemological naturalism, as contrasted with a primary or metaphysical naturalism?

Note what is occurring here. Though holding that the Bible is both a divinely inspired book and a writing produced by humans and thus possessed of full human characteristics, conservative scholars nevertheless proceed as if only the human aspect needed to be described and examined. It is as if one attempted to explain a human behavior by discussing only the physical cause—a genetic factor, the chemistry of the brain, or something of that type. This would certainly have to be regarded as at least implicitly a form of reductionism, and thus virtually a materialism.

To be sure, attempting to integrate one's view of divine supernatural origin and activity with an appreciation for the human means which were employed is not an easy undertaking. This is a task not unlike the attempt to relate one's view of miracles to natural law. It involves maintaining a balance between transcendence and immanence. If, however, there is no definite effort to bring these two together in some sort of integration, there will likely be gradual loss of belief in the Bible's supernatural character. For if we explain the Bible in strictly natural categories, we will come to regard it as natural. And this secondary naturalism will gradually extend to the primary level, so that fully natural explanations of the miracles recorded in the Bible will displace belief in divine activity.

Biblical Authority and Contemporization

Another major issue will have to be adequately resolved if belief in the inspiration and authority of the Bible is to be preserved. It is what I term the contemporizing of the biblical message. In 1937 Henry Cadbury wrote a book entitled *The Peril of Modernizing Jesus*.[25] Twelve years

---

25. Henry J. Cadbury, *The Peril of Modernizing Jesus* (New York: Macmillan, 1937).

later he published something of a sequel in the form of a journal article entitled "The Peril of Archaizing Ourselves."[26] Those two warnings need to be carried together. They point out the dangers of modernism and of fundamentalism respectively. A truly progressive conservative attempts to avoid both dangers by retaining the distinctive message of the Bible, but stating it in relationship to the present world, that is, translating it into what the Bible would say if it were being written today instead of in the first century.

If the liberal or modernist has erred by so restating the biblical message that Jesus sounds just like a twentieth-century person, the conservative has erred by making the form in which the biblical message was expressed normative for all time. It has sometimes been assumed that biblical theology can suffice for today. Yet in practice virtually everyone does some "translation" of the biblical message into contemporary forms. Very few persons, for example, insist that it is wrong to eat catfish (see Lev. 11:10), or that women should wear hats in church (see 1 Cor. 11:5). What is usually being done, often on an unconscious level, is to say that such regulations are not part of the essential meaning. Yet when we try to state the essential message, there is the problem that some object to the use of metaphysical terms, because the biblical message was presumably functional, and to the use of concepts such as "biblical inerrancy," on the grounds that they are not utilized in Scripture.[27] One of the tasks facing the church in the future, then, is to develop an adequate hermeneutic, in the broadest sense, so that the message of the Bible emerges faithfully in terms and concepts that are intelligible today.

Part of what is being said here is that biblical theology cannot stand alone. In 1970 Brevard Childs argued in his *Biblical Theology in Crisis* that the biblical-theology movement was crumbling.[28] The old consensuses and even clichés would have to be replaced. In the constructive portion of his book he in effect contended that biblical theology would have to become more like systematic theology. And that is the test of our understanding of the doctrine of Scripture. In our understanding, is the message of the Bible true to what was originally taught, yet expressed in a form that is intelligible today? Does our understanding make it clear that the Bible is inspired in such a way as to be the authority for belief and practice in all periods of the life of the church?

26. Henry J. Cadbury, "The Peril of Archaizing Ourselves," *Interpretation* 3 (1949): 331–37.
27. See, e.g., David Allan Hubbard, "The Current Tensions: Is There a Way Out?" in *Biblical Authority*, ed. Jack Rogers (Waco: Word, 1977), p. 168.
28. Brevard S. Childs, *Biblical Theology in Crisis* (Philadelphia: Westminster, 1970).

Contextualization of the Timeless Message

A closely related issue which will also determine the direction of the doctrine of Scripture is contextualization. In general, this is the question of how the teachings of Scripture are to be applied to later situations. A variety of approaches have been followed, some virtually reapplying the biblical statements unchanged, some seeking to "principlize" and then recontextualize the biblical texts. Still others, especially those most strongly influenced by anthropology, seem to reduce considerably the base of normative content in the Bible. Among those following this last approach is Charles Kraft, who contends that at least half of the teachings declared to be heresies by the early church councils were not that at all, but were legitimate attempts to contextualize the gospel for pagan groups of the time.[29] If this is indeed true, there must be considerable plasticity to the biblical statements.

On the other hand, Robertson McQuilkin asserts that we are to maintain the universality of every teaching of Scripture unless the Bible itself treats it as limited.[30] I anticipate that this view will come to be judged by most theologians and biblical scholars and eventually even most Christians as too rigid and restrictive. If it becomes the most prominent view on a short-range basis, it will lead to a long-range decline in confidence in biblical authority, for it will erode as sheer experience highlights the culturally localized character of many of the biblical commands. On the other hand, to the extent that the anthropologically based views continue to expand, there will be an erosion of belief in the normativeness of Scripture on any level of abstraction.

As these two rather diametrical alternatives struggle for supremacy, the intermediate position, which locates normativeness and universality in principles, will continue to grow in influence. This approach has the greatest potential for continued adherence to the authority of Scripture. This will be especially evident as the demand for pragmatic relevance amplifies.

The issue will probably narrow to the question of the nature, breadth, and generality of the principles. Consequently, the dispute will likely center on isolation, identification, and application of the principles rather than on methodology. Kraft has already spelled out a scheme of

29. Charles Kraft, *Christianity in Culture: A Study in Dynamic Biblical Theologizing in Cross-cultural Perspective* (Maryknoll, N.Y.: Orbis, 1979), p. 287.

30. J. Robertson McQuilkin, "Problems of Normativeness in Scripture: Cultural Versus Permanent," in *Hermeneutics, Inerrancy, and the Bible*, ed. Earl D. Radmacher and Robert D. Preus (Grand Rapids: Zondervan, 1984), p. 230.

interpretation and application based upon principles.[31] McQuilkin also focuses upon principles but tends to identify them more closely with biblical forms.[32]

Biblical Authority and Pragmatism in the Ministry

One other factor bearing upon belief in the authority of the Bible is the increasing pragmatism of those in ministry. This in itself would seem to have no direct effect upon the doctrine of Scripture, since it pertains to the methodology of ministry rather than its substance and content. In practice, however, there is a tendency to define even the message by the results, since what works is the most vital concern. There is less actual alteration of the formal content of doctrines than there is a change in which aspects are emphasized and which are minimized. In addition, while the Bible does not spell out in any detail the techniques of ministry, it does lay out some significant principles, and even these are in some cases being displaced by pragmatic considerations. There is also the whole general tendency to look somewhere other than the Bible first.

Pragmatic criteria are in many cases being drawn from studies utilizing the methodology of the behavioral sciences. This is notable in certain emphases in the church growth movement and in church planting. David Hesselgrave has noted a sharp increase in missiology articles drawing primarily on the behavioral sciences instead of biblical and theological materials, and observes that this trend is especially common among evangelicals.[33] He also notes that European missiologists tend to regard American missiology as strongly pragmatic in character.[34]

We find here both causes of concern and bases for hope for the future. Also emerging from our study are indications that the challenge of educating people regarding what the Bible actually teaches is both important and difficult.

---

31. Charles Kraft, "Interpreting in Cultural Context," *Journal of the Evangelical Theological Society* 21.4 (Dec. 1978): 365–66.

32. McQuilkin, "Problems of Normativeness," p. 221.

33. David J. Hesselgrave, *Today's Choices for Tomorrow's Mission: An Evangelical Perspective on Trends and Issues in Missions* (Grand Rapids: Zondervan, 1988), pp. 139–42, and appendix 2.

34. Ibid., p. 144.

6

The Doctrine of God

As for some time, surveys continue to indicate among all groups of Americans a high rate of belief in God. The Gallup figures for those who believe in God or a universal spirit have remained remarkably constant, varying only between 94 and 97 percent from 1944 to 1986.[1] The 94 per-

1. *Religion in America 1990* (Princeton, N.J.: Princeton Religion Research Center, 1990), p. 21.

cent figure in 1986 included 84 percent who believed him to be "a heavenly Father, who can be reached by prayers," while 5 percent thought of God as "an idea, not a being," and 2 percent believed God to be "an impersonal creator."[2]

The 1991 Barna survey posed a statement with some detail about the person of God, namely, "There is only one true God, who is holy and perfect, and who created the world and rules it today." This is more specific than the usual poll questions, which simply ask about belief in God. On this question 82 percent of the senior citizens as compared with only 69 percent of the baby busters agreed strongly; conversely, 2 percent of the seniors and 11 percent of the baby busters disagreed strongly. Among the intermediate generations there was a steady downward trend in strength of belief. From another viewpoint, however, the progression was not linear. For when the categories of those who agreed strongly and those who agreed somewhat are combined, baby boomers (88 percent) and those aged 55–64 (92 percent) slightly exceeded seniors (87 percent), and those 45–54 were only one point lower (86 percent). A rather large break came between baby boomers and baby busters (82 percent). We can probably anticipate some decline in belief in God, but more so in belief in his relationship to the universe, which entails both the doctrine of creation and, to a lesser extent, the doctrine of providence.[3]

Decline in belief in providence is also underscored by the responses to another statement, "There is a God who watches over you and answers your prayers." Here again an age pattern could be discerned. Among senior citizens 87 percent strongly agreed and 3 percent strongly disagreed, while 67 percent of baby busters strongly agreed and 8 percent strongly disagreed. We can anticipate a shift away from belief in a God who is actively involved in our lives and hears our prayers.[4]

The 1992 Barna survey, apparently with the intention of discerning finer variations in views, gave its respondents several options: A, "Everyone is God"; B, "God is the all-powerful, all-knowing and perfect Creator of the universe, who rules the world today"; C, "God is the total realization of personal, human potential"; D, "There are many gods, each with different power and authority"; E, "God represents a state of higher consciousness that a person may reach"; F, "There is no God." Overall the figures were: A, 2 percent; B, 73 percent; C, 10 percent; D, 2 percent; E, 6 percent; F, 1 percent; 6 percent did not know. Whites

2. Ibid.
3. George Barna, *The Barna Report: What Americans Believe* (Ventura, Calif.: Regal, 1991), pp. 200–203.
4. Ibid., pp. 207–9.

matched these figures almost exactly (7 percent selected option E and 5 percent did not know). Blacks were the most orthodox, with 81 percent selecting option B, and Hispanics the least orthodox, with only 64 percent. As might be expected, those with higher incomes and with more education were less likely to choose the orthodox option. In fact, those with household incomes above $60,000 registered a significantly higher than average degree of agnosticism: 15 percent did not know.

In terms of age we see a pattern similar to the previous year. The preboomers (46–64) and seniors (65+) show quite similar views, as do the baby boomers and baby busters. The seniors' responses included: B, 83 percent; C, 6 percent; E, 3 percent. The preboomers' figures for these alternatives were 82 percent, 8 percent, and 5 percent respectively. By contrast the figure for baby boomers included: B, 68 percent; C, 12 percent; and E, 8 percent. The responses of the baby busters were 64 percent, 11 percent, and 8 percent respectively. There was some increase in polytheism and henotheism (belief in several gods, each with a personal domain, usually geographical) among the younger generations: while 1 percent of the seniors and an even smaller number of preboomers selected option D, it was the choice of 3 percent of the baby boomers and 5 percent of the baby busters.[5] What we are probably seeing here are the inroads of secularism, relativism, and New Age religion upon the beliefs of younger persons. Barna calls attention to the rather surprising fact that 7 percent of the people classified as born-again Christians subscribed to nonorthodox views of God, 5 percent holding that God is the full realization of human potential, and 2 percent describing God as a state of higher consciousness that one can reach. Barna then makes an uncharacteristic statement for a pollster, one which could be construed as an expression of doubt about the objective value of the entire endeavor: "Let us pray that these people misinterpreted the meaning of the question posed."[6]

Factors Weakening the Doctrine of God

The Crisis in Metaphysics and the Doctrine of God

The doctrine of God has been in some ways a particularly troublesome doctrine in the twentieth century. But unlike the doctrine of the person of Christ, for example, the problems have not come primarily

5. George Barna, *The Barna Report 1992–93: America Renews Its Search for God* (Ventura, Calif.: Regal, 1992), p. 273.
6. Ibid., pp. 74–76.

from biblical studies. Rather, they have come primarily from philosophical difficulties, and in particular from a crisis in metaphysics.

Among the several reasons for the twentieth-century crisis in metaphysics is a simple doubt about the possibility of knowing anything about the nature of ultimate reality, the type of knowledge that metaphysics purports to give. In his *Critique of Pure Reason* Immanuel Kant had raised questions about the possibility of knowing anything of which we do not have sensory experience. His argument there was that true knowledge is a product of two factors, the content coming from sense data and the structure or logical order coming from the categories of the understanding. When one attempts to apply these categories (e.g., unity, negation, causality and dependence) to objects of which one has no sense experience, one gets only empty concepts. That is to say, one gets only hopeless contradictions, antinomies which are equally possible and for which there is no basis to judge between them.[7]

This issue was taken further by logical positivism, a form of empiricism. According to this school of thought, there are only two types of cognitively meaningful sentences. In analytical sentences, such as mathematical propositions, the predicate is contained within the subject. These are meaningful by definition, but in a sense trivial. In synthetic propositions the predicate adds something not present within the subject. The meaning of such a sentence is the set of sense data which would verify or falsify it. Propositions which no conceivable set of sense experiences could either verify or falsify are literally non-sense statements. Metaphysics as a whole has to be cast into such a classification.

As logical positivism somewhat mellowed, this movement together with its narrow, stipulative definition of meaningfulness was replaced by "ordinary language philosophy." This approach did not decree how language must work, but instead sought to inquire how it does work in practice. Metaphysics became the study of the language of metaphysics, of the meaning of the terms used in the discussion. Descriptive metaphysics replaced normative metaphysics. That is, rather than metaphysics what philosophers were engaged in was metametaphysics.[8]

A broader objection dealt with the whole concept of truth in traditional metaphysics. Metaphysics frequently worked with some form of the correspondence theory of truth, which holds that true propositions are those which describe correctly (or "correspond to") the state of affairs to which they purport to relate. This, however, leads to endless

7. Immanuel Kant, *Critique of Pure Reason*, I, second part, first division ("Transcendental Analytic"), book 2, chapters 1 and 3.

8. Frederick Ferré, *Language, Logic, and God* (New York: Harper and Row, 1961), pp. 18–65.

useless speculation in the case of metaphysical-type statements. They have no practical value, no bearing upon human life and behavior. What must instead be examined is the practical effects of a given belief or proposition.[9] This position, known as pragmatism, was as averse to metaphysics as was logical positivism.

There also was a strong theological objection to metaphysics. Karl Barth emphatically opposed any kind of natural theology, any attempt to know God from nature or in any way outside the revelation in Jesus Christ. The God that might be known by human reason is not God, but an idol. God is not known through the concepts of logic or by any kind of discursive reasoning. He is known in the direct personal relationship he initiates, which Barth identifies as revelation. What God reveals, however, is not information about himself, but himself. So, although Barth would abhor any idea that God is ineffable, there nonetheless is no body of objective propositional truth that can be accumulated and transmitted. Thus, although we know God in his revelation, it is God that is known, not something about God. On the other hand, to know that God is one or all-powerful, which might be described as an attribute or quality of God, is to know about him, but not necessarily really to know him. To say that he has such and such metaphysical qualities is not truly knowledge about him. We do not, after all, worship the prime mover, but the God of Abraham, Isaac, and Jacob.[10]

A very different approach is represented by process theology. Process theologians agree with traditional or orthodox theology that a metaphysical understanding of theology is needed, but believe the older approach outmoded. They contend that the world has changed, and in major ways. It is not actually the world as existent reality that has changed, although that also is true in a sense. It is the world of ideas, the understanding of the nature of reality, that is different. There is now a new understanding of God which involves less distortion of what he actually is than did the older understanding of him as static. The new view of God is part of the overall understanding of reality. The world or, more correctly, the universe is understood as growing, developing, evolving. The fundamental unit of reality is not substance, but event. Further, reality is organic, so that all of it is interrelated with everything else, and what is true of one segment of it is therefore also true of the entirety. Any change, development, or growth within the whole of reality is true of God as well. So while process theology is thoroughly meta-

9. William James, *Pragmatism* (New York: Meridian, 1955), pp. 41–86.
10. Karl Barth, *Church Dogmatics* (Edinburgh: T. and T. Clark, 1957), vol. 2, part 1, pp. 63–128.

physical, it is a metaphysic of process and event rather than fixed reality and substance.[11]

Process theology yields an understanding of God as basically similar to the rest of reality. Indeed, an earlier designation of this view was "naturalistic theism," for it emphasized that God is very much part of nature. This move toward an increasing understanding of God as immanent can be expected to continue in certain circles. In an extreme form, "God" will become simply a name for the ideals and actions of people. So Edward Scribner Ames once said that God is like Alma Mater or Uncle Sam. He is real, for he embodies all of the ideals of Christian people.[12]

The emphasis on immanence has a number of components and corollaries. One is that there is basically one level or type of reality. There is no supernatural realm outside of and apart from the observable realm of nature. Consequently, there are no miracles in the sense of actions contrary to or at least not explainable on the basis of the known laws of nature, for there is no realm from which such actions could derive. Further, since all of reality is of one type, it is all known by the same method. There is no special means of knowledge of religious or theological truth, as through revelation, for example. In this conception of God, everything is given a natural explanation. Prayer is often replaced by meditation or introspection or getting in touch with oneself.

The concept of the unity of all reality will also involve a diminution of the personal quality of God. Experiencing someone as personal involves a distinction of that person from all other persons and things. We do not know a group of persons in a personal fashion. It is only when someone is singled out from the group that distinctive characteristics and qualities can be known in such a way as to make one individually real. To be personal is, to a large extent, to be unique. That is part of why objects are experienced impersonally. To the extent that an object, such as an automobile, begins to take on distinctive qualities, it will begin to be treated quasi-personally, for example, by being given a name.

The weakening of the concept of God since the high point of neo-orthodoxy can be expected to continue. Among the contributing factors is that the intellectual problem of how to conceive of the relationship between God and the processes of nature will tend to be resolved by moving from a dualistic to a monistic scheme. A second factor will be the growing presence of Eastern religions, and the assimilation of some of their ideas into Christian theology. In general, these ideas tend to

---

11. Norman Pittenger, "Process Thought as a Conceptuality for Reinterpreting Christian Faith," *Encounter* 44.2 (Spring 1983): 111.
12. Edward Scribner Ames, *Religion* (New York: H. Holt, 1929), p. 133.

emphasize the oneness between "God," in whatever form, and the world, but especially between the human individual and ultimate reality, however that is conceived. What we are talking about here is not primarily intellectual or cognitive. It is more intuitive. Rather than a definite and clear understanding of the person of God and his relationship to the processes of nature, there is almost an emotion, a feeling about nature. The ultimate force or person is sensed more than known. A third factor is the growing pragmatic effect of science and technology. While the developments of modern science are not yet at the point where science is worshiped, there is a virtually reverential awe for its pronouncements. A widespread indication of this is the advertising world's appeals that utilize the authority of a "scientist" in a white jacket.

Feminism

Also weakening the doctrine of God is the growing impact of feminism, which has a paradoxical effect. On the one hand, it tends to depersonalize the conception of God by minimizing certain images in the revelation which give him particularity. Instead of God as Father, we have the father-mother god or the divine parent. This gain in inclusiveness is achieved at the cost of a certain loss of concreteness. On the other hand, we are enabled thereby to understand God as not limited to maleness, and thus to relate to God on a broader scope of experience. This inclusiveness especially helps women to personalize God to a greater degree and thus to have a closer relationship with God.

Popular Christian Music

When we turn to distinctly evangelical understandings of God, we find another interesting paradox. A leading indicator is the music of evangelicalism. An examination of its songs reveals a narrowing of the conception of God. On the one hand, there is a strong portrayal of God as powerful, giving victory over the forces of evil, and protecting and providing for his children. This emphasis upon the greatness and loftiness of God can be expected to grow. The idea is that God's capability is far beyond human capability. This might well be termed ontological transcendence.

Coupled with this ontological transcendence, however, is a diminishing of the emphasis upon God's holiness, righteousness, and his expectations of and demands upon his people. In the popular songs of today's church one finds very little about this aspect of God's nature, and virtually nothing about the idea of divine judgment. There is no reference to repentance and confession of sins, and very little mention is made of the need for cleansing and forgiveness.[13] The most crucial missing ingredient appears to be any indication of what Rudolf Otto called the *mysterium tremendum*, a sense of awe in the presence of the sacred.[14] Even the consciousness of the greatness of God in the forces of nature does not seem to evoke this emotion. Instead there is considerable indication of intimacy between the believer and God, suggesting moral continuity rather than discontinuity. Thus what we appear to have in the music of evangelicalism is moral immanence together with ontological transcendence.

It seems, however, that we can see the beginnings of a shift back toward greater emphasis upon God's moral transcendence. A comparison of the content of Integrity Music's *Hosanna! Music*, containing many songs written since 1983, with that of *Maranatha! Music Praise Chorus Book*, which was published in 1983, shows some interesting changes. Eleven percent of the songs in *Maranatha!* mention what could be termed the metaphysical transcendence of God and 2 percent refer to his moral transcendence. In *Hosanna!* however, the figures increase respectively to 38 and 15 percent. On the other hand, references to immanence also increase significantly, from 7 to 22 percent.[15] This probably indicates a generally heightened increase of interest in doctrine.

Technology in the Practice of Ministry

Paralleling what we have already seen of the evangelicals' growing sense of divine immanence is an indication from the practice of ministry. Conservative churches have in the past been relatively slow to adopt some of the new techniques available from the social and other sciences. There was a tendency to rely upon prayer and faith in God's direct action where change was desired. What God would do was considered relatively unpredictable. God might choose to act, but he might not. He was sovereign, so he was not bound to bless one particular program rather than another. In recent years, however, evangelicals have been at the forefront in employing technology, including nonmechanical procedures. Evangelicals have made extensive use of the popular media, such as radio and especially television, far outstripping the mainline denom-

---

13. See, e.g., the choruses in *Maranatha! Music Praise Chorus Book* (Costa Mesa, Calif.: Maranatha! Music, 1983).

14. Rudolf Otto, *The Idea of the Holy* (New York: Oxford University Press, 1958), pp. 12–40.

15. Kendal Anderson, "The Legacy of Kum Ba Yah: Heritage or Heresy?" (Unpublished paper, Bethel Theological Seminary, St. Paul, 1991), p. 10. See also *Hosanna! Music: New Songs for Worshipping Churches. Praise Worship Songbook 5* (Mobile: Integrity Music, 1991).

inations.[16] They have also developed highly refined, sophisticated forms of fund-raising.

One dramatic indication of the change in attitude is found in the area of church planting. Here again evangelicals are clearly taking the lead, while liberal churches are having difficulty maintaining their present situation. The sophistication with which evangelicals are planting churches belies the conservative nature of the message they present. The message is actually not so much conservative as radical, for it calls for and promises not merely some adjustments, but an extremely revolutionary change of one's life. It is a protest against the status quo, and in rather dramatic fashion. In selecting a location to plant a church where they can present this message, evangelicals make use of very sophisticated demographic studies. Then in the actual process of establishing the new congregation they use techniques such as telemarketing, which yields statistically predictable results. They explain these results as being the working of God—it is he who brings people to the services in the new location. But it is peculiar, is it not, that the way and degree of God's working are relatively predictable in this situation? Here God seems to have been virtually reduced to working immanently through technical procedures.

Church planting is not the only area in which this practical acceptance of the immanence of divine working is exhibited. Techniques of evangelism, counseling, and church management all show rather heavy indebtedness to social sciences. Whether or not the work of God can be programed, the results of these techniques can apparently be predicted. If the general thesis which we propounded in chapter 1 is correct, this strong emphasis on the immanent working of God will continue. At some point, however, a reaction back toward a more transcendent model will follow.

Factors Leading to a Strengthened Doctrine of God

Charismatic Christianity

At the same time as the growing sense of divine immanence, a diametrically opposite development is at work within evangelicalism. There is a renewal of belief in God's miraculous or unusual working, such as in the biblical phenomena of healing and speaking in tongues. In general, we have in view the charismatic movement that has been growing in influence within both Protestant and Catholic churches for

16. James Davison Hunter, *Evangelicalism: The Coming Generation* (Chicago: University of Chicago Press, 1987), p. 7.

some time. Beyond those who clearly identify themselves as charismatics, however, there is a similar trend in other circles as well. One of them is the phenomenon of "power evangelism" or the "signs and wonders" movement, which is based upon those passages in Acts according to which the apostles did "signs and wonders" as they bore witness to the resurrection of Christ (e.g., 2:43; 5:12; 14:3). In keeping with the use of the term *sēmeia* ("signs") for miracles, the central idea of the signs and wonders movement is that miracles accompanying the preaching of the good news are a major means by which God brings about faith. As in the time of the New Testament church, such miracles are occurring today as well and should be expected.[17]

Here is a view of God as thoroughly transcendent. Instead of working through natural processes in rather predictable ways, and thus apparently being subject to natural laws, God is seen as working in ways which transcend nature and its laws. This is a thoroughgoing supernaturalism.

Decline of Confidence in Technology

Another factor that will lead to a strengthened doctrine of God is the continuing erosion of belief in the efficacy of natural processes and technology for the solution to humanity's ultimate problems. The shortcomings of technology will become increasingly apparent on the pragmatic level. On the one hand, this is a time in which some of our global problems appear to be resolvable. The so-called Cold War between East and West is over, the Berlin Wall and other such obstructions gone permanently. The nations of Europe are coming together into an economic federation which promises to bring greater trust and cooperation. Steps are being taken to control and nullify the problems of pollution. These positive developments may well keep the optimistic emphasis on immanentism in place for a while longer. The end of the Cold War may have delayed the reversal in thinking which in some ways was far overdue.

There are, however, enough unsolved difficulties of a major sort that any kind of hope for a naturalistic solution to the world's problems seems empty. Indeed, many of these problems continue to grow. Although tensions between the superpowers seem to have eased, little progress has been made toward elimination of worldwide terrorism. The elections in Russia in late 1993 gave evidence of a resurgent nationalism there. Furthermore, domestic crime is on the rise. The use of drugs such as cocaine and the accompanying problems accelerate. Despite political and social progress, there are innumerable situations of injustice and exploitation.

17. John Wimber and Kevin Springer, *Power Evangelism* (San Francisco: Harper and Row, 1986), p. 50.

New diseases such as AIDS threaten to become epidemics. Natural disasters are invulnerable to any human attempts to combat them. In short, while modern science has succeeded in overcoming some of the serious problems which the human race faces, it has done very little with many critical ones. The realization that the view that God is working immanently in technological processes and progress is therefore inevitable does not fit the facts of life will be a significant factor in its decline.

Disillusionment with Eastern Religions

Another factor will be disillusionment with Eastern religions and their ideological offspring. Currently, New Age views are experiencing considerable popularity, especially among younger persons who are reacting against the relatively conventional religious backgrounds in which they were raised. There is a sense of novelty and intrigue about the Eastern religions, but they will gradually become less novel. At that point the actual substance of such religions, their conceptions and practices, will have to sustain them. Both rationality and practicality will prevail then, I believe. The result will be a reaction against views which tend to blur the divine and the natural, the divine and the human.

Strengthened Philosophical Resources

I believe another factor will enter in. For some time, an intellectually adequate case has not been made for a transcendent view of God. One reason is that its adherents did not possess the necessary resources. I am not here impugning anyone's intellectual capacities and abilities; rather, I am saying that preparation in metaphysics, and even the knowledge of the categories and arguments necessary to make the case, was inadequate.

As we saw earlier in this chapter, several different schools of thought rejected metaphysical thinking, and with it the idea of a metaphysically transcendent God. Then, when there was a resurgence of metaphysical thinking, it was process philosophy and process theology with its strongly immanent God that prevailed. In part this was because relatively few Christians, and especially conservative or orthodox Christians, were active in technical philosophy. It was difficult, if not impossible, thirty or forty years ago to find an orthodox Christian who was teaching philosophy at a major university. Consequently, the orthodox understanding of God was not being developed with the philosophical precision necessary to make it a viable intellectual option at the higher level of scholarly sophistication.

That situation has changed, however, and it appears that the change will continue and even accelerate. It is not uncommon to find several

Christians in the philosophy department of a major university; in many cases a Christian serves as the chairperson.[18] The Society of Christian Philosophers is perhaps the best indication of this phenomenon. Now numbering more than one thousand members, it has become an international organization.

The result of the increase in the number of Christians active in philosophy has been a literature giving competent treatment to some of the classical issues of theology. This production naturally lags the arrival of scholars in the field, so we can expect a growing body of literature in the years ahead. Whereas the options in metaphysics have seemed to be either process thought or some sort of Thomism, the possibility of an orthodox doctrine of God which combines his independence of the creation with his dynamic involvement in it is now greatly enhanced. The establishment of a genuine option should help change the direction of beliefs on this crucial subject.

In the realm of evangelical theology, we have noted the two relatively opposed tendencies. In some areas, however, there is a notable move of both extremes toward the middle. Quite likely the same will happen here as well. What is most needed is a more sophisticated treatment of the relationship between the supernatural and the natural, but that should be forthcoming as philosophical treatments of theological issues continue to develop.

Increased Acceptance of the Doctrine of the Trinity

It is my expectation that the doctrine of God will also be strengthened by a short-range trend on the part of professional theologians toward a greater acceptance of the doctrine of the Trinity. One of the reasons for this trend is the increased attention and exposition being given to the Trinity. Some of the most capable and insightful twentieth-century theologians have written major works on the subject.[19] They are providing options for understanding this seemingly enigmatic doctrine. Wolfhart Pannenberg recently said in private conversation that he believes the Trinity to be the most crucial doctrine at this time.

A second reason for increased acceptance of the doctrine of the Trinity is increased belief in the deity of Jesus Christ. This has always pre-

18. Kristine Christlieb, "Suddenly, Respect: Christianity Makes a Comeback in the Philosophy Department," *Christianity Today* 31.7 (April 17, 1987): 30–32.

19. Karl Barth, *Church Dogmatics*, 2d ed. (Edinburgh: T. and T. Clark, 1975), vol. 1, part 1, pp. 295–489; Jürgen Moltmann, *The Trinity and the Kingdom: The Doctrine of God* (San Francisco: Harper and Row, 1981); Eberhard Jüngel, *God as the Mystery of the World* (Grand Rapids: Eerdmans, 1983); Thomas F. Torrance, *The Trinitarian Faith* (Minneapolis: Augsburg Fortress, 1988); Karl Rahner, *The Trinity* (New York: Seabury, 1970).

sented one of the major problems for the doctrine of the Trinity. For the problems of the Trinity and the incarnation have been interactive with one another in a way in which the doctrine of the Holy Spirit, for example, did not interact with the doctrine of the Trinity. At some points difficulty with the Trinity resulted in doubt about the deity of Christ. More recently, the problem of establishing the ontological deity of Jesus has made the Trinity seem uncertain. But changes in biblical theology are now leading, or will lead, to a more widespread belief in the ontological deity of Christ. These changes have, at least in part, been a function of changes in form criticism of the Gospels, leading us to greater certainty regarding the historical Jesus.[20] As confidence has increased regarding the earliest strata of tradition in the Gospels, what has emerged is a picture of that Jesus as more clearly divine than had been previously thought.

A third reason for increased acceptance of the Trinity is a change in the very conceptions of biblical theology. It was popular, some thirty or so years ago, to draw a sharp distinction between biblical thought and Greek thought, the former being more definitely identified with Hebrew thought. Biblical thought at its purest was, according to this interpretation, nonspeculative, nonmetaphysical. It was not concerned with theoretical matters of an ultimate nature. Thus, when dealing with issues of Christology, biblical thought was not primarily interested in the question of who or what Jesus was, but what he did. Genuine biblical Christology, then, it was reasoned, does not concern itself with ontological questions, but with functional questions. Questions about natures and persons, such as were asked at Chalcedon, are not found in the Bible, and lead to unnecessary and perhaps even illegitimate additions to the biblical revelation. This type of thinking permeated many different Christologies.[21] While we will explore these matters in greater detail in the chapter on the person of Christ, we note here that they did not contribute to belief in an ontological Trinity.

The notion that biblical thought is nonmetaphysical has fallen on hard times, however. The very set of categories which underlay the division into Hebrew and Greek thought is now questionable at best. This was one of the walls of the biblical-theology movement which Brevard Childs described in 1970 as cracking.[22] For James Barr had demonstrated quite convincingly that the scheme did not rest upon a correct analysis

20. See, e.g., Craig Blomberg, *The Historical Reliability of the Gospels* (Downers Grove, Ill.: Inter-Varsity, 1987).
21. E.g., Oscar Cullmann, *The Christology of the New Testament* (Philadelphia: Westminster, 1959).
22. Brevard S. Childs, *Biblical Theology in Crisis* (Philadelphia: Westminster, 1970), p. 72.

of the semantics of the biblical languages.[23] Thus belief in an ontological deity of Christ became possible, and with it belief in an ontological Trinity. With the metaphysical puzzles of the components becoming more easily maintained, the feasibility of the whole has also increased.

The expansion in work by conservative Christian philosophers should be especially helpful as we try to develop our understanding of the Trinity, which has traditionally been one of the most difficult logical puzzles for theology.[24] While it is unlikely that the difficulties will ever be completely resolved, any reduction of the enigma should help strengthen the doctrine of God.

Remaining Issues for the Doctrine of God

Einsteinian Physics and Divine Transcendence

Important issues regarding God's relationship to the world remain to be dealt with. Here, it appears to me, there are a number of issues which have not been worked out in light of fairly recent developments in the nontheological realms. For example, we need to incorporate into our understanding of creation the full implications of the Einsteinian versus the Newtonian understanding of the universe. The Newtonian view carried a sort of absoluteness and finality to it. Laws were supreme. God's relationship to the creation consisted in his having brought it into being and given it the laws which are now to be found within it. Thus a sort of deism could be constructed which would fit quite well the Newtonian view. In the more dynamic view of the world found in Einsteinian physics, however, there is room for, and indeed there may be a necessity for, a more active and dynamic relationship of God to the world. I anticipate that a thorough and self-conscious application of the new developments in physics will result in a heightening of the concept of God as personal and active in the world.

One special area where continued work is needed, and where the new physics may be of special help, is the doctrines of transcendence and immanence. For our purposes here, the issue may be put in terms of the transcendence of God. How or in what way does God transcend, stand apart from, remain independent of the creation? In Newtonian physics this issue tended to be dealt with in spatial terms, as indeed it had for many centuries. The concept of space that was involved was understood

23. James Barr, *The Semantics of Biblical Language* (New York: Oxford University Press, 1961).

24. See, e.g., Peter Van Inwagen, "And Yet They Are Not Three Gods But One God," in *Philosophy and the Christian Faith*, ed. Thomas V. Morris (Notre Dame, Ind.: University of Notre Dame Press, 1988), pp. 241–78.

to be in some sense absolute. Thus God was thought of as "up there" or "out there." This mode of thinking of course resulted in certain absurdities which in its latter variety went beyond the problem which Rudolf Bultmann focused upon in his program of demythologization. At stake in part is the whole issue of how a spirit (an explicit designation for God in John 4:24) relates to the world of space and time. This is a problem which impinges upon a number of doctrines, including such issues in eschatology as the nature of resurrection and the nature of heaven and hell (i.e., are they "places" that can be plotted in terms of the present space-time universe?).[25]

Efforts have been made to recast the understanding of transcendence in terms other than space. Jürgen Moltmann, for example, makes it a function of time, so that God exists in the fullest sense primarily in the future.[26] He is the God who will be, so to speak. He awaits us in the future.

It appears to me that Einsteinian physics provides us with resources for rethinking the doctrine of divine transcendence. Topics like the convertibility of matter to energy, the relativity of time and space, and the conceivability of parallel universes present possibilities which have not been fully explored. I predict that exploration of such subjects will positively enrich the orthodox understanding of God.

The Problem of Evil

A second area which will and must continue to receive attention is the doctrine of providence as it is affected by the problem of evil. This problem is of course a perennial one for Christian theology and for all strong theisms. It will probably continue throughout the earthly history of the church. I anticipate an increasing awareness that real progress will be made only as the distinctive features of biblical theism are recognized and assimilated. Most attempts to handle the problem have used only the resources of a bare philosophical theism. Only when the doctrines of incarnation, resurrection, and eschatological judgment are taken into account, however, will real progress toward cutting the Gordian knot become possible. This in turn will strengthen belief in the biblical picture of God, and in fact in the authority or at least the relevance of Scripture itself.

One of the aspects of the biblical picture of God that are worth exploring in this connection is his passibility, to use an ancient term. The orthodox tradition frequently drew upon Greek and especially Aristotelian philosophy to construct a doctrine of God as unmoved, unaffected

25. John A. T. Robinson, *Honest to God* (Philadelphia: Westminster, 1963), pp. 11–44.
26. Jürgen Moltmann, *Theology of Hope* (New York: Harper and Row, 1967), pp. 37–94.

by anything which transpires within this world. It understood as imperfect a God who could be affected personally by what happens in the world; rather, God should remain aloof, above the fray. The orthodox tradition regarded all references to emotion on the part of God as anthropomorphisms (or, more correctly, anthropopathisms). More recently, process theology has constructed a view of God as participating fully in all that goes on in the world and as being greatly affected by it. Indeed, he is finite, if such terminology is appropriate in the context of process theology.[27] Sometime in the future there will be a blending or a synthesis of sorts between the two conceptions. There is a growing recognition, not primarily on philosophical but on biblical grounds, that while God is transcendent and immutable, he is also an active and involved being who actually feels the sufferings of his human children and is moved by them.[28]

The Rise of Experiential Religion

An additional factor which I believe will have an impact upon the theological understanding of God is the rise in experiential religion. In many circles a direct relationship to God is being experienced as it has not been experienced before. For example, the typical practicing Roman Catholic's understanding of Christian experience and of worship is rather different from what was the case twenty years ago. Instead of utilizing Latin and treating the worshipers as spectators, Catholic services now provide for more participation by the worshipers, and the mass is said in their language. Instead of preformed prayers read or recited, which always carried the danger of repetition without consciousness of meaning, prayers are now expressions of one's own thought in one's own words. This has the effect of making God more personal to the individual Christian.

There is another dimension. As the more evangelical understanding that the Christian life involves a personal relationship to Jesus Christ spreads, it also raises the question of the nature of prayer and its relationship to the providence of God. In short, a theology of prayer will become necessary, and especially when our prayers apparently go unanswered. We will have to consider whether praying affects what God does. And if so, how his will, decrees, and foreknowledge relate to our prayers. These issues will undoubtedly receive additional attention in the years ahead.

27. Pittenger, "Process Thought," pp. 112–17.
28. See, e.g., Bruce Ware, "An Evangelical Reformulation of the Doctrine of the Immutability of God," *Journal of the Evangelical Theological Society* 29.4 (Dec. 1986): 431–46.

The Decline of Authoritarianism

There is a well-documented trend away from authoritarianism in decision making toward a more democratic or participatory approach.[29] Everyone in a leadership role has discovered this—even the leaders of totalitarian Communist states, as Mikhail Gorbachev and countless others can attest.

We have noted in a number of areas the tendency of Christians, even evangelical Christians, to absorb and reflect the values of the broader society about them. If this is the case in this area as well, then what results might we see from the decline of authoritarianism? There may well be a tendency to minimize the idea of the absoluteness and sovereignty of God. For certainly the idea of a God of power who has the right to make decisions unilaterally conflicts with the recent trend. We may see on a popular and informal level the sort of view that some liberals advocated earlier in the twentieth century. Finding the concept of the kingdom of God offensive (today they might call it patriarchal), they spoke instead of the democracy of God.

The Need for Careful Definition

The poll data cited earlier suggest that in doing evangelism and, to a lesser extent, in teaching believers we must be extremely diligent to make clear what we mean by God. As one teacher of evangelism has cautioned: "When we say, 'God loves you,' to an unbeliever, we may assume he understands by those words the same thing we mean by them. Actually, his understanding of God may be the Force, if he has seen *Star Wars*, and his understanding of 'loves' may be, as the word is commonly interpreted, 'lusts.' Thus our statement 'God loves you' is heard as 'The Force lusts after you.'" So we must clearly teach what the Bible means when it speaks about God.

An Unresolved Tension

Finally, we will need to resolve the issues that have arisen from reliance upon the findings and techniques of behavioral sciences. An example is the use of telemarketing, especially in church planting. The advocates of this technique contend that the results are quite predictable. Peter Wagner, for example, asserts that one can predict with a high degree of confidence that if twenty thousand telephone calls are made, two thousand persons will ask to be put on the mailing list of the new

29. John Naisbitt, *Megatrends: Ten New Directions Transforming Our Lives* (New York: Warner, 1982), pp. 189–205; John Naisbitt and Patricia Aburdene, *Megatrends 2000: Ten New Trends for the 1990's* (New York: Avon, 1991), pp. 240–44.

church, and two hundred will show up at the first service.[30] At least on the surface this confidence in results appears to conflict with the idea of a transcendent God working in response to prayer in ways which cannot be predicted or, in a sense, even measured by human means. I would anticipate that an early practical effect of this idea would be a view virtually excluding God from any real influence upon the events of human history, in other words, a tendency to regard God as quite transcendent. Then there will follow a tendency to identify the use of technical methods as God's working, in other words, a view of him as more immanent. Eventually, however, the conflict between the two ways of thinking will force some type of dialogue and consequent resolution of the theological issues.

Ironically, one sometimes finds the two conflicting positions within the thought and writings of the same person. An example is Wagner, who advocates a very controlled form of church-planting ministry which will have very predictable results, but who also recommends that a Christian who travels to foreign countries and visits temples of non-Christian religions hold an exorcism upon returning home, since demons may have attached themselves to one's luggage or person.[31] Another example is Charles Kraft, who employs the methods and conceptions of modern anthropology in some of his writings,[32] but in another decries the closed scientific mentality, arguing instead for a view which allows ample room for the activity of demons.[33] It may well be that these men shifted their views, but they really ought to have indicated that a change in conviction had taken place. The tension or paradox cannot be maintained indefinitely. We will need to give our attention to it. I anticipate that this subject will be prominent in doctrinal discussions in the next few years.

30. C. Peter Wagner, *Church Planting for a Greater Harvest: A Comprehensive Guide* (Ventura, Calif.: Regal, 1990), pp. 107–9.

31. C. Peter Wagner, "Can Demons Harm Christians?" *Christian Life* 47.1 (May 1985): 76.

32. Charles Kraft, *Christianity in Culture: A Study in Dynamic Biblical Theologizing in Cross-cultural Perspective* (Maryknoll, N.Y.: Orbis, 1979); and idem, "Interpreting in Cultural Context," *Journal of the Evangelical Theological Society* 21.4 (Dec. 1978): 357–67.

33. Charles Kraft, *Christianity with Power: Your Worldview and Your Experience of the Supernatural* (Ann Arbor: Servant, 1989), pp. 37–49.

7

The Doctrine of Humanity

The doctrine of humanity occupies a prominent position in Christian theology and especially in popular thinking. Though, as we shall note, its special development has come relatively late in the history of Christian thought, it has received a great amount of attention in recent years. This is in part due to the fact that humanity is a doctrinal area about which everyone has a certain amount of knowledge. All of us, whether we know anything about God or even believe that he exists, nonetheless know and have contact with ourselves and other human beings. Further, all of us have a natural interest in humanity, what it is and what will happen to it, topics that concern and involve each of us directly and personally. In addition, the so-called human sciences or behavioral sciences have come to maturity only in relatively recent times. All these factors have generated a great amount of work at a time when some are altering or even abandoning the sources and framework of the doctrine.

The Classical Conception of Human Nature

Classical culture sought to identify the essence of humanity or human nature. This endeavor was simply an attempt to apply to humanity the same mode of investigation with which the early philosophers examined everything in their universe. Plato found the essences or pure natures of things in certain abstract forms or ideas. Individual existences were copies, shadows, or instantiations of these forms, and were less real than the forms. In Aristotle's thought the forms were united with matter, finding existence only within empirical instances. They were known through sense experience. Both varieties of Greek philosophy held that everything has an essence, a set of characteristics which makes it what it is. This understanding carried over to humanity as well. There was a search to determine the essence of human nature, to discover what makes a human being human. This search assumed an intrinsic or inherent set of qualities. A human being would be understood to be a human by virtue of possessing certain characteristics, rationality, for example.

In the Christian version, what made human beings distinctive was possession of the image of God, which had been conferred upon the human in the original creation (Gen. 1:26–27). What the image consisted of was variously conceived from theologian to theologian, although reason was a most common candidate. All were agreed, however, that the image was a substantive or structural element in the human person. They were also agreed that this objective quality or set of qualities had been received from God.

There also was, in the traditional Christian understanding, a definite conception regarding the relationship of humanity to the rest of the creation. The human was both one of many creatures, all having come from the hand of the same Creator, and the culminating member of the series. Thus there was a sense of being at home in the universe. It was not inherently foreign or hostile to humans. It represented a benevolent God's provision of an environment in which they were to live and be nurtured. Although there might be factors within the universe which at times worked to human disadvantage, this was not an intrinsic or intentional situation. Thus there was a certain comfort in the doctrine of humanity. God was in control of the creation, and nothing contrary to his will could occur.[1]

The relationship of the human to God was also crucial to the traditional Christian view. It was not simply that the human was finite; other views held that as well. Rather, humanity had been brought into existence as a finite being by the action of the infinite and perfect being. Thus both finitude and creaturehood were essential characteristics of the human. The human had been created to have fellowship with the perfect being, and was to serve, love, obey, and glorify that being. Finitude in itself was not understood as constituting a problem for the human.

The Christian view also identified one individual man as a paradigm for human nature. Not only was Adam the first human being, he was the entire human race. In him the human race was present in germinal or seminal form. He, as created, was the embodiment of what a human being is intended to be.

In addition, there was a definite social factor in the understanding of human nature. The man was not complete by himself. So God found it necessary to make a companion for him, which God did by taking a rib from the man and forming it into a female human being. Many conservative theologians infer from the second creation account (Gen. 2:18–22) the inferiority of the female to the male, and the necessity of her being subject to him. Though there is no explicit statement to that effect, they conclude from the priority of the male's creation that he was therefore inherently superior as well.

The social understanding of human nature carried over to broader applications. The entire human race, being derived and descended from that one man, was thought of as his family; Adam was their head and progenitor. This was to have significant implications when applied to the issue of sin.

There was, finally, in the traditional Christian understanding a bit of a paradox regarding human responsibility. Although God took the ini-

---

1. David H. Kelsey, "Human Being," in *Christian Theology: An Introduction to Its Traditions and Tasks*, ed. Peter C. Hodgson and Robert H. King, 2d ed. (Philadelphia: Fortress, 1985), pp. 168–69.

tiative—creating humankind, giving them a specific nature, and placing them within a setting prepared for them—he then turned over to the individual created human the responsibility for oneself. This sense of freedom and responsibility became clear with the temptation and fall (Gen. 3). Humankind could blame neither God nor the created world about them for their failings, which soon became apparent. Although God had given humans their nature, they were responsible for what they did with it.

Factors Changing the Understanding of Humanity

The Theory of Evolution

In the past two centuries, a number of influences have come to bear upon the understanding of humanity, and have in turn affected the Christian doctrine. One of these factors has been the theory of evolution as it applies to the origin and definition of humanity. Evolution has provided an alternative to the belief in the special divine creation of the human race. In the evolutionary scheme humans are not the highest product of God's creation, but of a process of development governed by immanent laws within the physical universe. In addition, monogenetic origin—the idea that the human race began with a single primal couple—is frequently denied.

The effects of the theory of evolution have been several. Humanity is defined not by looking backward to an original paradigm as its best example, but by looking forward to the end product which is to come. In addition, the fundamental affinity of the human with the animal is emphasized. This has the tendency to place more significance on the physical than on the other dimensions of human nature. And, given the absence of any special conferral of a spiritual nature, there is a strong emphasis upon the unity of the human. Humans do not possess a soul or spiritual nature which was given to them but not to any other creatures. While this emphasis upon the unity of the individual human increases, the emphasis upon the unity of the human race declines, since all humans do not necessarily derive from the same beginning.

Some varieties of the theory, such as that of Herbert Spencer, extend the concept of evolution to all aspects of reality. Even society is governed by the law of survival of the fittest. Social Darwinism sees humans in competition with each other, so that the stronger survive and prosper, while the weaker perish. This is good and not to be tampered with, since it strengthens and purifies the human race.

Existentialism

A second modern influence upon the understanding of human nature has been the rise of existentialism. This school of thought has strongly stressed individualism and the human will. Some forms include the idea that we create our own nature by willing what we are to be. There is a strong accompanying emphasis upon personal responsibility. External influences do not make us what we are. To argue that genetics, one's parents, national or racial origin, social, educational, or economic environment is responsible for one's being what one is, is at root an unwillingness to accept oneself and one's situation. It is what Martin Heidegger has called "inauthenticity." One must will to be what one is to be.

Deterministic Views

To a large extent existentialism developed as a reaction against the various social sciences and social theories which consider humans and their actions to be largely determined by outside factors. Some of these disciplines, such as behavioristic psychology, virtually eliminate the concept of human nature. Humanity is not something which individuals have or are. It is something which they do. Human nature is not a substance or a set of characteristics. It is nothing more than a collection of conditioned responses, tendencies to act in a certain way in the presence of a certain stimulus.

Determinism sees the human condition as defined by its relationship to certain natural factors. Some of these factors are geographical or racial. Economic status or social class can also be a major consideration. Reduced in significance are the human will itself and, to an even greater extent, the work of God, which includes his original creation and continued involvement and activity as the ruler of the world.

Decline of Theocentrism

What is happening in general is that God is no longer the focal point and the defining concept in the understanding of human nature. More and more, humanity is understood in reference to some earthly or natural factors. This means that human responsibility to God is de-emphasized. Moreover, people who want to make changes in human lives, whether in status or behavior, concentrate on earthly factors. If, for example, someone's antisocial behavior is viewed as being a result of economic or educational deprivation, then the cure for the problem is thought to lie in improvement of that individual's economic situation or in further education. Concentrating on these factors will likely have profound effects on one's view of the nature and source of salvation.

Relational Theology

One movement that reflects the growing tendency to define humanity basically in social terms is relational theology. Probably the chief ideological spokesperson for the movement has been Bruce Larson, an ordained Presbyterian minister. He attempts to mediate between, on one hand, socially sensitive but theologically somewhat indifferent liberalism and, on the other, theologically precise but sometimes socially insensitive conservatism. His writing, like that of Keith Miller (among others), tends to define the Christian (and presumably the ideal human) in terms of relationships with other humans.

In *Ask Me to Dance*, Larson spells out what he calls the "Jesus style in relationships." He offers a number of basic tenets or guidelines: be real (don't try to imitate any other Christian or even Jesus); identify with people; listen to people; affirm people; share decision making; don't try to change people (since this indicates that they are presently unacceptable); love specifically (one person at a time, and in particular ways); ask for help; love in terms meaningful to the other person (instead of in terms of how we think the other person ought to be loved); don't play it safe.[2] What we have here is ostensibly an emphasis upon the second commandment, the commandment to love one's neighbor as oneself. In the traditional understanding, however, this command was secondary to the command to love God with all of one's being. Real love for others, then, real concern for their ultimate welfare, would be defined by what God has established as right and wrong. In relational theology, however, humans are the primary consideration, and even others' conception of what is good for them. The pattern for behavior is not found in the commands or even the example of Jesus. Rather, fidelity to one's own nature and concern for others are the determining factors. Certain human and social factors are, then, the indicators of true or highest humanity. Likeness to God, which is linked to the concept of our having been created in God's image for the purpose of fellowship with him and service to his cause, has been considerably downgraded here.

Popular Psychology

The increased interest in popular psychology is another factor changing the understanding of humanity. Rather than consulting the Scriptures or the example of Christ to determine what to be and how to act,

2. Bruce Larson, *Ask Me to Dance* (Waco: Word, 1972), pp. 55–69.

some people allow psychology to establish the criteria for human healthiness. Authenticity, adjustment, self-fulfilment, and social adaptiveness are crucial considerations.

Increased Interest in the Individual

Within American society and, for that matter, within the world community there appears to be an increased interest in the individual.[3] Witness the protests against meaningless work, routine and monotonous labor that makes the individual seem little more than a machine. Or consider that when the United States weighed how to handle the situation in the Middle East in 1991, the value of individual lives was as forceful an argument as were the potential economic advantages and disadvantages of waging war. On the global scene, even nations whose communist ideology said that the individual was nothing and the state was everything have been forced by popular pressure to change their views.

In light of this interest in the individual, the anthropocentric orientation of much of theology has been growing. The idea of a God who sovereignly decides who will live and who will die, as well as who will receive salvation and who will suffer damnation, is repulsive to many persons today. It has always been the case, but is perhaps more noticeable today, that even Christians seem to feel that God is responsible to them. He is expected to supply their needs and even their wants, in short, to make them happy. Thus the tendency to blame God when all does not go well, when a loved one, especially one's child, dies. Humans have made their lives autonomous and their own values normative.

Nontheistic Views of the Purpose of Human Existence

Another factor changing the understanding of human nature is the modern tendency for definitions of what is good for the human being to ignore theistic considerations. Probably the most obvious form is the popular preaching that encourages us to "name it and claim it." If we ask God for something that we desire, God will give it to us. This is also known as the gospel of health, wealth, and happiness. Although somewhat discredited through the exposure of the practices of a few leading television preachers, this mentality still has a strong influence upon many people who call themselves Christians. Whether euphemized as "the good life" or as "gracious living," material prosperity and comfort are seen as the highest possible fulfilment of humanity.

3. John Naisbitt and Patricia Aburdene, *Megatrends 2000: Ten New Directions for the 1990's* (New York: Avon, 1991), pp. 322–35.

We are not so much interested in the exact nature of full human life as in the source on which people draw in trying to achieve it. Many have drawn on the teachings of Jesus and advocated a simpler lifestyle. For he said,"Watch out! Be on your guard against all kinds of greed; a man's life does not consist in the abundance of his possessions" (Luke 12:15). He then told the parable of the rich fool who stored up things for himself, but was not rich toward God. Jesus warned people not to store up for themselves treasures on earth, but in heaven, where they are not subject to deterioration and destruction. The problem with material things is that they distract one from devotion to God. Sadly, however, what we appear to have today is a temporal and mundane orientation supplied by society's standards of success. There is little understanding that humanity is to find its greatest fulfilment in fellowship with God.

In the 1960s there was a well-documented shift within American society toward subjectivity. It involved a virtual veneration of the self, shown in deliberate efforts to achieve self-understanding, self-improvement, and self-fulfilment. Has this large societal trend had any effect upon Christianity, including its doctrinal understanding of the meaning of humanity? James Davison Hunter offers some clear evidence that this has indeed taken place, especially within the younger generation of evangelicals. When presented with the statement "Self-improvement is important to me and I work hard at it," 87 percent of the evangelical-college students in his sample and 82 percent of the seminary students agreed, as compared with 87 percent of the public university students and 66 percent of the general population. In response to the statement "I feel a strong need for new experiences," 68 percent of the evangelical-college students, 52 percent of the evangelical-seminary students, 78 percent of the public university students, and 46 percent of the general population agreed. Perhaps the most telling response, however, was to the statement "For the Christian, realizing your full potential as a human being is just as important as putting others before you." Here 62 percent of the evangelical-college students responded affirmatively, compared with 46 percent of the evangelical-seminary students and 44 percent of the public university students (the statement was not posed to the general population).[4]

Indicative of the general understanding of the purpose of life are the responses to a statement posed by the Barna group: "The purpose of life is enjoyment and personal fulfillment." There were some significant differences between Christians and non-Christians, and between churchgoers and non-churchgoers. Yet among the born-again 25 percent agreed

4. James Davison Hunter, *Evangelicalism: The Coming Generation* (Chicago: University of Chicago Press, 1987), pp. 64–71.

strongly and 28 percent agreed somewhat, while 26 percent of the evangelicals agreed strongly and 30 percent agreed somewhat.[5] There was relatively little difference between age groups. It appears that the influence of the world's values is not restricted to the younger generation.

The pervasiveness of the values of general society is also seen in another item from the 1991 Barna survey. The respondents were asked how important different values were to them: "family; health; your time; having close friends; your free time; religion; the Bible; your career; living comfortably; money." As might be expected, there were some significant differences across age groups and between blacks and whites. Barna's closing comment gives real cause for thought:

> Perhaps most surprising, though, is the finding that if religion and the Bible are removed from the mix of factors, born again Christians and non-Christians have identical value patterns. These two groups of adults rank the other eight elements exactly the same.
>
> The only areas of true difference in relative priorities in life, among those measured, pertain to the importance of religion. How interesting that the influence of religious beliefs is not discernible in people's ranking of other factors.[6]

This suggests that the values and beliefs of Christians are more strongly influenced by the surrounding culture than we might wish to believe. Although there is quite strong formal commitment to religion and the Bible, that commitment appears to be largely restricted in practice to spiritual matters. More-general matters are culturally determined. Thus, gradually, even the understanding of the nature of humanity will come from sources other than special revelation.

Reasons for Growing Interest in the Doctrine

Past Neglect

It appears that in the years ahead the doctrine of humanity will get more attention than will some other doctrines. One of the reasons is the relative lack of attention given this doctrine in the past. The Apostles' Creed, for example, makes no statement regarding humanity. Like the Bible, which was simply drawn upon, humanity receives no direct and deliberate discussion. Presumably the subject was so familiar that no special treatment was required. It is implied in the statement about the

5. George Barna, *The Barna Report: What Americans Believe* (Ventura, Calif.: Regal, 1991), p. 94.
6. Ibid., p. 154.

forgiveness of sins, and to a lesser degree in the reference to Jesus' being born of a virgin, but that is the extent of the treatment.

Nor, for that matter, did the councils which met in the fourth and fifth centuries to discuss the issues of Christ and of the Trinity concern themselves specifically with the doctrine of humanity. The subject was once again implied in the discussion with the Apollinarians about the nature of Jesus' full humanity, but that was only an oblique and somewhat isolated treatment. It concerned the question of what makes up human nature, namely, the physical and the psychological, but not the issue of what the human being really is, or what humanity is. The dispute between Augustine and Pelagius was strongly involved with the question of human nature, but was primarily oriented toward the issue of the relative goodness and sinfulness of humans rather than toward the essence of humanity as such. Other treatments either isolated some aspect of human nature, such as the image of God, or merely touched on the general subject in connection with another topic, such as Christology. Even the Protestant-Catholic disputes connected with the Reformation and the Counter-Reformation tended to deal with questions like what constituted the image and what constituted the likeness of God, that is to say, which of God's qualities were natural to humankind and thus were retained, and which others were superadded and thus were lost in the fall.

Nor, for that matter, have recent surveys of religious conviction done much to illuminate the theme. The *Christianity Today*–Gallup poll of 1979 did not really pose any question on the topic of theological anthropology. There were questions about the validity of certain ethical principles and precepts, and the rightness or wrongness of particular practices, but nothing dealing directly with the nature of humanity itself. Similarly, Hunter's poll of young people did not directly address the nature and purpose of humanity, although there were a number of questions which in effect contained implications about the persons being queried.

I believe that the doctrine of humanity will come to play a more prominent role and will receive more thorough treatment than it has in the past. Part of the reason, as we have seen, is the simple fact that the subject is overdue for development. The time has come when theologians will turn their attention to this topic simply because it has not yet received the type of treatment that other doctrines have.

Legacy of the Evolution Debate

We have just examined what might be called the internal thrust toward increased discussion of the doctrine of humanity. In addition, there are several external factors which should evoke an accelerated treatment. One of them is the legacy of the debate over evolution. Although that discussion treated the origin of all living forms, and even of the entire universe, the real theological issue was the origin of humankind. Closely related was the issue of whether the human is merely a highly developed animal or is endowed with something distinctively spiritual. It remains for theologians to develop more fully the implications of these issues. For example, if humans are a special divine creation, what is the distinctive quality of humanity, and what should their consequent action be?

The Rise of the Behavioral Sciences

Beyond the natural sciences like biology, the social or behavioral sciences will have a major impact upon the understanding of human nature. It is only in fairly recent times that these disciplines have come into their own, and even more recently that Christians, and especially evangelicals, have attended seriously to them. When I was a student in seminary in the middle 1950s, for example, pastoral counseling was a very new subject. Very little course-work in that field was offered at that seminary, and much of what was offered was based upon rather commonsense approaches to counseling. When the seminary on whose faculty I served in 1970 sought for a qualified professor of pastoral care and counseling, the candidates available within our segment of Christendom were relatively few in number. In the ensuing twenty years, however, large numbers of evangelicals entered the field of counseling, and Fuller Theological Seminary even opened a graduate school of psychology, granting a Ph.D. in clinical psychology recognized by the American Psychological Association.

Growing problems and perhaps even crises within society and even within the church have led to greatly increased attention to issues like family relationships, child rearing, and marriage enrichment. Popular approaches have been multiplying extremely rapidly.[7] The sheer number and variety of these movements in psychology create confusion, calling for some way to evaluate them. As Gary Collins points out, many of the leaders of these popular movements have little or no training in psychology, and some are untrained theologically.[8] As a result, a considerable amount of attention is being focused on the theological implications of these movements, and especially on how they handle the

7. Gary R. Collins, "Popular Psychology: Short-cut Solutions?" *Christianity Today* 24.9 (May 2, 1980): 19–22.
    8. Ibid., p. 21.

issues of what in essence humans are, and what their purpose, role, or end in life is. I anticipate that this trend will increase.

Bioethical Issues

Another source that will stimulate theological discussion about the doctrine of humanity is the ethical issues which are forcing themselves upon us. Prominent among them is abortion. The question of whether the fetus is human is a crucial one. Yet that often resolves down into a temporal issue, since it is not possible to observe the fetus's activity directly. More pertinent perhaps is the matter of euthanasia. Here what is at stake in many cases is the definition of human life. When is it truly present, and what about the issue of the quality of life? Similarly, political debates often hinge in part upon the definition of humanity. We have in mind, for example, debates on the relative rights of the individual as opposed to the rights of the group. How does the value of individual freedom stack up against the community's need for security? With the growing interest and involvement in politics on the part of evangelical Christians, we can expect that theologians will become increasingly interested in the anthropological presuppositions of the arguments being used.

Future Directions

Efforts to Identify the Biblical Concept of Human Nature

But what directions will the heightened discussion of the doctrine of humanity take? Here a number of trends can be projected. I believe that one of the first will be a search for an understanding of human nature which does full justice to the range of biblical testimony. It will be necessary to incorporate the insights of exegesis and of the behavioral sciences.

Older theology often debated the relative merits of dichotomism and trichotomism: Is the human composed of body and soul; or of body, soul, and spirit? In some constructions body, soul, and spirit were virtually separate parts of the human person. In less extreme forms they were distinguishable aspects of the person. In either event they provided for a nonmaterial dimension capable of surviving death and thus of living on prior to the resurrection.

In the middle of the twentieth century, the conception of human nature as a composite of some sort began to come under rather heavy fire. The neoorthodox saw it as a manifestation of the liberal doctrine of the immortality of the soul. It was believed to reflect the dualism of Greek philosophy. While some thought there might be some basis in the

New Testament for drawing such a conclusion, there certainly was no such basis in the Hebrew Old Testament; and even such intimations of composite human nature as might be derived from the New Testament were regarded as reflecting the influence of Greek thought within the New Testament period.[9]

A number of factors have conspired to shed doubt upon the new consensus, however. First, it seemed to generalize regarding Greek thought. John A. T. Robinson's noted book *The Body*, for example, spoke much about Greek thought, but had not a single documentation from Greek sources.[10] Second, the sharp distinction between Greek thought and Hebrew (or "biblical") categories was called into question on semantic grounds.[11] Further, certain logical difficulties arose from the unitary conception of human nature. If the human is a unity, what is the nature of the unity? Is it material, immaterial, or what? In other words, what sort of metaphysic is to be assumed in dealing with human nature? While some branded the very raising of such questions as rationalistic, they were hard questions which would not go away. It even began to be suggested that the unitary conception might be a view read into the Bible, just as much as the composite view was read into the Bible, and perhaps more so. Indeed, modern behaviorism might have been a prime factor in establishing the monistic view of human nature.

It also has begun to be apparent that an excessive emphasis upon the unity of human nature creates difficulty for certain other doctrines. A prime instance is the neglected doctrine of the intermediate state, which deals with the status and location of the human being between death and resurrection. Several biblical passages seem to speak of an intermediate place or condition for the human. That would require some aspect of human nature able to have conscious existence without a body. Some of the exegetical attempts to interpret the passages in question as not requiring some sort of disembodied state are quite convoluted. There consequently has been doubt about the viability of the unitary view.

As theologians seek to deal with all of the considerations, there will be continued debate on the subject of the biblical concept of humanity. I anticipate that some form of nonmonistic view will begin to emerge, but the search for appropriate categories will require both diligent exegesis and self-critical philosophical endeavor. Ultimately a view which

9. Reinhold Niebuhr, *The Nature and Destiny of Man* (New York: Scribner, 1949), pp. 4–12.

10. John A. T. Robinson, *The Body* (London: SCM, 1952).

11. James Barr, *The Semantics of Biblical Language* (New York: Oxford University Press, 1961); Brevard S. Childs, *Biblical Theology in Crisis* (Philadelphia: Westminster, 1970).

expresses the permanent truth in appropriate categories for today will be constructed, although certainly not without protest from persons committed to nonbiblical presuppositions.

Growing Egocentricity

I anticipate as well a continued move toward egocentrism. This prediction is an extrapolation from trends already in place which will probably amplify. In addition, it appears from a number of studies, such as the *Christianity Today*–Gallup poll, the research done by Hunter, as well as Richard Quebedeaux's more informal studies, that the continued drift of the young evangelicals is toward a reduced separation from the thinking and practice of the secular world.[12] This mind-set is strongly oriented to the elevation of self and its needs and values over the more altruistic type of approach. In part influenced by existentialism and similar movements, there is also a strong emphasis upon freedom and autonomy rather than submission of oneself to an external authority, and particularly to God.

Decline of the Work Ethic

Among the results of the change that has taken place in the understanding of the human are, to borrow terms from the Westminster Catechism, a decline of the concept of work as a means of glorifying God and ascendency of the concept of enjoying God. The older Calvinists, and particularly the Puritans, understood work as a way of serving God and as a primary fulfilment of their purpose on earth. They especially had in view direct service of God, but also other forms of work, including one's livelihood. Work was often correlated with God's mandate that humans exercise dominion. Thrift and the accumulation of wealth, together with self-discipline and diligence, were frequently seen as special fulfilments of one's calling. Wealth was accumulated not necessarily for the sake of consumption, but almost as an end in itself, and as evidence of God's blessing. A part of laboring was to make one's "calling and election sure." Hard work, then, was not thought of as a curse, but as part of one's calling.[13]

Much has changed in that respect, however, at least in the West and especially in the United States. The decline in the length of the workweek and the highly developed leisure industry are signs of a major shift in the past three or four decades. When I was young, there was a

12. See, e.g., Hunter, *Evangelicalism*, pp. 71–75.
13. Georgia Harkness, *John Calvin: The Man and His Ethics* (New York: H. Holt, 1931), p. 183.

distinction between workaholics and hard workers. Hard workers often worked long hours and applied themselves diligently to their tasks, but they also took time off and enjoyed vacations. Workaholics, on the other hand, were compulsive about their work, did not enjoy their time off, and felt guilty if they were not doing something. Today, however, there is considerable difference in the connotation of these terms. People who apply themselves diligently, begin work on time, work until quitting time, do not take extended breaks, come to work unless ill, volunteer for assignments, and do more than what is expected of them, are no longer hard workers, but compulsive, driven workaholics. What we used to call lazy persons are now labeled well-adjusted and relationally oriented if they spend work time chatting with co-workers. Many people no longer consider work a high calling. The Japanese, the Swiss, and some other nationalities are the heirs of what was once American diligence. To some extent, this is a generational matter, as Hunter's data show,[14] and many employers and pastoral search committees have discovered.

This phenomenon carries over to Christians as well. There is something of a shift from the idea of serving God, carrying out his work, to enjoying him. This is reflected in the music of the time. Older hymns had considerable references to service and work. An outstanding example is the hymn "Work, for the Night Is Coming." One searches in vain, however, through current chorus books for similar themes. In *Maranatha! Music Praise Chorus Book*, for example, when one excludes the few older songs, the only real reference to service and work is the third stanza of "The Greatest Thing," which says, "The greatest thing in all my life is serving you," but only after "knowing you" and "loving you."

Short-Term Missions

The decline of the work ethic shows itself in other ways as well. One well-established trend in missions is toward short-term rather than career missionaries. Nearly half of all North American missionaries are short-termers. Although the number of missions with short-term programs is decreasing, the number of missions relying largely on short-term personnel has increased dramatically.[15] David Hesselgrave says that there is a consensus among missions that the benefits of short-term service are greater for the missionary than for the nationals. He

14. Hunter, *Evangelicalism*, pp. 50–75.
15. David J. Hesselgrave, *Today's Choices for Tomorrow's Mission: An Evangelical Perspective on Trends and Issues in Missions* (Grand Rapids: Zondervan, 1988), pp. 37–38.

believes that the trend results in part from the new approaches to self-fulfilment.[16]

The Charismatic Emphasis on Personal Benefits

One other trend calling for our attention is found in the "signs and wonders" movement and to some extent in the charismatic movement in general. The signs and wonders movement regards physical healing as a major dimension of the Christian life. There is a strong emphasis upon the benefit which the believer receives.

Perhaps even more significant is the profile of charismatics in the *Christianity Today*–Gallup poll of 1979. Sixty-seven percent of the charismatics polled were Protestants and 27 percent Catholics. In terms of some of the standard criteria of commitment and service, the charismatics consistently scored considerably lower than did three other groups, namely, "Tongues Speakers," "Conversionalists," and "Orthodox Evangelicals." The poll's measurements of commitment included contributing 10 percent (or 5 percent) of one's income to religious causes, reading the Bible at least once weekly, attending church at least once weekly, talking about faith at least once weekly, and doing volunteer work for church. In some of these categories the score for the charismatics was only a little higher than for the general public.[17] A possible explanation is the charismatics' tendency to rely more on direct guidance by the Holy Spirit than on the Bible. It appears that the Spirit's direct guidance regarding responsibilities may not be quite as explicit or extensive as the Bible's.

The poll also revealed a considerably larger number of charismatics than previous figures had indicated. There has evidently been, as some had predicted, a considerable outburst of Pentecostal and charismatic Christianity. If this trend continues, we can probably expect to find a shift toward a type of Christianity which emphasizes the benefits rather than the responsibilities of faith in Christ. Whether that trend is continuing and will continue, however, is difficult to determine. For some of the recent exposés which have struck Christianity involved preachers from the charismatic wing of the church. It is too early to detect whether a decline of charismatic Christianity will follow.

There do, however, seem to be increasing indications that a shift is taking place within our society with respect to the matters of self-discipline and self-indulgence. Some of the members of the me gener-

16. Ibid., pp. 83–84.
17. Kenneth S. Kantzer, "The Charismatics Among Us," *Christianity Today* 24.4 (Feb. 22, 1980): 27.

ation are now moving toward a simpler lifestyle.[18] Some young people are also expressing a desire for greater discipline. To the extent that this continues and increases, as I believe it will, we should also see a growing conception that the fullest expression of humanity is realized through focus upon God and service, and especially through sacrificial service for him.

Emphasis on Self-Determination

An interesting issue, although somewhat difficult to interpret, pertains to the belief in self-determination. The 1991 Barna survey posed the statement "Every person has the power to determine his or her own destiny in life." Of the total sample 56 percent agreed strongly and 26 percent agreed somewhat, there being relatively little variation from one age group to another. Nor did the responses of born-again Christians and evangelicals vary to any extent from the total sample.[19] It is difficult to know how to interpret these responses. As Barna observes, "It is possible to argue that believers would respond affirmatively to this statement because they believe that through the acceptance of Christ as their Savior they have the power to determine their eternal destiny."[20] This is one of those instances where theological refinement and testing out the question before the survey might have helped to reduce the ambiguity.

Noting that self-determination is one of the guiding principles of the New Age philosophy, Barna wonders whether the responses to the statement on self-determination indicate the influence of that movement.[21] It should be pointed out, however, that self-determination is not unique to the New Age philosophy. It is also found in existentialism, which has had a longer and more pervasive influence upon our society through various art forms and media. Regardless of the source of the influence, what does seem apparent is that the general mood of the populace and of Christians in particular is more favorable to an Arminian view than to a strongly Calvinistic view.

---

18. For example, by the fall of 1990 the percentage of college freshmen for whom being well off financially was very important (74 percent) had dropped slightly for the second straight year after seventeen consecutive years of increase, and the number of those interested in a career in business (18 percent) had also dropped for a second consecutive year. Indications of a growing social concern also were present. See "Record Number of Freshmen Plan to Join Protests on Campuses, Survey Prior to Gulf War Shows," *Chronicle of Higher Education* 37.20 (Jan. 30, 1991): A32.

19. Barna, *What Americans Believe*, p. 216.

20. Ibid., p. 214.

21. Ibid.

8

The Doctrine of Sin

Closely related to the doctrine of humanity is the doctrine of sin. While the former deals with humanity in its ideal state, the latter deals with actual humanity, or humanity as found in real life. Here we have some rather clear data which should be of considerable help to us in assessing current trends and future directions.

Indications of a Changed Situation

Popular Moral Reposturing

One indication of change in the general understanding of the doctrine of sin is the attitudes among evangelical young people toward practices once thought to be wrong and sinful. With regard to smoking, drinking, and theatergoing, there has been quite significant shift. On some other matters, however, there has been very little real change. On such matters as premarital and extramarital sex and homosexuality, there have been only rather negligible changes.

What is perhaps most significant for our purposes is the shift in the nature and tone of the commentary on the traditional taboos. James Davison Hunter terms this shift "moral reposturing." For example, focus on the virtues of abstinence and temperance has shifted to discussion of the problem of alcoholism in the church and society. Similarly, condemnation of sexual permissiveness and loose morals has given way to attempts to understand the human vulnerability to sexual temptation. And even though homosexuality is rather clearly rejected, the psychological anguish of the homosexual is treated with greater sympathy.[1] Though still considered practices in which a Christian should not engage, the status of the traditional taboos has changed. The conception of what they are has undergone alteration. They tend to be regarded less as sins, actions that are wrong because they disobey God and displease him. Now the emphasis is more upon their dysfunctional or unwise character than upon their inherent evil.

In part the change in approach is a matter of shifting from the categories of theology to those of social sciences the evaluation of practices once considered sinful. Instead of being viewed as subject to one's control, these practices have come to be explained in terms of certain social determinants. Because the people involved are no longer considered responsible for their actions, they need to be understood and sympathized with rather than being condemned. To be sure, there should be a proper compassion for sinners. The old adage urged us to "hate the sin, but love the sinner." Now, however, there seems to be a tendency not only to love the sinner, but also virtually to condone the sin.

On the other hand, it appears that, within the general public, belief in sin is not obsolete. The 1992 Barna survey posed the statement "The whole idea of sin is outdated." Perhaps somewhat surprisingly, a strong majority rejected this statement. Only 10 percent agreed strongly and another 10 percent agreed moderately, while 19 percent disagreed moderately and 57 percent disagreed strongly. The breakdown into groups did not show many meaningful patterns, the major exceptions being Catholics, Hispanics (many of whom would of course be Catholic), men, and the single, who showed considerably more agreement with the statement than did other groups. In addition, 25 percent of those who

---

1. James Davison Hunter, *Evangelicalism: The Coming Generation* (Chicago: University of Chicago Press, 1987), pp. 59–62.

did not consider themselves born again agreed with the statement that the idea of sin is outdated; this compares with only 11 percent of the born again.[2] Overall results with respect to the statement "The Ten Commandments are not relevant for people living today" were very similar. Relatively little difference was found among the subgroups, the only really significant factor being that people with lower income and lower education were approximately twice as likely to agree with the statement.[3]

Also of interest is the degree to which the respondents felt that they obeyed the Ten Commandments. With regard to most of the commandments a majority of the respondents felt that they obeyed completely, the exceptions being the prohibitions against working on the day of worship (25 percent), swearing (40 percent), and lying (48 percent). When the numbers of those who satisfied a command either completely or mostly are combined, however, only the command not to work on the day of worship received less than a majority response (45 percent).[4] Thus people tend to think that they are keeping the Ten Commandments. To put it differently, although the concept of sin is still meaningful, people tend to think that they do not break specific commandments or commit the major sins. And, as we shall see in the chapter on salvation, they tend to think that others are doing quite well also.

Barna feels that the 1992 figures regarding the understanding of sin must be combined with the data in his 1991 survey regarding absolute truth.[5] There 28 percent of the overall sample agreed strongly and 39 percent agreed somewhat with the statement "There is no such thing as absolute truth; different people can define truth in conflicting ways and still be correct."[6] To Barna this suggests a widespread belief that what one person considers sinful may not be sinful in someone else's view. We noted earlier (p. 38) our reservations about Barna's alarm. Nevertheless, his interpretation of the responses does fit the overall indications of individualism (see chap. 2) and Hunter's conception of civility.

Ironically, Barna himself seems unconsciously to pick up on the tendency toward individualistic thinking. In one of his "action steps" he says that we must "studiously avoid the temptation or the trap of becoming legalistic in our faith and life style." The Ten Commandments were "provided to help us negotiate the snares of life." We must help people

2. George Barna, *The Barna Report 1992–93: America Renews Its Search for God* (Ventura, Calif.: Regal, 1992), pp. 48–50, 260.
3. Ibid., p. 259.
4. Ibid., pp. 263–72.
5. Ibid., p. 50.
6. George Barna, *The Barna Report: What Americans Believe* (Ventura, Calif.: Regal, 1991), pp. 83–85.

see that God's commands are not outmoded and irrelevant today; we must "help people comprehend the value of knowing and following the basic rules God intended for us to follow—for our own best interests."[7] Sin, by this reasoning, is wrong not so much because it is an offense against God, but because it works against one's own best interests. But if sin is based, as many theologians have thought, upon selfishness, then avoidance of sin out of one's own self-interest may itself be sin.

Perhaps another statement posed in the 1991 survey will be of some help in attempting to understand the general conception of sin. There respondents were given the statement "People are basically good." In the general sample 37 percent agreed strongly and 46 percent agreed somewhat. Only 9 percent disagreed somewhat and 6 percent disagreed strongly. Even among born-again Christians, 77 percent agreed while only 22 percent disagreed; among those in evangelical denominations 74 percent agreed and 26 percent disagreed.[8] This may, of course, simply indicate a positive feeling toward other people; Hunter does speak of civility, unwillingness to speak ill of others.[9] But if the responses are in any sense to be taken literally, they suggest that while believing in the reality of sin in the abstract, most people do not think it very common among their fellow humans. In other words, people may sin, but they really are not sinners or depraved.

Changes in Preaching and Evangelism

One of the accompanying signs of the revamped understanding of sin is a change in the nature of preaching, and even in the strategy of evangelism. It used to be fairly common to refer to certain actions as sins; this created a sense of sin and guilt in the person with whom one was dealing. Recently, theology in the broader sense has tended to speak more of estrangement than of guilt. The idea is that one is maladjusted. Rather than being out of conformity with God's will, or out of relationship with God, one is out of alignment with one's own true nature. Instead of being against God, sin is against oneself, or one's highest possibility, or something of that type. This is in part why an increasing amount of preaching deals with the problems of human life. Sin, if it is to be called that, is not so much the wrong as it is the unwise or the imprudent. Not wickedness but indiscretion is the nature of the problem.

The popular self-help teachers and writings contribute to the self-oriented understanding of sin. Many of these approaches assume that happiness and success come when people focus their attention and

7. Barna, *America Renews Its Search*, p. 120.
8. Barna, *What Americans Believe*, pp. 89–91.
9. Hunter, *Evangelicalism*, p. 47.

efforts upon themselves. Bruce Shelley writes, "Ministries appeal to self-interest because they know that is what moves people. But in such a climate, how can people possibly repent? If church members themselves breathlessly pursue happiness, when will they discover the meaning of 'taking up your cross,' or find that God's strength is, in fact, 'made perfect in weakness'?"[10] The idea today is that the meaning of life is found through a direct search for it rather than as the by-product of a more altruistic approach.[11] Accordingly, there has been in recent years a great deal of emphasis upon self-esteem.[12] This concept seems, at least on the surface, to be in contradiction with the tradition that views selfishness as the essence of sin.

Some who encourage self-esteem do not neglect the importance of recognizing human sin and the need for divine grace. Here the emphasis is upon having sufficient self-respect to be able to understand and accept grace. In an evangelical context the emphasis is that each person has value, first because of having been created and loved by God, and second because of the redemptive work of Christ in behalf of each person. In other cases, however, the gospel involved seems to treat low self-esteem as being the fundamental human problem. The "I'm O.K., you're O.K." slogan sometimes becomes virtually "I'm O.K., I'm O.K." Here the emphasis is often simply that one has value because one is human and because one believes oneself to have value. But if one is inherently morally good, there is no need for change or turning away from what one is. This perspective will actually encourage what formerly was thought of as sin.

Relative Silence Regarding Sin

Also noteworthy is the lack of discussion of and attention to the topic of sin. I discovered this recently when searching for popular doctrinal books to recommend to laypersons. I began by consulting the catalogues of certain evangelical publishing houses, the very publishers most likely to produce books dealing with this doctrine. I found an absolute paucity on the subject. I then went to my seminary library. Whereas row upon row of books were available on most doctrines, I could find only two shelves dealing with the doctrine of sin. Significantly, 80 percent of the books in this library have been purchased within the last twenty-

10. Bruce L. Shelley, "The Seminaries' Identity Crisis," *Christianity Today* 37.6 (May 17, 1993): 44.

11. Gary R. Collins, "Popular Psychology: Short-cut Solutions?" *Christianity Today* 24.9 (May 2, 1980): 21.

12. See, e.g., Robert H. Schuller, *Self-Esteem: The New Reformation* (Waco: Word, 1982).

five years. This confirms that sin has not been a popular subject for evangelical authors in recent years. Compare, for example, the number of volumes written in the past ten years on human sin and sinfulness with the number on self-esteem and how to achieve it.

The question of human sinfulness did not even enter into the *Christianity Today*–Gallup poll. No questions dealt directly with that issue. In a sense the subject was somewhat implied by some of the questions, such as those about the basis of salvation (grace versus works) and the continuing validity of the Ten Commandments. For some reason, however, those who commissioned the survey did not think the theme worth pursuing in any detail. That the leadership of *Christianity Today,* which was founded for the purpose of being a major voice of evangelical Christianity, did not think sin important enough to ask about may be a signal of how far evangelicalism has come in its neglect of the subject.

Contemporary Christian Music

Neglect of the topic of sin is very evident as well when one considers the Christian music favored by today's young people. There are an abundance of references to the greatness of God and the wonderful character of Jesus; there are a great many expressions of praise and love for him. Extremely conspicuous by its absence, however, is any reference to sin, any confession of sin, or any repentance for sin. One searches almost in vain for any such themes in the *Maranatha!* chorus book. Among the few exceptions are "Surely Goodness and Mercy," which is an older song, and "Zion Song," but in each case there is just a one-word reference to sin rather than any extensive development of the subject. In the entire book of 185 songs words like "sin," "guilt," and "wicked" appear only ten times, and there are no expressions of confession or repentance.[13]

It is surprising, in light of the popularity of the psalms in the praise-chorus movement, that the fifty-first psalm is omitted, as are all the psalms which speak of God's wrath or of evil deeds. It seems that this is not part of the religious experience or conceptions of the younger generation. We seem to be dealing with a variety of religion different from that of Moses in Exodus 3, Isaiah in Isaiah 6, or Simon Peter in Luke 5. The sense of awe, of sinfulness, of unworthiness, of guilt, is absent from today's positive religion.

Before leaving the subject of contemporary music we should notice what segment of Christianity sings these songs. They are not so much the repertory of the more liberal circles, where sin has not been taken

13. *Maranatha! Music Praise Chorus Book* (Costa Mesa, Calif.: Maranatha! Music, 1983).

seriously for some time. Rather they are most popular with evangelicals, whose belief in human sinfulness has been the basis for their gospel of the need for supernatural regeneration by divine grace.

Epistemological Pelagianism

One of the most unusual and interesting developments among evangelical biblical scholars is what might be termed "epistemological Pelagianism." The great dispute in the late fourth and early fifth centuries between Augustine and Pelagius concerned the moral and spiritual condition of human beings, and the effect of the fall upon human nature. That dispute was to a large extent concerned with the question of guilt, the issue of whether all persons are wrongdoers and thus deserving of divine condemnation. To a lesser but genuine extent the debate also concerned the issue of depravity, that is, whether and to what extent human nature is spoiled or impeded by the effects of sin.

The orthodox position came to be known as total depravity, by which was meant that the negative effect of sin upon human persons is complete. This did not ordinarily signify that all persons are as evil as they can possibly be. Rather, it meant that sin affects all parts of human nature instead of just one part of the person. Consequently, humans in their natural condition are unable to do any genuinely good works which would win God's favor and thus give them some spiritual standing with him. In addition, humans in their natural condition are unable to understand divine truth and thus to construct correct beliefs, especially in relation to the most important issues of life. Thus unbelievers cannot understand the Bible as well as can believers, and spiritually mature, sanctified believers have an advantage over less mature believers with respect to biblical understanding.

A different approach to this issue has been expounded by Daniel Fuller, professor of hermeneutics and Bible at Fuller Theological Seminary, the school founded by his father and named for his grandfather. His concern grows in part out of a desire to avoid a mistake of Origen and some of his latter-day followers. Origen held that just as the biblical writers wrote under the influence of the Holy Spirit, so the reader of the Bible must be taught by that same Spirit. The reader who interprets the Bible merely in terms of the way the writer intended the words will surely miss the true meaning. To discern the spiritual meaning requires the illumining work of the Holy Spirit. This perspective led Origen to allegorical interpretations far from the more obvious or literal meaning of the text. In more recent times, those who have relied upon a special illumining work of the Spirit to get at the spiritual meaning have tended to neglect the hard scientific exegetical work necessary to get at the author's intended meaning. Fuller's quarrel is with the notion that humans in their natural condition cannot understand the biblical message.

Fuller focuses his attention especially upon 1 Corinthians 2:14—"The unspiritual man does not receive the gifts of the Spirit of God, for they are folly to him, and he is not able to understand them because they are spiritually discerned" (RSV). Fuller seeks an interpretation which will urge the reader always to acknowledge complete dependence upon the Holy Spirit and at the same time to utilize valid exegetical means to determine the meanings intended by the author.[14] In Fuller's interpretation of the verse, "receive" means to "welcome," and "understand" refers not to grasping the meaning of what the author has said, but to seeing its worth. Consequently, the work of the Holy Spirit is not to impart some new information to counter the person's ignorance, but to work upon the heart of the individual to instill a love for the meaning of the text, which one has derived from the historical-grammatical data. Thus possession of the Holy Spirit does not excuse one from the responsibility of doing the hard exegetical work required to arrive at the meaning.

The problem for nonbelievers is not inability to understand the meaning of the biblical text, but unwillingness to accept it. The biblical message conflicts with their own self-centered approach to life. For that reason they say that the Bible is foolishness. This judgment on their part does not, however, negate the merits of their epistemological and cognitive processes. "Naturally, the conclusion that the Bible is foolishness will not affect the accuracy of the exegetical results of those whose only concern is the academic task of describing what the biblical writers intended to teach. An agnostic or an atheist, whose concern is simply to set forth, say, a description of Pauline thought, can make a lasting contribution to this subject, if he has achieved a high degree of exegetical skill."[15]

Even more noteworthy is the conclusion to Fuller's discussion of what makes acceptance of the Bible's meaning difficult for the believer. The meaning of the Bible, when understood, frequently conflicts with the desires of our egos. Thus there is a temptation, because we regard the Bible's teachings as true and authoritative, to modify the intended meanings of the biblical writers to fit our egos.[16] This, however, is not a problem for the unbeliever, nor even for the atheistic student of Scrip-

---

14. Daniel P. Fuller, "The Holy Spirit's Role in Biblical Interpretation," in *Scripture, Tradition, and Interpretation: Essays Presented to Everett F. Harrison by His Students and Colleagues in Honor of His Seventy-fifth Birthday*, ed. W. Ward Gasque and William Sanford LaSor (Grand Rapids: Eerdmans, 1978), p. 190.

15. Ibid., p. 192.

16. Ibid., p. 197.

ture, who regards the meaning of the Bible as merely a matter of curiosity or interest, but not as true and binding. Their exposition therefore has no bearing upon their ego desires:

> Of course these doctrines will present no problem to those whose only concern in biblical interpretation is to give an accurate description of biblical theology. Their desire to gain ego-satisfaction leads them to regard the biblical teachings as foolishness. But since they are concerned only to describe biblical theology and not also to say that the biblical message is true and beneficial, their exposition of the Bible does not clash with their desire for ego-satisfaction. So they have no need to modify the teachings determined by the pertinent historical-grammatical data of the Bible, and to the extent that they are skilled in exegesis, their exposition of what the biblical writers intended to say will be accurate.[17]

There are many aspects of Fuller's interpretation which we might want to discuss and evaluate, such as the adequacy of his exegesis of 1 Corinthians 2; the restriction of consideration to one passage, ignoring other potentially pertinent passages like Romans 1:18–23 and 2 Corinthians 4:4; the underlying faulty psychology dividing human personality; and the ignoring of the difference in meaning between "A did X" and "A did X, *and A is a historical person who actually did X.*" For our purposes here, however, it is sufficient to note that the direct effect of sin is apparently restricted to the human will; it does not impede the mind or the reason. That is why the ability to understand the message is not affected, only the willingness to believe it.[18]

We can expect to see continued tension between the two approaches that Fuller attempts to bridge. On the one hand, we have the professional exegete, the learned pastor who, with knowledge of the original languages and of the best techniques of exegesis, obtains the message of the Scripture and declares it to the laity. On the other hand, small lay study groups in the same congregation may use minimal study helps. The participants sit in a circle and discuss the meaning of the Bible, often giving commonsense explanations of the text, sometimes reading aloud from different translations of the Bible and choosing the one that satisfies them most. If asked how they obtained their interpretation, they would probably declare that the Holy Spirit gave them the understanding. This schism between the intellectual and the spiritual approaches to biblical interpretation will probably tend, at least among some exegetes, to accentuate the type of stance Fuller takes.

17. Ibid.
18. Cf. Alfred Glenn, "A Worthy Successor," *The Standard* 74.1 (Jan. 1984): 51.

Fuller's view is not widespread at present. There are some signs of a similarly objectivized approach, however. A number of evangelical theological schools place great credence in E. D. Hirsch's *Validity in Interpretation*.[19] The primary value of his work is that he emphasizes from the standpoint of a literature specialist the objective meaning resident within the text rather than any subjective meaning brought in by the reader. It is notable that Hirsch does not anywhere mention the role of the Holy Spirit in interpretation. This is not surprising given his presuppositions. Hirsch's impact on increasing numbers of evangelicals is a tendency toward Fuller's perspective that sin and depravity have no direct effect upon one's ability to comprehend the text. The views that are emerging do not diminish the degree or intensity of depravity, but its extent: certain facets of human personality are affected, but not others.

Factors Influencing the Future of the Doctrine

On the basis of what we have observed, I would anticipate that the movement toward a weaker and less pervasive understanding of sin will continue. If, for example, Christian people continue to sing songs which make no mention of sin, guilt, or repentance, they will become decreasingly receptive to sermons on those subjects. The pressure, overt or tacit, on preachers to avoid guilt-inducing sermons will be great. To the extent that people are exposed to the positive and self-esteem-inducing messages of preachers in the popular media, their conception of sin will be diluted. There was a time when the pastor of one's church was the only preacher the typical Christian heard. That pastor's teaching was therefore quite influential in determining what the people believed. Now, however, many Christians hear one or more sermons even before arriving in church on Sunday morning.

The Grace Controversy

There is also a development on the level of official or professional theology which I believe will have an increased effect on the understanding of sin, at least in certain circles. There has arisen what is sometimes termed "pure grace theology." The most extensive treatment has been given by Zane Hodges, formerly a professor at Dallas Theological Seminary. Other advocates include Charles Ryrie and the Grace Evangelical Society.

Initially the movement developed in terms of the issue of whether to be saved one must accept Jesus Christ as both Savior and Lord, or

19. E. D. Hirsch, *Validity in Interpretation* (New Haven: Yale University Press, 1967).

whether belief in him simply as Savior is sufficient. That issue has extended to a discussion of whether to be saved one must agree to give up certain sinful practices. To require persons to do so appears to the theologians in the school of pure grace to be legalism. That raises further the question of the necessity of repentance. Hodges contends that repentance is not needed for one to be saved. Only belief is required. He points out the number of cases in the Bible where only faith, not repentance, is specified for salvation.[20]

Note the implications. Unless prepared to redefine the nature of God with respect to holiness, the school of pure grace will have to reassess the human condition. If would-be Christians are not required to repent, then it follows that they are really not very sinful. Their condition does not require too great a change. Their less desirable actions will not have to be abandoned for conversion and regeneration, but only for discipleship. As these ideas become the basis for preaching, the belief in sinfulness, or at least in its seriousness, will diminish. To be sure, conversion from sin will no doubt continue to be preached as a prerequisite to discipleship. But with increasing numbers of persons in the church who have not undergone true regeneration, the appeal to discipleship will tend to go unheeded. If people are invited to accept Jesus Christ just to have their needs met, it will be difficult to expect something more of them later. It should be noted that this need-centered preaching and evangelism are becoming more prominent in conservative Christian circles, and especially in churches that seem the most successful.

The grace controversy should not be thought of simply as another expression of the difference between Calvinism and Arminianism. For Arminianism, at least in its conservative form, has always believed in the reality of sin and the necessity of its being overcome. Some Arminians have taught that prevenient grace is needed to negate the effect of sin so that the person can undergo conversion. All have required repentance. The Holiness variety of Arminianism has emphasized mastery of sin, and even the eradication of it. The position of pure grace, by contrast, is something more extensive in import, actually modifying belief in the sinfulness of unregenerate persons.

Pure grace theology is especially interesting because, as we noted, it is developing within segments of Christianity which have been among the most conservative and have emphasized evangelism that calls for a radical change of life. Dallas Seminary has been the source of much of this teaching, although it is not the viewpoint of all of the faculty. Dallas has supplied pastoral leadership to many very conservative churches,

20. Zane C. Hodges, *Absolutely Free! A Biblical Reply to Lordship Salvation* (Grand Rapids: Zondervan, 1989), pp. 25–33.

especially independent ones. Thus it may well be that some of the most conservative churches, or those which in the past have held most consistently and emphatically to a radical view of sin, will change the most sharply on this matter.

Exposure to Situations of Extremity

Eventually, however, a reversal of direction toward a more radical understanding of sin will occur. One of the factors in that reversal will be the geographical shift of the center of Christianity from the Northern to the Southern Hemisphere, from the developed world to the Third World. It is in the North American branch of Christianity that positive or "healthy minded" Christianity, as William James termed it, has especially flourished. In part this is due to the fact that the United States has had prosperity and peace. There has not been a war fought on American soil in well over a century, so most Americans have not seen that type of destruction at first hand. The only Americans who have observed it saw it occurring to other peoples' homes, churches, schools. It was civilians of other countries who were killed or maimed. Further, there was at least enough prosperity that very few people actually starved to death. Health care and education were at such levels that some of the major problems were avoided.

In a situation of peace and relative prosperity it is possible to believe in the goodness of human beings. Although shortages were known to exist elsewhere in the world, and there were ample evidences of crime and evil in the United States, they did not really have a strong impact. This is not surprising. A most revealing book on this subject is Langdon Gilkey's *Shantung Compound.* As the son of the dean of Rockefeller Chapel at the University of Chicago, Gilkey had grown up in a cultured environment. Then, too, as a student at Yale University he found everyone very gracious and generous, willing to provide a guest bedroom and a meal. When there was an adequate supply of the necessities of life, people were always willing to share. Gilkey's whole estimation of human nature changed, however, when he found himself imprisoned in a Japanese prisoner-of-war camp in China during World War II. There, in the midst of hardship and with everything in short supply, people behaved quite differently from what he had earlier observed. Gilkey was the housing officer, responsible for assigning quarters to individuals and to families. He discovered the lengths to which people would go to obtain some advantage that others did not have; he was amazed at the rationalizations they would give to justify their request for special or favored treatment. Some persons would move their bunks a fraction of an inch during the night to gain additional living space. The Christian missionaries in the group do not fare especially well in Gilkey's description of human selfishness. He reflected on this "just plain human cussedness" which he had discovered.[21] What he had discovered was, of course, the Christian doctrine of total depravity; he had arrived at it experientially. If we should begin to experience extremity in our country, or to be influenced by people who live with it, we may take more seriously the idea of human sinfulness, especially as revealed in selfishness. More to the point, when more theology is written by persons from poorer cultures, the place of sin in theology will be magnified.

Globalization and Diversification of Theology

There is a further dimension. In our enlightened culture, with its highly developed form of society, evil takes subtle forms. People in the Third World, however, are brought into regular contact with powerful expressions of evil. In some of the African cultures, evil takes on particularly vivid and dramatic forms of expression. In such societies people have a greater sensitivity to the reality of sin, both in others and in themselves.[22] The same is doubtless true of Christians in countries formerly behind the Iron Curtain. Now that they are able to move and to practice their Christianity more freely than before, they will certainly be able to communicate their ideas and feelings more fully. Our hope is that they will also grow in strength and eventually in theological production. Their theology should reflect a stronger sense of sin than is usually found today.

The sense of sin will no doubt grow even stronger with the participation of some other groups currently underrepresented in the theological discussion. As some liberation theologians have pointed out, theology is frequently written in the comfort of endowed chairs at prestigious institutions of learning. As more and more minority and female theologians speak and write (particularly if they are what James Fowler has termed theologians of balance), theology will give more expression to first-hand encounters with evil.[23]

Emphasis on the Individual: Freedom and Responsibility

There are two contemporary trends which would seem to have canceling effects. One is the strong individualistic movement, which has

---

21. Langdon Gilkey, *Shantung Compound: The Story of Men and Women Under Pressure* (New York: Harper and Row, 1966), pp. 89–96.

22. John S. Pobee, *Toward an African Theology* (Nashville: Abingdon, 1979), p. 100.

23. James W. Fowler, "Black Theologies of Liberation: A Structural-Developmental Analysis," in *The Challenge of Liberation Theology: A First-World Response,* ed. L. Dale Richeson and Brian Mahan (Maryknoll, N.Y.: Orbis, 1981), pp. 83–84.

tended to foster a sense of independence. Considered the final and most important unit of being, the individual is not answerable to anyone. Indeed, in the existentialism of Jean-Paul Sartre, God cannot exist, because he would encroach upon human freedom.[24]

Martin Heidegger, however, emphasizes instead the responsibility of the individual. Excusing one's behavior on the basis of some supposed conditioning factors is "inauthenticity."[25] This accent of Heidegger is in some ways being picked up in the current stress upon the individual. John Naisbitt and Patricia Aburdene see the emphasis upon the individual as involving responsibility: each of us is responsible for preserving the environment, preventing nuclear war, and eliminating poverty.[26]

There is evidence of a general belief in responsibility. The 1990 Gallup poll asked people to indicate their reaction to the statement "We will all be called before God at the judgment day to answer for our sins." In the national sample 52 percent said they completely agreed and 28 percent mostly agreed. The figures were highest among evangelicals and black Protestants. Although there was relatively little difference among age groups, older persons were more likely to agree completely.[27] Thus it appears that a majority of persons believe that we are ultimately responsible to God for our lives. We shall see in the chapter on salvation that most people believe that they and most others will fare quite well in the judgment.

Some political straws in the wind are also signaling an increased accent on responsibility. In the past, discussion of certain societal issues centered on the theme of victimization, which seemed to preclude fixing responsibility on anyone but the majority group. One area where this theme dominated was racial matters. Since Daniel Patrick Moynihan's controversial government paper "The Negro Family: The Case for National Action" (1965), which reported on the apparent breakdown of the black family, and for which he was subsequently denounced, it has been customary to regard blacks as victims exclusively and whites as the victimizers. There are, however, some indications of change. One is speeches made on the Senate floor by Bill Bradley of New Jersey and John Kerry of Massachusetts, both Northern white liberal Democrats. Another is the reception being given to Andrew Hacker's book *Two*

24. Jean-Paul Sartre, "Existentialism Is a Humanism," in *Existentialism from Dostoevsky to Sartre,* ed. Walter Kaufmann (Cleveland: Meridian, 1956), pp. 289–95.

25. Martin Heidegger, *Being and Time* (New York: Harper and Row, 1962), p. 68.

26. John Naisbitt and Patricia Aburdene, *Megatrends 2000: Ten New Directions for the 1990's* (New York: Avon, 1991), pp. 322–23.

27. *Religion in America 1990* (Princeton, N.J.: Princeton Religion Research Center, 1990), p. 21.

Nations. Their theme is that blacks must be given and must take a larger measure of both credit and responsibility for their own liberation.[28]

In addition, we are seeing the privatization of the welfare state, as Naisbitt and Aburdene term one of their megatrends. Citing Margaret Thatcher as one of the truly significant persons of the later twentieth century, they see a genuine shift from liberal welfare states. Evidences include requirements that welfare recipients take jobs whenever possible and the demise of the socialistic societies of Eastern Europe.[29] To the extent that this emphasis on personal responsibility, even despite adverse conditioning factors, spreads to other areas of society, we may well see a return to belief in human sinfulness. For where people are held responsible for their own actions, the concept of sin again becomes meaningful.

The Failure of Optimism in Human Ability

It may also be instructive, in seeking to anticipate when and how the reversal will come, to note a somewhat parallel situation earlier in the twentieth century. Classical liberalism in Germany and elsewhere in Europe had developed an understanding of the human as essentially good, having great affinity with God and possessing considerable potential. Karl Barth had been trained in that liberalism, and had begun his ministry preaching that sort of message. A number of circumstances combined, however, to alter his outlook. One was his observation of the inability of Christians to distinguish good from evil, the secular from the divine. A manifesto endorsing the war policy of the kaiser was signed by ninety-four German intellectuals. Among the names Barth recognized some of his own theological mentors. This was an indication to him of the bankruptcy of liberal theology. In addition, Ernst Troeltsch, who had taught theology, switched to the discipline of philosophy. Barth interpreted this move as Troeltsch's admission that theology really had nothing to say. In a very real sense, August 1914 was the end of the nineteenth-century optimistic view of human nature.[30]

Barth also received a sort of empirical confirmation of the validity of his new insights. This may sound paradoxical, as if the archenemy of natural theology were relying a bit upon natural theology. Barth, almost in desperation for something to preach to his people, began preaching from the Book of Romans. Whereas formerly his preaching had seemed

---

28. Andrew Hacker, *Two Nations: Black and White, Separate, Hostile, Unequal* (New York: Macmillan, 1992); John Leo, "Straight Talk About Race," *U.S. News and World Report,* 20 April 1992, p. 27.

29. Naisbitt and Aburdene, *Megatrends 2000,* pp. 157–83.

30. Karl Barth, *God, Grace and Gospel* (Edinburgh: Oliver and Boyd, 1959), pp. 57–58.

unrealistic to his congregation, now they sensed that he was really speaking to them, really describing them. Their own unexpressed self-understanding was considerably more negative than the theology he had been taught. Out of the practical ministry of a small pastorate was forged the theology which he would hold and preach in the years ahead.[31]

The First World War did much to make the liberal view of human nature obsolete in Germany. A firsthand exposure to the ravages of war had a devastating effect. Nonetheless, a return to a positive assessment of human nature soon seemed irresistible. So the church found itself again making the very mistake it had made a generation earlier. A group of German Christians issued a statement in 1933 hailing Adolf Hitler as God's way of bringing about his will and bringing in his kingdom.[32] That optimism was rather effectively quenched, however, by World War II. Hitler's imperialism and the genocide of approximately six million Jews showed the depths of what human nature is capable of perpetrating.

In North America the reversal occurred somewhat later. The century had begun on a positive note, so much so, in fact, that one Christian periodical changed its name in the belief that the twentieth century would indeed be the *Christian Century*. It was in the United States that the social gospel developed. Although its advocates were quite aware of the depth of the problems with society, they were quite optimistic about the possibility of effecting changes, for they did not really believe anything was seriously wrong with human nature. The First World War, although it involved the United States in the later years, took place a long way from home, and long before modern communications exposed people in the homeland to the vivid reality of war. Bear in mind that there were not even home radios at that time. Nonetheless, that war was a disturbing matter to Walter Rauschenbusch, the father of the social gospel.[33]

The great economic depression that began in 1929 affected not only the United States, but the entire world. It called into question society's ability to Christianize its structures and also created shortages of the type that tend to produce conflict. The labor-management disputes of the 1930s, often accompanied by violence, added to the sense of frustration of those who had hoped to see society restructured on more equita-

31. Thomas F. Torrance, *Karl Barth: An Introduction to His Early Theology, 1910–1931* (Naperville, Ill.: Allenson, 1962), pp. 35–36.
32. Karl Barth, *The Church and the Political Problem of Our Day* (New York: Scribner, 1939).
33. Walter Rauschenbusch, *A Theology for the Social Gospel* (New York: Macmillan, 1917), pp. 74–76.

ble and cooperative bases. And then the Second World War brought about total disillusionment with the optimism of liberal theology.

It is ironic that the positive view should return in our time. There really has been little of a political, economic, or cultural nature that would encourage this optimism. Yet optimism seems to be one of the philosophies that keep recurring within society. Perhaps the present impetus has come, not from positive accomplishments within society, but from the rise of various explanations of human behavior which seem to take the responsibility away from the individual. Thus, instead of blaming ourselves for the problems we experience, a perspective that would sway us to believe that we must be inherently evil, we blame certain social variables that we assume can be altered fairly easily.

It should be noted that great progress has been made by the human race in a number of areas. Health has seen remarkable advances. Smallpox, for example, has been eliminated worldwide. Life expectancy has increased significantly. Infant mortality has been greatly reduced. The general educational and economic levels have been elevated considerably. Thus, superficially we appear to be doing very well. Yet some of the most basic problems seem to be the most intractable. Poverty, crime, drugs, violence, unemployment, and war all seem to be as prevalent as ever, if not more so. The areas in which we have made the greatest progress seem to be in some senses the least important, for they involve human nature the least.

It seems that we have failed in our attempt to transform human nature. The usual reply is that there has not been enough time to evaluate the situation, but this cry has been heard since the beginning of the century. If indeed we are moving in the wrong direction, then the elapsing of time will simply take us further from, not closer to, our desired goal. At some point there should be, at least among Christians, a recognition of the accuracy of the old doctrine of original sin, if only as an empirical description of human behavior.

I believe that any change in the understanding of moral human nature will come to pass through factors similar to what changed the optimistic theological liberalism of a century ago. Some historical developments like the wars and economic problems earlier in the twentieth century will shake our confidence in ourselves. This should really not be needed, given the current situation we have described above, but a characteristic of our society seems to require it, namely the enchantment with the spectacular or the sudden, what I refer to as the "home run complex." More-gradual occurrences seem to evade notice. It may well be essential that some major catastrophic event, such as war or economic disaster, occur. The gradual spread of AIDS has the potential of reversing the positive view, but an outbreak of a major epidemic would bring swifter and stronger results. Unfortunately, it will probably take some major event to bring about a reversal of the public's estimation of human nature. There is, however, the possibility that the growing incidence of violent crime in the United States will have the effect of awakening awareness of the reality of personal and societal evil.[34] In fact, the neglected and avoided topic of hell has experienced a recent resurgence of interest even at such unexpected places as secular university campuses.[35]

The Pragmatic Effects of Positive Preaching

Another possible impetus for change is a pragmatic reassessment of positive preaching. We are reminded here of what occurred in Karl Barth's ministry. In the present situation, positive philosophy is being taught to and practiced by people from a basically evangelical or "conversionalist" background. For them, preaching that focuses on healthy mental attitudes is a supplement to, not a substitute for, conversion and regeneration. I anticipate, however, that gradually this philosophy will come to take the place of the gospel of supernatural transformation. Then the basic constituency of the church will no longer be regenerate persons attempting to apply the positive philosophy, but "good" though unregenerate people; and the result will be a deterioration of the quality of church life and service. At some point preachers will again recognize the need of speaking out against sin, of proclaiming the essentiality of new birth. That will be the sign that the reversal has begun.

It may well be that the reversal, when it comes, will not be spearheaded by preachers and people from within the evangelical tradition. For it may take them longer to feel the effects of softened theology which those from a more liberal tradition have already been experiencing for some time. To the extent that evangelicals in their pragmatic drive for success in ministry ignore human depravity, they may forfeit their opportunity to reverse the diluting of the doctrine of sin. There are some indications that those of a more liberal orientation are beginning to take the Bible more seriously, in some cases more so than are the evangelicals. David Hesselgrave reports on one missiologist who attended a missions conference sponsored by the World Council of Churches (conciliar) and immediately thereafter one sponsored by the Lausanne Committee for World Evangelization (evangelical). The liberal confer-

34. Ted Gest et al., "Violence in America," *U.S. News and World Report*, 17 January 1994, pp. 22–42.

35. Judith Valente, "Hell Reconsidered: Perdition of Tradition Is All the Rage Again," *Wall Street Journal*, 27 December 1993, pp. 1, 34.

ence had devoted considerable time to regular small-group Bible studies. The evangelical conference had featured no such studies, and only a very few of the major addresses had dealt with the biblical text in any serious way.[36] Perhaps God will choose again to work in surprising ways and through surprising channels.

36. David J. Hesselgrave, *Today's Choices for Tomorrow's Mission: An Evangelical Perspective on Trends and Issues in Missions* (Grand Rapids: Zondervan, 1988), p. 146.

9

The Doctrine of Christ

The doctrine of the person of Christ has, like the doctrine of God, been affected by changes in the conception of the nature and possibility of metaphysics. It has also been strongly impacted by historical criticism of the Gospels. In recent years, however, the external considerations which most affect the doctrine of Christ tend to come from social developments. A number of considerations internal to the theological enterprise have also exerted substantial influence.

Social Developments Affecting the Doctrine of Christ

Globalization

One major factor affecting the doctrine of Christ is the globalization of our consciousness. By this we have something very specific in mind.

Until the present century, and even within the early portion of this century, the different segments of the world population, together with their different cultures, were relatively isolated. They each functioned and developed with relatively little effect from the other cultures. Christianity was especially localized in Europe and North America. The interpretation of its theological content was worked out by persons whose perspective reflected Western categories. Protestant theology was largely done from the perspective of the German and Anglo-American cultures. These cultures and their intellectual categories were regarded as the correct way of viewing things. The people in the rest of the world were looked upon as prospective converts to the Western Christian view. The religions of those other people and cultures were simply in error. Part of the purpose of Christian missions was to correct these erroneous understandings. The intellectual perspective of Western Christianity was not merely one way of looking at things, it was the correct way or simply *the* way. It was not a view of how things are, it was the way things are.

Cultural anthropologists, by contrast, have long asserted their opinion that other cultures, their philosophies and religions, should not be considered odd, or even wrong, simply because they are different from Western culture. Anthropologists have recognized the value of those cultures in their own settings and considered them alternative ways of approaching reality. Other cultures are to be judged on their own merits, not on the degree to which they agree with Western conceptions and practices.

Until fairly recently, it was not common for the average Westerner to have extensive contact with other cultures. A number of developments in the latter half of the twentieth century have changed that, however. One is the increased travel, both for pleasure and for business, of Westerners to other parts of the world. Similarly, increasing numbers of persons from other cultures have come to the West, either as visitors or as immigrants. This has exposed us to very different ways of thinking and acting. In addition, television, particularly with the use of communications satellites, has enabled us to visit other countries via the screen. It is possible to see news events as they happen in other countries, and hear the actual words of the leaders of other nations as they are interviewed. We can see that people in other cultures are sincere in their religious practices. They are able to testify to what their faith means to them, much as Christians do.

As contact with other cultures grows, certain questions are raised and will continue increasingly to be raised. One of them bears upon the uniqueness and exclusiveness of Jesus Christ and faith in him. Is he really the unique incarnation of God, divine in a way in which no other human being ever has been, the only means to a proper relationship with God; or is he simply the Western Christian way of understanding reality, made absolute by persons of limited perspective?

We can expect that this question will continue to increase in prominence as contact with other cultures grows. While we will examine its implications more fully in the chapter on salvation, it does have relevance here. As appreciation for persons of other cultures and respect for their religious beliefs and practices grow, we can expect to find some leveling effect between Jesus and other humans, especially other religious leaders. This may take the form of an "inspiration Christology," which holds that the presence of God within the person of Jesus is an influential presence that may possibly be found in others as well.[1]

It should be noted that in some senses the impact of cultural diversity is really just beginning, especially in evangelical circles. We may expect to see more persons taking the anthropological data to their logical conclusions, as John Hick and Paul Knitter have already done. We may also expect some on the left wing of evangelicalism to expand somewhat the concept of Jesus' uniqueness. Clark Pinnock, for example, while continuing to insist that Jesus is the only way, opines that he may have a variety of modes to which people can relate.[2] It is quite possible that Pinnock or his followers will at some point modify the understanding of the uniqueness of Jesus Christ.

At the same time other persons are reacting against this tendency toward universalism and doing so rather vigorously. Carl Braaten, for example, takes strong exception to the relativizing of Jesus.[3] We may expect a reaction at some point from Catholics and mainline Protestants who are faced with the dilemma of either absolutizing their view of Jesus or seeing their view drift off into something not greatly unlike Bahaism. They will find themselves in a situation similar to that of the liberals or modernists in the fundamentalist-modernist controversy, who were caught in the cross fire between conservatives on the right and humanists on the left, both of whom accused the liberals of failure to carry through consistently on their original agenda. There will also be a reaction on the part of a majority of conservatives, who will insist

1. John Hick, "An Inspiration Christology for a Religiously Plural World," in *Encountering Jesus: A Debate on Christology,* ed. Stephen T. Davis (Atlanta: John Knox, 1988), pp. 5–22.
2. Clark Pinnock, "Toward an Evangelical Theology of Religions," *Journal of the Evangelical Theological Society* 33.3 (Sept. 1990): 361.
3. Carl E. Braaten, *No Other Gospel! Christianity Among the World's Religions* (Minneapolis: Fortress, 1992).

169

upon the uniqueness of Jesus Christ and the necessity of recognizing it. At stake here is the definition of globalization.

The Association of Theological Schools in the United States and Canada, the professional accrediting agency for seminaries, has made globalization a high priority for the years ahead. Several definitions of globalization exist, however:

1. Dialogue with other religions
2. Ecumenical cooperation
3. Concern with world issues of hunger, poverty, and justice
4. Evangelization of the world

Member schools were asked to indicate which definition best reflected their fundamental purpose. The response was enlightening: the first three possible definitions were in order designated by 5, 21, and 23 percent respectively, while 51 percent designated "evangelization of the world."[4] The executive summary of the report of the task force on globalization commented: "In light of the preponderance of 'evangelical' schools in the association, the assumption that one of these other definitions should be followed should probably be reexamined."[5]

The responses of the seminaries and the comment of the task force suggest that there may well be a movement to reaffirm the unique deity and saviorhood of Jesus Christ and thus to redefine the concept of globalization in that light rather than vice versa. The odds favoring such a movement become even higher when one takes into account not only the number, but also the size of the schools selecting the fourth definition. With one or two possible exceptions, all of the large schools in the Association of Theological Schools in the United States and Canada (those with enrolments of seven hundred or more) are classified as evangelical.[6] We may, then, expect a progressive movement back toward absolutizing the person of Jesus.

There will need to be special effort to establish the uniqueness of Christ in a demonstrable way. This effort will probably go in two directions. One will be a close examination of Jesus' teachings, contrasting them with those of other great religious leaders in such a way as to show clearly the unusual character of his words. There is a tendency in some circles to regard the teachings of all religious leaders as basically the

4. "Addendum: Executive Summary, Report of the Task Force on Globalization" (Report delivered to the Thirty-seventh Biennial Meeting of the Association of Theological Schools in the United States and Canada, Montreal, 1990), p. 82.

5. Ibid., p. 83.

6. Association of Theological Schools in the United States and Canada, *Bulletin* 39 (1990), Part 4, *Directory for the Academic Year 1991–92*, pp. 4–65.

same, to find parallels, for example, between Jesus' Golden Rule and Confucius's Silver Rule ("What you do not want done to yourself, do not do to others"). Scrutiny will be the order of the day as scholars of all theological persuasions seek to determine whether there are genuine parallels.

The second factor which will become even more prominent in the future is Jesus' resurrection. Since it sets him apart from everyone else, any success in establishing the historicity of this crucial event in Jesus' life will be of great importance. In recent years there has been considerable treatment of its historicity, and we are now seeing more discussion of the nature of the resurrection and of the resurrection body of Jesus. This trend can be expected to accelerate. Some of the attention has been given to the Shroud of Turin as a possible evidence, and that will probably continue.[7] There may even be some scholars who tend to make the shroud the pivotal evidence for the resurrection. In so doing, they risk the credibility of the resurrection upon the authenticity of one relic.

Current Music

When we look at the current music within evangelicalism, we get a view rather different from what we have just seen in connection with the evangelical seminaries. Here we find a somewhat detheologized view of Jesus. One rather striking observation is the marked preference for the use of "Jesus" as compared to "Christ." In the chorus book *Marantha!* for example, "Jesus" appears 222 times, as compared with only 21 occurrences of "Christ," a ratio of more than ten to one.[8] This is almost six times as great as in the Bible, where the ratio between occurrences of "Jesus" and "Christ" is approximately 1.8 to one. Furthermore, when some of the more traditional songs, including Christmas carols, are eliminated, the count in the chorus book changes to 206 to 15, a ratio of nearly fourteen to one.

A number of possible interpretations could be drawn from these data, of course. We must attempt to determine precisely what "Jesus" and "Christ" mean to the persons who sing from the chorus book. In general, "Jesus" is usually understood as referring to the historical personage of Nazareth, while "Christ" is often understood to refer to his deity.[9] The

---

7. Gary R. Habermas, in Gary R. Habermas and Antony Flew, *Did Jesus Rise from the Dead? The Resurrection Debate*, ed. Terry L. Miethe (San Francisco: Harper and Row, 1987), pp. 27–28; and William Lane Craig, *Knowing the Truth About the Resurrection* (Ann Arbor: Servant, 1988), pp. 57–61.

8. *Maranatha! Music Praise Chorus Book* (Costa Mesa, Calif.: Maranatha! Music, 1983).

9. I once asked an adult Sunday school class in a suburban evangelical church what the two words represented to them. Overwhelmingly, they indicated that "Jesus" represented humanity and "Christ" deity.

name *Jesus* frequently appears in songs that place a strong emphasis upon his humanity. Jesus is beautiful, wonderful, great; he is the friend and helper who meets our needs. But the name *Jesus* rarely appears in contexts that refer to his divine origin and virgin birth. This being the case, we can expect that continued singing of the current songs will tend to underscore the reality of the historical Jesus and of his humanity at the expense of emphasis on his deity. The upshot is that in the years ahead we can expect to find evangelicalism encountering some difficulties with belief in the deity of Christ. It is my expectation that there will be, at least on the popular level, a movement toward belief in a Jesus who is human, and in some sense a very unusual human, but not fully divine.

The Gallup data indicate a shift in this direction. From 1952 to 1983 the numbers of those who subscribed to the idea that Jesus is God declined from 74 to 70 percent, while those who considered him the Son of God or something similar (rather than a mere religious leader like Muhammad or Buddha) increased from 3 to 6 percent. In a 1978 survey of how sure people were that Jesus had risen from the dead, 64 percent indicated that they were absolutely certain (10 on a 10-point scale), while another 11 percent thought that it was highly probable (8 or 9 on a 10-point scale).[10]

The Political Objections

We have noted the growing global sense, which has the effect of bringing Jesus into comparison with other religious figures. One issue is whether Jesus is the object of faith of only one specific segment of Western society. At stake here is not merely Jesus' uniqueness but, in a different sense, his universality. Political objection is made that Jesus, as understood in conventional theology and in some interpretations of the biblical picture, is simply the embodiment of the ideals of white Western middle-class males. The image in which he has been constructed meets their needs. So he is not a proper object of faith for those of other cultures or even other subcultures of Western society. Accordingly, the more radical forms of feminist and black theology reject the usual picture of Jesus.[11]

One development which will probably follow from the political objections is an effort to show the universal appeal and applicability of

10. *Religion in America 1990* (Princeton, N.J.: Princeton Religion Research Center, 1990), p. 23.

11. Mary Daly, *Beyond God the Father: Toward a Philosophy of Women's Liberation* (Boston: Beacon, 1973), pp. 71–79; James H. Cone, *A Black Theology of Liberation*, 2d ed. (Maryknoll, N.Y.: Orbis, 1986), pp. 120–23.

Jesus. This will require a close scrutiny of our picture of Jesus, to determine which of the features attributed to him are genuinely biblical, and which are cultural overlays. Those who wish to make Jesus the universal object of religious devotion and the universal expression of incarnation will look for his universal qualities. While they will not pay any less attention to or show less appreciation for Jesus as a specific individual, they will try to identify those qualities of his which transcend his individual situation. Here it will become apparent that the lack of specific biographical detail about Jesus is not totally disadvantageous; it actually helps focus us upon the fact that he is indeed a universal figure.

Internal Theological Developments Affecting the Doctrine of Christ

The Accent on the Work of Christ

A tendency to approach the person of Christ through the work of Christ, or to base Christology upon soteriology, has been in place for a number of years and continues to the present time. In Lutheran theology this goes back especially to Philipp Melanchthon, who wrote, "To know Christ is to know his benefits."[12] Emil Brunner gave this approach more definitive form, emphasizing that we must first examine what Jesus did if we would know who he was.[13] This theme has been repeated in many ways in recent years.

A popular evangelical version of approaching Christ through his work is found in the emphasis upon Jesus as the friend who meets our needs. This is the point that interests most people; it is thus the necessary beginning point in evangelism, however that may be understood. The object of faith is Jesus as we know him in our personal experience, not as he is in some absolute or unrelated fashion.

What we are encountering here, at least in the popular variety, is a version of the emphasis upon personal or subjective experience that is so prevalent in our culture. Taken to extremes, this becomes a matter of "getting high on Jesus," a vivid emotional experience of great personal satisfaction. A mundane parallel is the use of various stimulants to get high. In milder forms, the subjective religious experience may be simply finding Jesus to satisfy one's needs, whether they be for a sense of peace and security, or for resolving family conflicts.

12. *Melanchthon and Bucer*, Wilhelm Pauck, comp., Library of Christian Classics 19 (Philadelphia: Westminster, 1969), pp. 21–22.
13. H. Emil Brunner, *The Christian Doctrine of Creation and Redemption* (Philadelphia: Westminster, 1952), pp. 271–74.

There are some indications in society in general, however, that the emphasis on personal experience is beginning to reach a peak and thus the point of reversal. The long-term consequences of relying heavily upon immediate experience and sensation are becoming apparent in the lives of drug addicts, many of whom have forfeited their future through neglect of academic studies. Thus we can expect something of a general decline in the anti-intellectual or antirational approach. This will be reflected in inquiry about the nature of the Christ who makes certain experiences and benefits possible.

There will also be a turning away from the theological emphasis upon the work of Christ as contrasted with his person and nature(s). The attempt to determine the person by investigating the work assumed that it was somehow possible to scrutinize the work objectively. There is, however, increasing awareness that one's very perception of the work is affected by one's understanding of the person. What Jesus did is surely related to what he could do, and what he could do is to a large extent a function of what he was and is.

The Status of Biblical Studies

One of the major influences upon christological belief is the status of biblical studies. This is especially true of New Testament critical studies, and in the greatest degree Gospel criticism. In the chapter on Scripture we noted some diverging tendencies. Here we wish simply to review them a bit and draw some implications for the doctrine of Christ.

A continuing development today is postmodernism, which in the area of biblical studies is often referred to as "reader-response criticism." There had been a progressive movement from source to form to redaction criticism. Eventually, however, this progression came to certain dead ends, occasioned by the extremes of its conclusions. Instead of a reversion to more confidence in the basic historicity and reliability of the Scriptures, biblical studies moved onto a different track. In a sense the basic assumptions of the critical endeavor were abandoned. Instead of looking for specific historical meanings, scholars focused on structural exegesis, which was oriented to finding deeper universal themes within the biblical passage. This was almost a Jungian approach to the Scriptures. It sought a deeper and broader authorship of the Bible. Though the expressions of specific authors, the books of the Bible were, so to speak, the work of the human race.

All of this was still tied to the assumptions of the modern period, however. As the modern consensus began to give way to postmodern assumptions, conceptions, and methodology, biblical study also changed. The shift came in terms of moving from the objective approach, from looking for meaning resident within the text, to a more subjective approach, to asking what meaning or experience the text evokes from the reader. Thus, in a certain sense, the reader creates the meaning. The meaning of the passage is what it means to me, although "meaning" may be too strong a word in that it implies cognition.

The shift toward subjectivism carries over into the doctrine of Christ. Now the question is not so much what Jesus said and did, or who Jesus was. Instead, Jesus is what he does to me, or what emerges in me as a result of an encounter with him. Here, however, we have the basic problem that plagued Friedrich Schleiermacher and those who adopted his emphasis upon human subjectivity. The question becomes whether Jesus was an objective person who lived in the first century and who perhaps in some way is alive and active today as well, or whether "Jesus" is simply a symbol for our subjective experiences.

I believe that this trend toward subjectivization of the Christian experience will continue as the postmodern mood amplifies. This means that increasingly Jesus will be a figure, a symbol of certain religious values or emotional elements. Less and less will the Gospels be sources of data or norms controlling the religious experience. The only exception will be those biblical incidents and sayings which relate particularly to experiences which one values on other grounds.

Concurrent with the trend toward subjectivization is an opposite type of development—a growing sense of the reliability of the Gospels. Evidence of early dates for the writing of the Gospels, their satisfaction of several standard criteria of authenticity, the accuracy of their topographical references, and the breakdown of some of the tenets of the more skeptical criticism, have all contributed to the conviction that we can get close to the Jesus of history and know with considerable confidence some of what he said and did. The result has been an increased awareness of the full humanity of Jesus, as we are able to rely upon those statements by and about him which show that he had the same needs, weaknesses, and problems we have. Those statements are seen as accurate reports rather than what human authors attempting to depict him as one of us, or reading their own human experiences into his life, might manufacture.

Significantly, this growing confidence in the Gospels, with the accompanying strengthened belief in Jesus' humanity, has resulted in a stronger, not a weaker, belief in his deity. Growing confidence in the accounts of his miracles yields greater surety of his deity.

We can expect the conservative approach to the Gospel accounts to continue gaining momentum and to contribute increasingly to the understanding of the person of Christ. This trend will continue both because of the growing skepticism of liberal scholars regarding the tenets of the more radical biblical criticism, and also because of the growing number and competency of conservative, evangelical biblical scholars.

The "Third Wave"

One trend that has been with the church in varying forms and to varying extents throughout its history has manifested itself in a special form which bears upon the doctrine of Christ. I am referring in general to the charismatic movement, but specifically to what is variously called "the Vineyard," the "signs and wonders" movement, "power evangelism," and the "third wave." Whereas the two previous Pentecostal movements in the twentieth century had emphasized the practice of speaking in tongues, the third wave stresses the miracles of healing and the "word of knowledge," by which the healer can identify a particular physical problem that needs healing. The word of knowledge is a type of new revelation and appears to be closely related to the biblical gift of prophecy. The third wave, identified especially with John Wimber and the School of World Mission of Fuller Theological Seminary, rests its claims on the biblical reports that the preaching of the gospel message was accompanied by signs and wonders (miracles) which helped certify its truth to the hearers. This was an effective aid to evangelism in New Testament times, and, say the spokespersons for the third wave, it can and should also serve a similar end in our time. Miracles, especially healings, are to be expected and sought.

In light of the third wave's accent on miracles, one might well expect a strong emphasis upon the deity of Christ. Ironically, however, the result has instead been an increased concern for his humanity. The reason is that if Jesus is thought of as simply divine, then his miracles are a function of his deity. They are inaccessible or unavailable to us humans. If, on the other hand, we think of Jesus as human, then the miracles are something we humans may expect to perform as well. Consequently, we find Charles Kraft decrying the tendency of much conservative Christianity to emphasize the deity to the neglect of the humanity. Kraft, by contrast, holds to a thoroughgoing kenosis: "It is clear that he [Jesus] laid aside his divine prerogatives to become human (Phil. 2:6–7). Though in some mysterious way Jesus continued to be God, he became human in such a way that he expects us to be able to imitate his works (Jn. 14:12)."[14]

14. Charles Kraft, *Christianity with Power: Your Worldview and Your Experience of the Supernatural* (Ann Arbor: Servant, 1989), p. 174.

Kraft holds that Jesus, like us, lived in a powerless state until his baptism. Then he received power by the Holy Spirit to do the wonderful things which he did in his later life. This, however, was not a power of his own. Consequently, we should be able to emulate various acts of Jesus which evangelicalism has traditionally attributed to his deity, but which are now understood as works of the Spirit through him.[15] For example, Jesus' knowledge of what people were thinking had traditionally been understood as a function of the fact that he was God. Kraft himself had held to that interpretation, but now has come to understand Jesus' knowledge in these instances as being like the word of knowledge which he and others experience.[16]

It is interesting to note this aspect of Kraft's thought, for as we pointed out in the chapter on the doctrine of God (p. 120), the theology of the signs and wonders movement is strongly transcendent. There is a great emphasis on the miraculous working of God in healing rather than on his immanent employment of medicine.[17] Yet here we have a strong emphasis upon immanence in the sense that great effort is made to show the similarity between Jesus' humanity and ours, and to insist that God will work through us just as he did through Jesus.

It seems likely that some of the implications of the third wave for the doctrine of Christ will be drawn in the future. For example, if the word of knowledge is similar to Jesus' knowledge of what people were thinking, will there not be a tendency to expect knowledge beyond the level of what physical ailments a person has? And if what Jesus accomplished during his ministry was entirely through the working of the Holy Spirit in his life rather than some inherent power or capacity, will there not be a move in the direction of an inspiration Christology which maintains that God was dynamically present in Jesus?

It is not easy to tell how long the strength of the signs and wonders movement will continue. It certainly does not give any indication at this point of having passed the peak of its popularity. It seems likely that its rise will continue for some time. That would suggest a continued emphasis on Jesus' humanity to the relative neglect of his deity.

The Understanding of the Atonement

We noted earlier in this chapter the issue of whether the person or the work of Christ should receive priority. Regardless of one's conclusion on this issue, there is little doubt that the two concerns are very intimately related. What Jesus did and indeed could do is very much a func-

15. Ibid.
16. Ibid., p. 73.
17. Ibid., pp. 37–47.

tion of who and what he was. Our understanding of the atonement cannot really be in conflict with our understanding of the person of Christ. For instance, if we hold the example theory of the atonement, we must believe in the humanity of Jesus; and if that theory is the primary dimension of our understanding of the atonement, we will tend to believe in the humanity to the exclusion or at least minimization of the deity. The reason is that Jesus' example would be of little value if he were only divine, and not human, for then we could scarcely be expected to imitate him. Conversely, we can scarcely hold to the penal-substitution understanding of the atonement unless we believe in the deity of Christ, for unless Jesus is divine, his death could not have the value which that theory specifies. We can then say that each theory of the atonement presupposes an understanding of the person of Christ. Epistemologically, commitment to one view of the atonement is also, logically, a commitment to the corresponding view of Christ's person.

When we examine the contemporary repertory of praise choruses, one striking feature is the lack of emphasis on and, indeed, the virtual absence of any references to the atoning work of Christ. The *Maranatha!* chorus book includes just six songs which refer to the death of Jesus or his atoning work even in general or oblique fashion. One of them, "Our God Reigns," includes words based upon Isaiah 53: "It was our sin and guilt that bruised and wounded him. It was our sin that brought him down. . . . His life ran down upon the ground like pouring rain, that we might be born again."[18] The communion song "We Remember You" refers to the cup as "your blood that was shed, Lord Jesus."[19] Other songs include the following lines: "Then the blood of Jesus Christ, it cleanses every sin"; "Holy is the Lamb that was slain"; and "I've been redeemed by the blood of the Lamb."[20]

Note, now, the content of these references. The basic assertions are the historical fact that Jesus shed his blood and died, and the theological interpretation thereof, that his shed blood cleanses us from our sin. There is, however, no indication of how this cleansing is effected by his death. Jesus is to be loved, praised, worshiped, followed, obeyed. But the idea that he is a substitutionary sacrifice on our behalf and in our place is not to be found in these songs.

We have here another indication that contemporary popular evangelicalism is moving toward an emphasis upon Jesus' humanity to the neglect of his deity. It is likely that this trend will continue and even expand until a reversal takes place. It should be noted, however, that

18. *Maranatha!* no. 2.
19. Ibid., no. 16.
20. Ibid., nos. 53, 56, 77.

this is not primarily an intellectual emphasis; the main focus is not on the cognitive dimension of religious experience. We have here something of a conflict between the more official theology of evangelicalism, that held and taught by the seminary professors, and the unofficial theology implied in the popular songs. Important to the future of the doctrine of Christ is whether the official theology will alter the popular theology, or whether the popular conceptions will transform the scholarly understanding. The underlying key here may be the point at which the popular emphasis upon experience and emotion will be reversed. If this occurs before official theology is transformed by popular theology, the former's emphasis upon objectivity and definition will prevail, accompanied by a renewed attention to the teachings of the Bible and, with it, a greater awareness of the doctrine of the deity of Christ.

Some Waves of the Future

Popular Music

It appears that a reversal of the trend in popular Christian music may already be under way. Comparison of the lyrics of popular Christian songs written before 1983 with those written since that time suggests that a shift is taking place. In the *Maranatha!* chorus book (1983), 13 percent of the songs refer to Jesus' deity and 16 percent to his humanity. In *Hosanna! Music* (1991) the figures are 17 and 6 percent respectively. We can therefore anticipate that with greater utilization of the latest songs there will be a relative increase in emphasis on Jesus' deity and a relative de-emphasis of his humanity.[21]

The Universalizing of Jesus

Another development significant for Christology is making its impact from a number of different directions. This is what might be called the social universalizing of Jesus. There has been a tendency to think of Jesus as a white male with Western and middle-class values. In part this is due to the fact that white Western middle-class males dominated Christianity. They were in a position to define Jesus and to teach others the right view of him.

A change is taking place, however, with the increasing production of theologies written from other perspectives. For example, theologies have been written that see Jesus as much more willing to accept women

---

21. Kendal Anderson, "The Legacy of Kum Ba Yah: Heritage or Heresy?" (Unpublished paper, Bethel Theological Seminary, St. Paul, 1991), p. 10; *Hosanna! Music: New Songs for Worshipping Churches: Praise Worship Songbook 5* (Mobile: Integrity Music, 1991).

on virtually the same basis as men than was the typical rabbi of his time. The qualities of God which he revealed and the qualities of humans which he commended are not restricted to masculine characteristics. A case has been made and is being made by a number of theologians, both male and female, that Jesus was a feminist.[22] Study will undoubtedly continue on this subject because of the wide disparity in opinion regarding the extent to which women can identify with Jesus. On one extreme Mary Daly sees Jesus as inseparably linked with the hierarchical structure of society and therefore rejects him.[23] Others agree with her that he absolutized the traditional male-oriented society, but find justification therein for continuing its hierarchical structure. It is my expectation, however, that a more feminist-oriented conception of Jesus will gradually emerge.[24]

A similarly wide range of opinion exists on the issue of Jesus' relation to ethnic groups other than Anglos. While within American society these groups might be considered minorities, in a worldwide context they of course are not. Jesus has often been pictured as a North American or North European. The reason is that Northern Europe and North America have generally enjoyed a position of control and power in the world, and in particular in those societies with large Christian constituencies. This situation is beginning to change as well, however. Some blacks and Latin Americans have seen in Jesus a representative of the white Anglo values. Others, however, have seen in him an advocate of the oppressed and exploited. In this conception he advocates the values of the Third World rather than those of individualistic Westerners. Still others, such as James Cone, even see him as being for blacks and against whites. If he is white and not black, according to Cone, he is an oppressor and we must kill him.[25]

The continuing contact between Christians from the majority and minority segments of American society will in all likelihood lead to a broadened conception of Jesus, as will the continuing contact between believers from traditionally Christian parts of the world and those from Third World countries. As Christians from the Third World become more theologically active, it is likely that they will develop their views more thoroughly and thus become more influential.

22. E.g., Leonard Swidler, "Jesus Was a Feminist," *Catholic World* 212 (Jan. 1971): 177–83.

23. Daly, *Beyond God the Father*, p. 71.

24. See, e.g., Rebecca D. Pentz, "Can Jesus Save Women?" in *Encountering Jesus: A Debate on Christology*, ed. Stephen T. Davis (Atlanta: John Knox, 1988), pp. 77–91.

25. Cone, *Black Theology of Liberation*, p. 111.

10

The Doctrine of Salvation

In regard to the doctrine of salvation there is an unusual diversity of issues. Developments in the years ahead will determine whether present trends continue or reverse.

Current Issues

The Extent of Salvation

A major issue presently in flux is the extent of salvation, or the number of persons who will be saved. Here we are seeing a considerable growth in openness to the idea that all persons will ultimately be saved. By contrast the traditional position, both in Protestant and Roman Catholic circles, has been that only those who have explicitly exercised saving faith in Jesus Christ are saved. Roman Catholics added the stipulation that to be saved a person must be a communicant member of their church.

There has been a considerable erosion of exclusivism, however. This erosion has taken two forms. The first, inclusivism, is the view that indeed only Christians are saved, or only the work of Christ provides salvation, but that the concept of Christianity and the saving work of Jesus Christ are much broader and more inclusive than have previously been thought. Thus there may be those who identify with Hinduism, Buddhism, or some tribal religion, who actually participate in the benefits of Jesus Christ without being aware of that fact. Christianity is still the true religion, and Jesus the only Savior, but their applicability is broadened.[1]

The second form of the erosion of exclusivism is pluralism. Closer to universalism than is inclusivism, this approach contends that Christianity is not a uniquely true religion, but that all religions lay hold upon the same truth, which they express in somewhat different ways. The basic argument for pluralism is the similarity of religious experience and testimony found among the adherents of different faiths. It is contended that they are obviously speaking of the same reality, laying hold upon the same truth. This is what one theologian has termed "ecumenical ecumenism," that is, commonality not on the level of Christian denominations, but of various religions.[2]

Quite remarkably, tendencies toward universalistic views have begun to appear in places which one would have thought the least likely. For example, the Roman Catholic Church, which for much of its history was the most exclusivistic denomination, and used its power of excommunication to cut persons off from saving grace, has since the early 1960s shown cracks in this position. Vatican II showed an openness by speaking of degrees of membership in the Catholic church. Communicant Roman Catholics are fully incorporated into the church. Non-Catholic Christians, who used to be spoken of as heretics and schismatics, and later as "separated brethren," are now thought of as "linked" to the church. Finally, other religious persons who are not part of any Christian group are "related" to the church. In varying degrees all three of these categories participate in the grace which Christ conveys to his church and thus participate in salvation.[3]

Contemporary Roman Catholicism also includes Karl Rahner's concept of the "anonymous Christian." This term refers to persons who, while they have not made an explicit commitment to Jesus Christ, and

1. John Hick, *Problems of Religious Pluralism* (New York: St. Martin's, 1985), pp. 32–33.

2. J. Deotis Roberts, *Black Theology in Dialogue* (Philadelphia: Westminster, 1987), p. 17.

3. "Dogmatic Constitution on the Church," in *The Documents of Vatican II*, ed. Walter M. Abbott (New York: Herder and Herder, 1966), pp. 30–35, sections 13–16.

consequently are not thought of as Christians by others or even by themselves, are yet, without being aware of it, indeed Christians, anonymous Christians, if you please.[4]

Relevant to the present-day understanding of the extent of salvation is the attitude of Americans toward the gods of other religions. The Barna survey of 1991 posed the statement "Christians, Jews, Muslims, Buddhists, and others all pray to the same God, even though they use different names for that God." A surprising 37 percent of the entire sample agreed strongly, and 27 percent agreed somewhat. There was relatively little variation on the basis of age. Even 30 percent of born-again Christians agreed strongly, and 18 percent agreed somewhat. Among those affiliated with evangelical denominations, 28 percent agreed strongly, and 18 percent agreed somewhat. Even 50 percent of Catholics, traditionally the most exclusivistic, agreed strongly, and 33 percent agreed somewhat; this compares with 37 and 33 percent from mainline denominations.[5] While the statement posed in the Barna survey did not directly relate to the matter of salvation, the responses suggest that there will be an increasing openness to inclusivism and pluralism. There seems to be an accumulated reservoir of tolerance or broad-mindedness with respect to the gods of various religions. The implications have not yet been drawn in most cases, but probably will be soon. At that point additional universalistic soteriological conceptions will probably emerge. It is especially instructive to note how far contemporary Catholics depart from the exclusivist view long held by their church.

Even some evangelicals, traditionally considered very conservative and exclusivist in regard to the possibility of salvation for those not explicitly confessing faith in Christ, have begun to show openness to a broader view. One who has done so is Clark Pinnock. Pinnock argues that it is not fair that God should condemn those who have never heard the gospel or had an explicit opportunity to believe in Jesus Christ as Savior. Although he does not hold that everyone who rejects the gospel will get a second chance, he does believe that everyone must have a first chance or a genuine chance. And so, those who have not heard during this life will have an opportunity beyond this life. This is, of course, not true universalism, since there is no guarantee that all who hear in the afterlife will believe, and, indeed, many who have heard during their earthly lifetime did not accept Christ. Nonetheless, there is at least a

4. Karl Rahner, *Theological Investigations*, 20 vols. (Baltimore: Helicon, 1961–81), vol. 6, pp. 390–98.

5. George Barna, *The Barna Report: What Americans Believe* (Ventura, Calif.: Regal, 1991), pp. 210–12.

universalizing tendency in Pinnock's approach, which he bases on texts like 1 Peter 3:18–20 and 4:6.[6]

If we are to determine whether and to what extent the universalizing trend will continue and expand, we must investigate its underlying causes:

1. *Increased contact with persons of other cultures and other religions.* It was fairly easy in the past to think of people from other cultures as unsaved pagans engaged in bizarre and exotic practices and holding to peculiar beliefs. These were people whom most of us had never met, and ignorance enables us to believe almost anything. In recent years, however, this has changed. Increased business and tourist travel has brought many Westerners into contact with Hindus, Muslims, and Buddhists. Television, including satellite transmissions, has brought the East much closer than in the past. Perhaps most telling, however, has been the presence of people of other cultures right within our own country. Some of them have come as refugees, others were part of a more normal immigration process. The resulting increased contacts have all had a somewhat similar effect. Instead of seeing people from other cultures as strange and perhaps immoral, we see them as very decent, civilized people, not too different from the good Christians whom we have known. In some ways the moral behavior inculcated by their religion may prove equal or superior to our own.

Upon examining the religious beliefs and practices of other cultures, some theologians find considerable similarity to what characterizes Christians. John Hick, for example, quotes from prayers found within the Muslim, Hindu, Sikh, Jewish, and Bhakti religions, and notes the similarity of expression. Although the form of worship may vary—the prescribed attire of worshipers differs; some religions use musical instruments, others do not—these are not essential differences. All of the worshipers are dealing with and relating to the same reality.[7] Hick also believes there is a comparable spirituality found within the several religions. Each has its own saints, prophets, and martyrs analogous to those within other religious traditions.[8]

2. *The emotional factor.* Many sensitive Christians are bothered by the idea that large numbers, perhaps even the majority of all the persons who have ever lived, are condemned to eternal hell without any opportunity for deliverance. How, they ask, can a loving and just God con-

6. Clark Pinnock, "The Finality of Jesus Christ in a World of Religions," in *Christian Faith and Practice in the Modern World: Theology from an Evangelical Point of View*, ed. Mark A. Noll and David F. Wells (Grand Rapids: Eerdmans, 1988), pp. 152–68.

7. John Hick, *God Has Many Names* (Philadelphia: Westminster, 1982), pp. 13–19.

8. John Hick, *God and the Universe of Faiths: Essays in the Philosophy of Religion* (New York: St. Martin's, 1973), p. 130.

demn people to eternal damnation if they have never had a real opportunity to believe? This is a powerful consideration.[9]

3. *Christianity's relative lack of evangelistic success vis-à-vis other world religions.* Most missionary success is, in Hick's term, "downwards," that is, conversions from primitive tribal religions. When matched against the more sophisticated world religions, however, Christianity does not fare so well. At best, it is barely holding its own on the mission field. Further, other world religions are now sending missionaries to evangelize in predominantly Christian nations and are beginning to achieve real headway. The result of these developments is a tendency toward universalism. One of two factors may be involved. There may be a simple conclusion that the lack of conversions reflects the lack of any real difference between the religions, so that conversion would be inappropriate and unnecessary. Or we may have here a highly sophisticated version of "if you can't beat 'em, join 'em." If Christians are not successful in convincing Hindus and Muslims to become Christians, it is comforting to think they may actually already be Christians or, at any rate, what Christians also already are.

We must now ask whether these three factors are likely to increase or diminish. The answer will go far toward enabling us to judge whether the universalizing tendency will itself continue and grow.

1. Contact with persons of other cultures and other religions is not likely to decline. Indeed, it will probably expand. World travel, communications, and immigration are not likely to be reversed, nor should they be. Thus this factor can be expected to be even greater in the future than in the immediate past. I believe, however, that its influence will change and perhaps even reverse direction. With increased contact will come greater familiarity, as contrasted with what at this point is still rather superficial acquaintance. It is easy, under circumstances of casual contact, to conclude that there are no real differences between the different religious groups. Under closer scrutiny, however, we may well begin to see that the similarities contain some quantitative and even qualitative differences. Further, differences which were not noticed will begin to appear.

In time we will also reevaluate the spiritual and ethical quality of the lives of the adherents of other faiths. Most of us present our best side to those whom we have just met. Under these conditions, we tend to see just the best side of people, much as we see people at their best in church on Sunday. As acquaintanceship becomes closer, however, we begin to see other aspects, some of them less attractive. To say that other

9. Pinnock, "Finality of Jesus Christ," pp. 164–65.

religions have points of weakness which may not immediately appear upon initial examination is not to deny their genuine ethical quality. In the intense scrutiny of closer contact, our idealized understanding of other religions may fade somewhat.

Another consideration here is the "rurbanization" described by Russell Chandler.[10] Many people in rural settings have had no real contact with other religions. That is changing. On first encounter there may well be an idealization of people of different faiths. But there will eventually follow a realization of their shortcomings as well.

2. The emotional factor seems to be inspired by a sense that some of the people being deprived of salvation have not really done anything deserving of such a severe treatment. Barring some drastic change of personality or outlook, that feeling ordinarily would not be expected to decline. Yet, upon closer contact, we may discover that people of other faiths have refused to respond to the available light, which may even have contained an explicit message. And beyond that, we will discover that these people do not live consistently by the teachings of the religion which they espouse. Thus our pity and sympathy for the supposedly innocent may be somewhat diminished by extended contact.

On the other hand, some research data suggest that the emotional factor will remain strong. The 1992 Barna survey asked respondents to complete the statement "When you die, you will go to heaven because. . . ." Of the general sample 62 percent chose "because you have confessed your sins and have accepted Jesus Christ as your Savior." Only 6 percent selected "because you have tried to obey the Ten Commandments"; 9 percent, "because you are basically a good person"; and 6 percent, "because God loves all people and will not let them perish."[11] The majority, then, had a correct understanding of the basis of salvation. But this seems to be belied by the responses to the statement "All good people, whether they consider Jesus Christ to be their Savior or not, will live in heaven after they die on earth." Of those who said they had made a personal commitment to Jesus Christ (65 percent of the total sample), 25 percent agreed strongly and 15 percent agreed moderately; 16 percent disagreed moderately and 33 percent disagreed strongly; 11 percent did not know. Thus, of the Christians who would hazard an opinion, those who disagreed outnumbered those who agreed by less than a 5 to 4 ratio! Even 29 percent of the born-again and 26 percent of the Baptists agreed, either strongly or somewhat. Those most opposed were the charismatics

10. Russell Chandler, *Racing Toward 2001: The Forces Shaping America's Religious Future* (Grand Rapids: Zondervan, 1992), pp. 20–23.

11. George Barna, *The Barna Report 1992–93: America Renews Its Search for God* (Ventura, Calif.: Regal, 1992), pp. 76–78, 294–95.

and Pentecostalists, with 18 percent agreeing and 78 percent disagreeing.[12] It appears that while a strong majority agree in theory on what qualifies a person for entrance into heaven, a significant portion of the sample take a very different view when the question shifts to who will actually get there. Probably what has happened here is that the emotional factor has overwhelmed the rational.

3. The relative lack of missionary success is another question, however. Here I believe we will see different effects with different theological groups. It is well known that liberal denominations have been reducing their missionary activity.[13] Part of this reduction is due to a decline in membership and a corresponding decline in giving. This has made it very difficult at best to maintain the missionaries in the field. Another consideration, however, is the lack of success of those missionaries. For the message which is proclaimed by missionaries of mainline denominations has not proven to have great appeal; it does not produce any greater responsiveness on the mission field than it does at home.

On the other hand, the response to the message of evangelical missionaries has been more positive. This is not surprising, since the effectiveness of the ministry of conservative churches in the United States was documented some time ago by Dean Kelley.[14] The success here is paralleled by the effectiveness of foreign missionaries. This being the case, while there will be an increasing trend toward universalism on the part of the more liberal groups, there will be a reinforced exclusivism among conservatives and evangelicals.

Annihilationism

A somewhat related issue can be expected to receive increasing attention, particularly among evangelicals. As their allegiance to the teaching of Scripture is brought to bear on their concern for the welfare of persons outside of Christ, the idea of universal salvation will not be a real option. But if the idea that everyone is saved is not acceptable, there may be a compromise solution—the idea that no one is lost, at least in the traditional sense of that term. Those who die without having found salvation in Christ will not live on forever in the endless punishment of separation from God. Rather, they will pass out of existence. While there are many variations of annihilationism, one of the more common

---

12. Ibid., pp. 50–52, 262.

13. James Leo Garrett, Jr., "'Evangelicals' and Baptists—Is There a Difference?" in James Leo Garrett, Jr., E. Glenn Hinson, and James E. Tull, *Are Southern Baptists "Evangelicals"?* (Macon, Ga.: Mercer University Press, 1983), p. 81.

14. Dean M. Kelley, *Why Conservative Churches Are Growing: A Study in Sociology of Religion* (New York: Harper and Row, 1972).

is that death is simply the cessation of being. It is death, rather than suffering, that is endless; so that having died, those who are not saved will never come back to life again. Clark Pinnock believes that if this view is not espoused, large numbers of sensitive Christians will choose universalism rather than the concept of endless punishment.[15] Other evangelicals who have endorsed annihilationism are John Stott and Philip Edgcumbe Hughes.[16]

There are some indications that annihilationism is growing in popularity. At the Consultation on Evangelical Affirmations that was held at Trinity Evangelical Divinity School in May 1989, debate broke out on this very point, with the result that the statement issued by the consultation did not address the issue.[17] The research done by James Davison Hunter also indicates a shift toward annihilationism.[18]

The Nature of Salvation

A still more basic problem concerns the understanding of the nature of salvation. Traditional orthodox Christianity had understood the human predicament largely in terms of the broken relationship between the human individual and God. Thus sin and guilt, separation from God, were the major problems. This was not an issue between the factions in the Reformation dispute. Both Luther and the Catholic church agreed that the problem of human sin and the resulting guilt must be dealt with. The real question was how that problem was solved. Was it by works, including acts of penance, or was it by faith alone?

Note that in the traditional orthodox perspective it is God who has the complaint. It is he who has been wronged, and the wrong done to him must be redressed. Further, he has the prerogative to determine what must be done to set things right. He prescribes, in other words, what salvation is and must be. Although the state of lostness is a serious problem for the human, in a very real sense God's problem is what must be addressed.

There has, however, been a continued shift in identification of the basic problem. In general the move has been from a theocentric toward an anthropocentric view. Addressing the injury done to God is no longer the issue. Now it is more a question of caring for the human's need, dif-

15. Clark Pinnock, "Fire, Then Nothing," *Christianity Today* 31.5 (March 20, 1987): 40.
16. John R. W. Stott, "Judgement and Hell," in David L. Edwards and John R. W. Stott, *Evangelical Essentials: A Liberal-Evangelical Dialogue* (Downers Grove, Ill.: Inter-Varsity, 1988), pp. 312–29; Philip Edgcumbe Hughes, *The True Image: The Origin and Destiny of Man in Christ* (Grand Rapids: Eerdmans, 1989), pp. 398–407.
17. *Christianity Today* 33.9 (June 16, 1989): 62–63.
18. James Davison Hunter, *Evangelicalism: The Coming Generation* (Chicago: University of Chicago Press, 1987), pp. 38–39.

ficulty, distress. Salvation, in the ultimate sense, is for the sake of the human, not the sake of God.

Attempts to resolve the human dilemma have taken many forms. In an earlier part of this century the social gospel was thought of as the answer to the human predicament. Advocates of the social gospel believed that individual sin was an effect, not the cause. The cause was the dislocation of society, the deprivation of many of its members. The group as a whole was considered sick, and the individual would never be well until the society was transformed or rearranged. This meant revamping economic, social, and political structures.

More recently, we have seen growing emphasis upon various types of liberation. Feminist theology, black theology, and Third World liberation theology all believe there has been injustice in the form of deprivation and oppression of their own social group. They have consequently argued that the church be involved in altering the structures which are producing injustice. This development, which derives in large part from the secularizing movement within our society and our world, might be termed a horizontalizing of the concept of salvation. Life and its quality here and now have become relatively more important in comparison with eternal salvation in heaven.

The horizontalizing of salvation is more obvious among liberal groups than among evangelical groups. Although evangelicals have shown a growing concern for the church's social ministry, they ordinarily see it as secondary to the primary issue of the individual's eternal standing in relationship to God. Is there any other evidence, however, that evangelical circles are horizontalizing their understanding of salvation?

Understandings of the doctrine of salvation may be plotted on two coordinates. One is the individual/group coordinate. This is a measure of the relative emphases given to salvation of the individual and salvation of the group. The social gospel placed its emphasis upon the group, while revivalism concentrated upon the individual. The other coordinate is a measure of the relative emphases given to salvation understood as fulfilment of the divine command regarding righteousness and salvation understood as satisfaction of the perceived needs of its recipient. On this coordinate the liberation theologies of the latter part of the twentieth century have made a slight shift away from the social gospel of the early part of this century. The social gospel seemed to put more stress on the prophetic dictum that "righteousness exalts a nation." Although the present protest against exploitation and injustice does draw upon the biblical prophets and other portions of Scripture, especially in Latin American liberation theology, the accent is on the experience of oppression. This shift in emphasis is even more noticeable with some evangelicals. Here the shift has been from holiness to wholeness, or from concern with pleasing God to concern with satisfying one's own perceived needs.

The shift among evangelicals is not difficult to document. One can note it in the topics of their sermons. Comparison of recent sermon topics with sermon topics in the same churches some thirty years ago would, I believe, show a significantly increased emphasis upon life situations. The preaching and programs of many churches center upon human needs (even exercise classes are available). In many cases the idea is that ministry to perceived needs will eventuate in ministry to more directly spiritual needs. This idea is not new, for the church has been putting it into practice for some time and in various cultures. Thus Japanese churches offer English classes; and one Japanese pastor, a golf professional, gives golf lessons on Sunday afternoons. Yet the connection between the initial point of contact and the ultimate objective of a personal decision of faith seems to be becoming less clear. While the new emphasis upon ministry to the whole person, not simply the spiritual aspect, is commendable, because the emotional and even the physical aspects of human nature must be attended to, there may in the process be a new maldistribution, the spiritual becoming somewhat neglected.

I anticipate that the new emphasis on giving attention to the perceived needs of the individual will grow. It should be noted, however, that the nature of the message which evangelicals are presenting to Christians is quite different from that being proposed by the liberation theologians. The liberation theologians appeal to Christians to give themselves, perhaps even sacrificially, to the alleviation of others' needs. In most forms of liberation theology the object of concern is not only oneself or the underprivileged in one's own group, but all persons who suffer deprivation. In the evangelical message, however, there seems to be less altruism in the Christian life to which people are called. Moreover, the needs to be addressed are not limited to basic requirements like food and shelter. The evangelical message focuses on more-advanced needs, such as personal fulfilment, meaningfulness in life, and social adjustment.

A potentially serious problem lies in the fact that ministry to the needs people feel requires individuals who are quite altruistic and sensitive to the needs of others. They are willing to give of their time and money, forgoing personal satisfactions that could otherwise be pursued. Currently, such a ministry is being performed by persons who became Christians under a gospel that called for self-sacrifice more than self-satisfaction. What will happen, however, when these people die or become inactive? Will those who have been taught that the gospel is intended to fulfil all of their needs learn to serve and give sacrificially? This may not be among the needs that they feel. Already some indications are beginning to surface that churches are struggling in this regard, as the older generation of servers and givers either have passed from the scene or have come to feel that they are not really needed and welcome, the church's program and appeal being geared almost exclusively to baby boomers and younger generations.

At some point the problem will become critical; ministries geared to meeting people's needs will no longer have the internal resources to sustain themselves. At that point there may be a sharp decline of such ministries; they may virtually go into eclipse. Another possibility is that some people will see the weaknesses of the majority conception of the Christian life and rally to a new call to dedication and sacrifice. That message, however, has traditionally been tied to the supernaturalistic view of salvation as a transformation of life involving faith and repentance and leading to sanctification.

The Blurring of the Popular Understanding of Salvation

An additional factor that is presently at work is a general blunting or blurring of the popular understanding of salvation. Witness, for instance, the trends in popular Christian music. Earlier generations of evangelicals, reared on their denominational hymnals, were exposed in song to the rich meaning of the Christian experience. For example, "To God Be the Glory" declares that "The vilest offender who truly believes, / That moment from Jesus a pardon receives." In "Complete in Thee" the worshiper sings in the chorus, "Yea, justified! O blessed thought! / And sanctified! Salvation wrought! / Thy blood hath pardon bought for me, / And glorified, I too shall be!" "All My Sins Have Been Forgiven" puts it clearly: "My account is closed forever; / Jesus Christ has paid it all; / Shed His blood my sin to cover, / Paid the price to save my soul; / There is now no condemnation, / I am fully reconciled; / What a wonderful salvation, / For a sinner so defiled." Numerous other songs, such as "There Is a Fountain Filled with Blood," "Free from the Law, O Happy Condition," and "And Can It Be That I Should Gain," give expression to a rich and complex doctrine of salvation. To be sure, the presence of such songs in the hymnal does not establish a complete doctrine of salvation, for there are countless songs which are merely sentimental references to relationships between the believer and Christ. Furthermore, we would have to determine just how frequently the songs we have cited were actually used. The point, however, is that they were available as expressions of a rich doctrine of salvation.

In many cases, the repertory of songs available today does not express the full traditional doctrine of salvation. Take, for example, the *Maranatha!* chorus book. In a song entitled "I Confess You as My Savior," one would probably expect to find doctrinal content more complete than "I confess You as my Savior; / Jesus, You're all that I need. / Holy One, chosen One, / Lamb of God, I believe." But that is the entire content of the song. "I Am Crucified with Christ" consists only of the words of Galatians 2:20. The popular conception of the Christian life seems to be epitomized in "Living Bread": "Living Bread, You're all I need; / Living Word, on You I feed; / Living Water, You satisfy; / Living Jesus, You are my life." A more detailed expression is found in "Spirit Song": "O let the Son of God enfold you with His Spirit and His love, / Let Him fill your heart and satisfy your soul. / O let Him have the things that hold you, / And His Spirit like a dove will descend upon your life, and make you whole. / O come and sing this song with gladness, / As your hearts are filled with joy; / Lift your hands in sweet surrender to His name. / O give Him all your tears and sadness, / Give Him all your years of pain, / And you'll enter into life in Jesus' name. / Jesus, O Jesus, come and fill Your lambs. / Jesus, O Jesus, come and fill your lambs."

A generation that sings the current popular repertory almost exclusively will tend to have a considerably narrowed understanding of salvation. It will be something like, "Come and follow Jesus; / Let Him fill your life with joy. / Praise Him, He's so wonderful." This understanding of the Christian experience is different from what is found in "Complete in Thee." In an earlier period today's conception of salvation would have represented the ascendency of mysticism over reflection, but it seems to have even less focus upon the object of belief than did traditional mysticism.

We will probably see a continuation of the detheologizing of the Christian experience until there come a recognition of and reaction against the shallowness of this form of Christianity. At that time there will occur a new reformation of sorts, with a reemphasis upon doctrinal preaching, upon evangelism which calls people to a deep Christian experience, and upon songs which express the full spectrum of biblical truth. Persons hungry for intellectual content of the faith will respond eagerly.

Unresolved Issues

There are some topics pertaining to the doctrine of salvation which either have not been adequately resolved or on which new controversy has recently developed. Attention to these issues will provide some of the theological agenda for the years ahead.

Faith and Works

One major area of doctrinal controversy will probably require considerably more debate before there is settlement. There has always been a bit of tension between the role of faith and the role of works in the Christian life and experience. Indeed, if we accept the theory that the Letter to the Galatians was sent to the churches of South Galatia and is thus the earliest book in the New Testament, this issue may have been the first major dispute within the Christian church. To those who emphasize grace, understandings of faith which require works as evidence of the genuineness of faith seem to fall into legalism. But to those who argue, as did James, that faith without works is dead, exclusive emphasis on grace appears to fall into antinomianism.

In recent years a tension has arisen within evangelicalism over this issue. On the one hand, Zane Hodges, a former professor at Dallas Theological Seminary, has defended the position that salvation must be completely free. Faith does not entail repentance or any commitment to obey Christ. If it did, faith would be a form of legalism requiring an intention to perform works. But if such an intention were necessary, then it would not be faith alone that produces salvation.[19]

On the other hand, John MacArthur, pastor-teacher of the Grace Community Church of Sun Valley, California, has argued that Christ must be accepted not only as Savior but also as Lord, or he is not accepted at all. True faith includes acceptance of discipleship. A person who is not living in obedience to Christ, or at least attempting so to live, has not experienced regeneration.[20]

Each of these positions, as representative of a larger school of thought, considers the other view defective and even heretical. Both sides are right in considering the discussion and debate important. Part of what is involved is the nature of conversion. Does it consist simply of faith, or is repentance also involved? A further question concerns the nature of faith itself. Can it be simply an acceptance of the promises and provisions and gifts of Christ, or does it also involve assumption of the obligation to follow and obey Christ? Then, too, there is the matter of assurance. Can we, on the basis of a one-time commitment to Christ, rest

19. Zane C. Hodges, *Absolutely Free! A Biblical Reply to Lordship Salvation* (Grand Rapids: Zondervan, 1989).

20. John F. MacArthur, *The Gospel According to Jesus* (Grand Rapids: Zondervan, 1988).

confident of our salvation; or must there be accompanying fruits, works of obedience, to demonstrate the reality of our regeneration?

The fervor of the discussion of this issue will probably increase. Each position views the other as falling into heresy. Thus the theologians who emphasize free grace believe that the position that acknowledgment of Christ's lordship is necessary for salvation espouses and advocates legalism.[21] Conversely, the theologians who assert that Christ must be acknowledged as Lord consider the school of free grace to be advocating antinomianism or "cheap grace," to use Dietrich Bonhoeffer's term.[22] I anticipate that the two sides will continue to react to each other and to harden their positions. As they continue to react, they will at some point actually fall into the view they are accused of holding. It will then be necessary for them to work their way back to a more moderate position.

Sanctification and the Secular World

Another major issue relates to what might be broadly termed the matter of sanctification. It involves specifically the question of the Christian's relationship to the secular world. Does being a Christian mean separation from the observable world? Or, on the contrary, does spirituality involve actually affirming the world, becoming one with it?

Over the centuries the church has taken different stances with respect to this issue. It is probably safe to say that for a majority of its early history the church saw itself as in opposition to the prevailing order of things. This is understandable in light of the fact that for much of that time the church was actually under persecution. At other times the church thought of itself as in danger from the contaminating influence of the world. In order to preserve what was considered most genuine and important about the Christian faith, the church withdrew in some fashion. The medieval church did so in the form of the monastic orders. Here the church was separated *representatively*. Through the withdrawal of this one segment of the church into the seclusion and isolation of the monastery, the purity of the Christian life was preserved.

Other eras saw different forms of separation. The radical wing of the Reformation sometimes withdrew from normal participation in social and political life, refusing to vote, hold public office, or pay taxes. More extreme elements, such as the Amish, still reject modern technological developments and adopt attire distinct from that of the prevailing culture.

21. Hodges, *Absolutely Free!* pp. 167–77.
22. MacArthur, *Gospel According to Jesus*, pp. 196–202.

The late-nineteenth- and early-twentieth-century variety of evangelicalism that was known as fundamentalism had a distinctive understanding of separation. Taking their cue from 2 Corinthians 6:17–18, the fundamentalists worked out a definite code of behavior with negative emphases. Christians, according to this understanding, were to dissociate themselves from the behavior patterns of the world. This meant abstinence from certain activities, such as smoking, drinking, dancing, attending movies, and card playing. In addition, there was to be an avoidance of entangling and compromising relationships with non-Christians. A Christian should not marry or even date a non-Christian. One should not engage in business partnerships with non-Christians. And one should avoid membership in non-Christian organizations, such as secret societies or political parties. Because the world was under the devil's control, it should be abandoned to him, lest one fall under his power. This principle sometimes even led to "secondary separation": believers not only lived separated lives themselves, but also separated themselves from those who did not. Thus some fundamentalists refused to participate in Billy Graham's evangelistic crusades, because liberal churches were also involved.

The antithesis between the spiritual and the worldly was believed to rest on an adequate biblical basis. This included Paul's injunction in Romans 12:1–2 to be renewed inwardly rather than conformed to the world. There was also the sharp contrast in Galatians 5 between the "works of the flesh" and the "fruit of the Spirit." The antithesis has been replaced in some circles, however, by an emphasis upon "worldly Christianity." The believer is to be actively involved in the ordinary affairs of this world and to endeavor to influence it.[23] This new perspective has resulted in part from a breakdown of the distinction between the sacred and the secular, which in turn is in part a logical inference from the recent emphasis that God has become immanent within the world. Thus religious activity is not a matter of a different realm, but of this present, visible realm. This idea was highlighted in works like Harvey Cox's *Secular City*, and in the writings of the Death of God theologians, who insisted that theology would not advance and the sense of the divine presence would not be recaptured in the cloister or the study, but instead in the civil rights movement and similar settings.[24]

23. Richard Quebedeaux, *The Worldly Evangelicals* (San Francisco: Harper and Row, 1978).
24. William Hamilton, "The Death of God Theologies Today," in Thomas J. J. Altizer and William Hamilton, *Radical Theology and the Death of God* (Indianapolis: Bobbs-Merrill, 1966), p. 48.

Another manifestation of the replacement of the antithesis between the spiritual and the worldly has been the return of conservative Christians to participation in the political process. Groups like the Moral Majority, which was organized and headed by Jerry Falwell, have been the most conspicuous but not the only instances of such activity. Among others, pro-life Christians have entered the political arena, a realm which conservative Christians had formerly left to the more liberal and the social gospel. Conservatives have also adopted several secular activities as proper for themselves. As early as 1978, Richard Quebedeaux documented the move toward greater involvement in practices formerly considered taboo by many Christians, and even the use of four-letter words. For the younger evangelicals, being a Christian did not necessarily mean conduct markedly distinct from the world.[25]

Underlying the changes in practice there is, or there will come to be, an altered understanding of the nature of sanctification. The Christian life is no longer considered sharply distinct from the behavior of the world. I anticipate that this trend will continue until at some point there emerges a call to separation which is heard and heeded. It may well be that this call will be sounded not by Christian leaders, but by some outside the church, proclaiming the necessity of a marked distinction from the dominant pattern. If so, the usual roles of the church and of those outside the church will be reversed. This will lead to a challenge to reexamine the basis of the Christian understanding of life, and then to a new and deepened understanding of sanctification.

---

25. Quebedeaux, *Worldly Evangelicals,* pp. 118–19.

11

Influencing the Direction of Theology

A Proper Attitude
   Seriousness About the Issues
   Focus on the Bigger Issues
   Willingness to Be Prophetic
Values Requisite to Influencing Theology
   An Ethical Lifestyle
   A High Priority for the Theological Enterprise
      Research Professorships
      Striving for Excellence
      Provision for the Preparation of Future Theologians
      Establishment of Theological Think Tanks
Improved Communication of Doctrine
   Christian Education
   Drama
   Music
Penetration of Influential Social Spheres
   The Media
   The Teaching Profession
   College-Age Christians
   The Home Schooling Movement
   Senior Citizens
The Tasks of Seminaries
   Integration of Theory and Practice
   Research for the Church
   Identification and Development of Needed Leadership Qualities

One of the earliest characterizations of Christians was that they had "turned the world upside down." I take it that this was a dramatic first-century way of saying that they were agents of change. They did not simply react to the world about them or bemoan conditions there; they transformed it. This seems to be the thrust of some of the imagery used by Jesus in his preaching as well: his references to Christians as the salt of the earth and the light of the world. At its best the church has been an active force, taking the initiative and going on the offensive as a potent influence upon its environment. While the exact form of this initiative may be a subject of considerable difference of opinion among us, the underlying principle is sound.

As we noted in the first chapter, there are three possible ways in which people relate to change: some make it happen, others watch it happen, and the third group wonder what happened. All too often, I fear, we have been in the second of the three groups, and perhaps sometimes even the third. We also observed that theology develops within a number of contexts, so that several different forces are at work influencing the ultimate product. This chapter will suggest just how we as the church can be agents influencing theology in the years ahead. I am somewhat hesitant to use the term *change agents*, since it suggests that theology must necessarily become different from what it now is, a suggestion that seems to connote a liberal rather than a conservative orientation. What I would hope for is that, while the basic contours of our theology remain the same, there will be ever deeper expressions of it and a continual updating of timeless truths in forms that are clear and appealing for the current time. We will consider how we, who believe we have a correct understanding of divine truth, can be used by God to help determine what theology will be in the years ahead. I recognize that there is a tone of virtual arrogance in that statement, for it could be construed as a claim to somehow possessing all truth. All of us, however, consider our own views to be the most nearly true views, or we would not hold them. We may do that while yet maintaining a healthy measure of humility in light of our fallibility.

A Proper Attitude

Seriousness About the Issues

The ability to shape the directions which theology takes in the future depends in large measure on a proper attitude. We must, first of all, presuppose that we are indeed able to make a difference. And we must take seriously the issues which face us and will face us. We must be aware of the potential, either for good or for ill, of the trends which we can already identify. At this point we must be willing and able to break away from the crowd. In general, the public tends not to think about problems until they become really serious or have personal impact. Then people often complain about the state of affairs and wonder how "they" (frequently the government is in view) could have allowed it to happen, and who is going to do something about it. There may be a demand for an instant solution to problems which have accumulated and worsened for years, together with the sense that someone else should do something. Examples of these problems include environmental pollution, the depletion of natural resources, and overpopulation. Some of us who taught social ethics twenty and more years ago (about the time of the first Earth Day) pled with our students and others to become concerned about these problems. I once expounded some of my concerns to a colleague, who was very impressed and commented, "Feeling as strongly as you do about these matters, you are going to be very effective when you teach about them." A substantive issue had been transmuted into a methodological one. On the other hand, a student stopped me in the hallway shortly thereafter and said, "After that lecture you gave on population last week, I went home and talked about it with my wife. We decided that our present child is the only child that will be born to us. If we want more children, we will adopt. We have not figured out yet what to do about the lifestyle and consumption question, but we are working on it." I was pleased, but surprised, that a student had taken the matter more seriously than simply as material to be mastered for an examination; in fact, he had gone beyond relating it to his future ministry to relate it to his own life. Such persons constitute the hope of the church, both in theology and in other areas.

Focus on the Bigger Issues

A proper attitude also entails breaking free from pragmatic and individually centered concerns to concentrate on the bigger issues and their ramifications. Shortly after the 1991 Barna report appeared, a seminary dean took the latter part of a faculty meeting to share some of the more significant and even disturbing contents of the book. When he called for discussion, the first comment was that the faculty should agree as to which courses would use the book. The conversation then turned to a question about faculty benefits, which had been an earlier item of discussion. No other comments were forthcoming (perhaps the faculty were thinking about their dinners). The dean adjourned the meeting. Pragmatism had prevailed!

Willingness to Be Prophetic

We simply must be aware of and willing to wrestle with the big issues facing the world and the church. We must also be willing to be prophetic, even at the cost of some personal popularity if necessary. Fortunately, books calling attention to some of the issues that will be crucial to the future of the church and of theology are beginning to appear in larger number. Among them are *No God but God*, *Power Religion*, and *Selling Jesus.*[1] We must pay more attention to such volumes than to the sports section and the comic pages of our daily newspaper, and we must watch television programs more serious than sitcoms.

Leaders willing to be prophetic are a necessity because of the danger that we will go with the easiest way, the way of least resistance, which may be the way a majority of the church is going. In the type of situation we are now facing and will be facing, however, the easiest way may well be the wrong way. For there is profound truth in the saying "To every complex problem there is an easy solution, and it is usually wrong!"

Among those calling attention to the danger is David Wells, who contends that the church has been unconsciously influenced by the world and has taken on its characteristics. He calls for a reversal of the trend: concern for the truth and fidelity to the theological heritage of the church are needed.[2] George Barna, on the other hand, has likened the church to a frog in a heated kettle, unaware of the changes that are taking place in its environment.[3] Ironically, however, if Wells's analysis is correct, it may be that some who are following Barna's suggestions are themselves the frog in the kettle, unaware until too late of the way in which the church is changing, becoming so much like the world that it will eventually lose the ability to bring change to the world.

Values Requisite to Influencing Theology

Values are at the heart of what we do and even who we are. What we consider important, what ends and objectives we prize, have a strong influence upon our lives. The real value system of a church, denomination, or other religious institution is not found in its statement of pur-

---

1. *No God but God: Breaking with the Idols of Our Age*, ed. Os Guinness and John Seel (Chicago: Moody, 1992); *Power Religion: The Selling Out of the Evangelical Church?* ed. Michael Horton (Chicago: Moody, 1992); Douglas D. Webster, *Selling Jesus: What's Wrong with Marketing the Church* (Downers Grove, Ill.: Inter-Varsity, 1992).

2. David F. Wells, *No Place for Truth, or Whatever Happened to Evangelical Theology?* (Grand Rapids: Eerdmans, 1993).

3. George Barna, *The Frog in the Kettle: What Christians Need to Know About Life in the Year 2000* (Ventura, Calif.: Regal, 1990).

pose or mission; it is found in its budget. What we are willing to pay for shows what is really important to us.

An Ethical Lifestyle

My first suggestion for making sure our values are such as will enable us to influence theology may come as a bit of a surprise, not that I mention it, but that I put it at the head of the list. It is that we watch very carefully our ethics and lifestyle to assure that they are genuinely biblical and Christian. Ideally, our beliefs and practices should flow from the avowed source of our faith. Thus we should formulate our doctrines from the Bible and then draw ethical implications from them. That is to say, we should use the Bible to develop some standards of Christian behavior (my terminology here may be a bit too formal and legalistic) and then seek the Holy Spirit's help to conform our behavior to them. But while theology should have priority over subjective elements, it frequently is affected to some extent by noncognitive factors. Human beings are not as rational as we may think them to be or as we might wish them to be. We sometimes form our ethical convictions to fit what we want to do, and then construct a theology to justify or rationalize them.

I am reminded of a woman in the first church I served as a pastor. She asked me to come to her home to counsel with her regarding a decision she had to make. In reality, she had already made the decision. She had earlier sought the counsel of all four pastors at a large and prestigious church where she was employed as a receptionist. They as well as her fiancé's pastor all agreed with her. I asked her if she had done any studying about what the Bible said on the subject, and she recited every reference dealing with it, including some I had not thought of. I then suggested that she summarize what they said, and she eloquently stated a position opposite from what she wanted to do; asked for her reaction, she replied, "I don't believe that applies to me." When I told her that I had no authority as a minister to give her advice contrary to the Scriptures, she said, with tears in her eyes, "You were the one person in the whole world that I wanted to hear say that it was all right." Her case is an illustration of the fact that heteropraxis frequently precedes heterodoxy. It is crucial, then, that we live correctly. Perhaps the reason why I put this principle first is that at heart I am a pastor before I am a theologian, a professor, or a seminary administrator. An ethical lifestyle will not suffice alone, but it is extremely important.

The tendency to mold our theology to fit our conduct is a subjective reason why correct ethics and lifestyle are so important; there is also an objective reason. The credibility of our theology will depend at least in part upon the integrity of our lives. The non-Christian world may not regard very highly the convictions which we profess, but they do expect us to live by those convictions and will respect us only if we do. They may think us mistaken, but that is less serious than if they think us dishonest or hypocritical. I often recall the comment made on "Washington Week in Review" by Haynes Johnson of the *Washington Post* after describing the lavish lifestyle of Jim and Tammy Bakker, which included gold-plated bathroom fixtures: "It's not what you usually think of as piety." We must live in ways that are above reproach.

Sometimes in our desire to demonstrate our Christian liberty, or to prove that we are not legalists who slavishly go by the book, we fail to live up to the standards the secular world sets for itself. Not too long ago, an administrator was fired from a public institution for using its equipment and employees for his private business affairs, while a few miles away a Christian institution tolerated much more extensive activities of the same type by one of its employees. Consider also the remark of a man who after a lifetime in public service joined a Christian institution: "If in the public sector I had handled funds the way they are handled here, I would have been in jail within a week!" In business matters, interpersonal relations, and consideration of intellectual issues, our standards will need to be the highest. In the final analysis, we must be the type of individuals from whom people would not be afraid to buy a used car. If we are not, they will not be willing to consider our ideas.

The Gallup poll has given evidence that our behavior affects the church's ability to influence the world. For example, the scandals of the 1980s affected negatively the public's perception of the televangelists. Not only were Oral Roberts, Jim Bakker, and Jimmy Swaggart less favorably perceived in 1987 than in 1980, but so too were other television ministers, namely, Jerry Falwell, Pat Robertson, Robert Schuller, and Rex Humbard. Only Billy Graham was unaffected, his figures being identical in 1980 and 1987, with the exception of a 1 percent shift from mildly unfavorable to strongly unfavorable. In addition, far fewer respondents in 1987 believed that the televangelists cared about people, were honest, had a special relationship with God, and could be trusted with money. Moreover, the number of persons who said they would be likely to vote for a born-again evangelical for president declined from 19 percent in 1980 to 15 percent in 1987, and the number who said they would be unlikely to do so increased from 9 to 29 percent in the same period.[4] These figures suggest that the image, and thus presumably the

4. *Religion in America,* Gallup Report 259 (Princeton, N.J., April 1987), pp. 57–58.

potential influence of evangelicalism, were adversely affected by the actions and reputations of three or four highly visible persons.

There are other indications that the scandals have had a broad negative effect. One is the public's rating of the ethics of the clergy. In 1977, 61 percent of the respondents rated the ethics of the clergy as high or very high; that figure rose to 67 percent in 1985, before declining to 60 percent in 1988 and 55 percent in 1990.[5] Another revealing statistic is the general public's opinion of whether the influence of religion is increasing or decreasing. In 1985, 49 percent of the people thought the influence of religion was increasing, as did 48 percent in 1986. By 1988, however, that figure had dropped to 36 percent; in the same time span the number of people who thought religion's influence was decreasing had increased from 39 to 49 percent. The following year 33 percent saw it as increasing and 49 percent as decreasing.[6] The reports of the polls do not suggest any explanation of this rather sharp change of opinion. One cannot help speculating, however, whether it does not reflect the 1987 scandals. The correlation is certainly present. It would seem, then, that we must work hard at improving the ethical images of prominent Christian leaders if we are to shape the thinking of the world outside the church as well as of those within it.

A High Priority for the Theological Enterprise

The church must give the theological enterprise high priority in its planning and work. All too often this has been thought to be relatively unimportant. Those activities which produce direct and immediate results and are more spectacular in nature, such as world missions, evangelism, and church planting, even Sunday school, have frequently been given more prominence. I want to make clear that I consider all of those areas to be extremely important. In the long run, however, if we do not have good theology, our efforts in those other areas will fail. Success in missions depends upon a sound theology of mission, evangelism upon a correct doctrinal understanding of the human predicament and the divine provision for meeting that predicament.

I suspect that we in the church are simply victims of a general cultural disposition for the spectacular. Baseball fans are much more impressed by a long bases-empty home run than by the combination of a walk, stolen base, error, and sacrifice fly, although in each case the result is one run. Consider also that we become more upset by the loss of lives in an airplane crash than by an equal or greater loss of lives on

5. *Religion in America 1990* (Princeton, N.J.: Princeton Religion Research Center, 1990), p. 57.
6. Ibid., p. 60.

American highways on any given weekend. Despite this predilection we must recognize that theological study and education, though not spectacular, are vital to the future health of the church.

If the theological enterprise is to receive priority, the church must support theological education well. There is a popular theory that certain denominations have drifted away from the gospel because their seminaries lost their faith. In actuality, the truth is quite otherwise. The schools did not abandon the churches; rather, the churches abandoned the seminaries, failing to support them. Willingness to support theological education at the level necessary to guarantee excellence is a prerequisite if theology is to advance.

When we say that the theological enterprise must have priority, we have in view the study, discussion, and publication of theological ideas. Teaching, committee work, denominational service, public relations work, all are important, but if we neglect theological scholarship we will put ourselves at the mercy of what others produce. There are secular universities where the faculty must publish or perish. I doubt we would want to go to that extreme, but we certainly do not want to have a situation where publishing is not encouraged. We need to realize that those who write the books that students, pastors, and theologians read will have a considerable influence upon the theology of the church in the next generation. They will help shape the convictions of theological students, the preaching in our pulpits, and the beliefs of the people in the pews.

Failure to encourage theological scholarship risks our future. I grew up on a small, general-purpose farm. We raised dairy cattle, pigs, chickens, grain, potatoes, and hay. Much of the crops we grew went to feed the cows, horses, pigs, and chickens, some of it after grinding at the local mill. We were careful not to use in this way or sell all of what we raised, however. We always saved some of the grain for seed for the next year's crop. The theological scholarship which we are engaging in today is the seed that will produce the next generation's crop of belief, and some of that crop may grow not only in our fields, but in those of our ecclesiastical neighbors as well.

Research Professorships

One way to encourage the theological enterprise is for individual institutions to create research professorships primarily geared to persons productively pursuing scholarship. Their teaching, committee, and administrative responsibilities would be limited. Such a position would, of course, have to be clearly designed and involve strict performance standards. It might be awarded in the last decade of the career of someone who has proven extraordinarily productive. A potential problem is jealousy on the part of colleagues who do not receive such an opportunity. There would have to be safeguards guaranteeing that worthiness is the sole consideration in awarding research professorships, but the concept does have merit.

Business and science have, of course, long recognized the value of research. Many university faculty positions involve little actual instruction. I have a friend who received a Ph.D. in marketing from Northwestern University some years ago. He received a number of offers from universities, all as an assistant professor, and all with a comparable starting salary. He selected the offer that permitted him to teach one course if he wished. While we would not want such to be the norm in our seminaries, it is time that the church begins to be as wise as industry and science in realizing that the quality of its work a decade from now depends upon the quality of its research and creativity now. I am well aware of the travails which chief executive officers of theological schools have in attempting to convince churches of the importance of supporting theological education at all, let alone something as esoteric as scholarship. The churches, however, need to be far-sighted enough to invest in their future theology.

Striving for Excellence

Whatever form the emphasis upon theological scholarship takes, those of us who have a sense of calling to the theological enterprise will need to recognize its great urgency. This will mean taking no shortcuts, especially in our preparation for and continued practice of our ministry. We will strive for excellence in what we do, and will not misrepresent or overstate our activities and accomplishments. The objective of excellence is to be one of the great controlling purposes of our lives. Here we in the United States are swimming against the stream of a decline of pride in workmanship and quality. We may need to find our models in cultures other than our own.

I think sometimes that we Protestants are in this respect somewhat less well situated to fulfil our task than are our Catholic brethren. About twenty-five years ago, I was involved in a Friday afternoon talk show on a radio station in the northern suburbs of Chicago. There were four of us: a Lutheran process theologian, a conservative Catholic theologian, an independent Baptist fundamentalist pastor, and myself. Each week we had a different topic, such as Jesus Christ, the Bible, miracles, the church. For the first hour or so we would interact among ourselves in response to questions posed by the show's moderator. Then the telephone lines would be opened for questions from the radio audience. After the program we would have dinner together and then go our separate ways. Three of us would go to our homes, to our wives and children. Father Campbell, however, would return to the rectory, where he had no family responsibilities, did not need to cook or keep house, maintain an automobile in good repair, or any such chore. Because he had taken a vow of poverty in addition to chastity and obedience, he was not tempted to spend his time moonlighting. He could give himself to scholarship and publication.

I am not prepared to recommend the monastic life to theologians. I believe that God placed us in the world to be human beings and Christians before being theologians, and that family and church responsibilities are not burdens, but part of the joys of life. I do believe that the well-rounded human being will be a better theologian, all other things being equal, than will a recluse. At the same time I am aware that it is possible to become so caught up with some secondary matters that they displace the primary directive which we have from God. As a husband and father, I have a responsibility to provide adequately for my family. If I become unduly preoccupied with the pursuit of an ever-increasing standard of living, however, I will fail to do my best as a theologian. Willingness to sacrifice some material prosperity and some ease in life will be one mark of those who shape the future direction of theology. We are engaged in a spiritual battle, and combat duty calls for dedication to the task.

Provision for the Preparation of Future Theologians

We must be grooming the very best of our young people to carry on the theological enterprise. It has been wisely said that "success without a successor is failure." No matter how well we have done our tasks, we must sooner or later surrender them to others. It is tragic to work hard to build something only to see it crumble because of poor handling by the next person to take up the task. I am reminded of a pastor who returned to visit a church he had served about two decades earlier. Now there were fewer persons at the one morning service than there had been at the less well attended of the two services when he had concluded his ministry. One of the older members of the church noticed tears in the pastor's eyes as he left.

One of the most important things we can do to guarantee the quality of theology in the future is to assure the quality of the next generation of theologians. That means that we who are now in a position to do so need to be on the lookout for bright, talented, dedicated young people who have all of the gifts to be the theologians and teachers of theology in the future. We need to place before them the challenge of theological scholarship. This is what wise pastors do with prospects for the ministry; in fact, I entered the ministry rather than a career in science in large part because my pastor placed the idea before me. We must engage in a similar practice. We must also, of course, be willing to let go of our promising young people, much as parents do with their children. That is, we must not insist that they enter our discipline, attend the graduate school which we attended or the one which we recommend for them, or continue to hold our view on every matter. A word of encouragement is in many cases the best approach.

Once we have encouraged suitable prospects, the church needs to be committed to facilitating their preparation. Graduate study is a long and expensive process these days, especially if, as I believe, our future professors should also acquire some full-time ministerial experience. One way for the church to assure that it will have the right kind of theology in the future is to establish a fund devoted to assisting persons of outstanding promise to complete their graduate study. Christians will have to see such a cause as vital even when some of the needs of home and foreign missions are not being met. The fund will have to be carefully controlled. To exercise good stewardship in its distribution, we must protect the fund from political pressures and at the same time seek to guarantee that we assist such students as will become the type of theologians we desire to produce. We may even need a program operating outside regular denominational channels. Good News is a fellowship of persons from the United Methodist Church who share a set of evangelical goals and values. One of their major endeavors is AFTE (A Foundation for Theological Education), which helps evangelicals prepare themselves to occupy the teaching chairs of the church's seminaries.[7]

In fostering graduate study we must be careful to have a broad sense of mission. We are not talking simply about selecting our own students to come back and teach at their alma mater some day. That type of ingrowth is not always helpful nor smiled upon by accrediting associations, although some of it is certainly desirable. A school is especially vulnerable if it offers graduate study leading to the terminal degree for teaching. We may need to think of our mission as helping to prepare future theologians not so much for our seminaries as for one another.

Establishment of Theological Think Tanks

I believe that there also need to be theological think tanks. They would be somewhat similar to the centers which already exist for study of a number of subjects; the Hastings Institute and the Brookings Institution are examples of such centers. The establishment of think tanks would be another way in which the church could say that theology is important enough to underwrite financially. One of their objectives

7. Ken Sidey, "A Call for Renewal Pays Off," *Christianity Today* 37.6 (May 17, 1993): 92.

would be the underwriting of individual scholarship, the funding of leaves of absence to free academicians for concentrated periods of study.

As important as is individual effort, it is vital to realize the value of interaction on the issues of theology. Thus the second objective of theological think tanks would be to promote group interaction on given subjects. We have in view small groups working together for a series of fairly short but intensive sessions over a relatively long period. Some models that come to mind are the Institute for Advanced Christian Studies, the Council on Biblical Inerrancy, the translation work sponsored by the International Bible Society, and the topical seminars within the Society of Biblical Literature and the American Academy of Religion. Perhaps an even better example is the so-called Pannenberg Circle, the small group of graduate students from different theological disciplines at the University of Heidelberg who met regularly to do a sort of team theology. The individuals involved in such a group must be compatible, with sufficient coherence of interest and perspective to be able to work together over the years, but enough difference to challenge and stimulate one another's thinking. A long-term commitment to the group is essential.

Predicting and influencing the future of theology are areas that require a particularly broad set of competencies, more than can be found in any one person. In group endeavor there is a synergistic effect that ideally results in the whole's being considerably greater than the sum of the parts. Theologians have sometimes functioned without access to the kind of data produced by social science research, so that their theorizing may tend to be armchair sociology. Conversely, social science researchers need the insight and analysis of theologians. We have noted the problem with the ambiguity of the theological questions posed by James Davison Hunter, George Barna, and even the Gallup poll at times. Submitting to focus groups questions that had been nuanced by theologians would have been helpful.[8] Barna moves from his role as researcher to being a virtual preacher in his "action steps" at the end of each chapter, drawing conclusions which follow from the research data only with the addition of unexamined and sometimes unsound assumptions. His qualifications in the former role do not necessarily mean that he meets the standards for the latter role.

Improved Communication of Doctrine

In addition to the theological enterprise we must commit ourselves to serious education of lay people regarding the content of the Bible, the

8. See, for example, Donald G. Bloesch, "What Think Ye of Christ? A Test," *Christianity Today* 24.15 (Sept. 5, 1980): 25.

meaning of doctrines, and their relationship to practical issues of life. It appears that one of the problems which is becoming more acute is the hiatus between what I term "official theology" (what we subscribe to in our official or quasi-official creeds and confessions) and "unofficial theology" (what we show in actual practice to be our theology). Part of the problem is making firm the linkage between the biblical content of our preaching and present-day living, between the Scriptures written so long ago and their actual application. We are good either at explaining the biblical passage and the formal doctrine or at discussing practical problems of the present. The greatest challenge, however, is to show how the biblical narrative or the doctrine relates to contemporary living.

Christian Education

We certainly must continue to teach biblical content. Even though a high percentage of persons believe strongly in the Bible's authority, their knowledge of its contents leaves much to be desired. As I was once quoted as saying, "It is no surprise that those who have had a conversion, read their Bible frequently, attend church frequently, talk often about their faith, and tithe, derive a great deal of consolation and help from their beliefs. Christianity works for those who practice it."[9] We need to help people understand what they say they believe, and the implications of those beliefs, including how they are to be put into action.

To help people understand the Bible and its implications, we must develop new and creative methods of Christian education. In many circles the Sunday school has fallen on relatively hard times. The 1992 Barna research, for example, indicated that whereas 76 percent of adults attend church in a given month, only 30 percent attend Sunday school.[10] This decline is not yet so evident to persons in evangelical churches and in certain parts of the country, such as the South, where the problem is not yet acute, but historical precedent suggests that it will also be increasingly experienced there. Yet it would seem that there still is considerable knowledge of the Bible that most people have not attained. I am not suggesting abandoning Sunday school, though it is not of eternal duration. It was begun in 1780 by Robert Raikes.[11] Since it did not exist before, it may not need to be present now, or at least it

9. Walter A. Elwell, "Belief and the Bible: A Crisis of Authority?" *Christianity Today* 24.6 (March 21, 1980): 23.

10. George Barna, *The Barna Report 1992–93: America Renews Its Search for God* (Ventura, Calif.: Regal, 1992), pp. 126–27.

11. J. D. Douglas, "Sunday Schools," in *New International Dictionary of the Christian Church*, ed. J. D. Douglas, rev. ed. (Grand Rapids: Zondervan, 1978), pp. 940–41.

need not be the exclusive or even primary means of education in the future. I do not know what new thrusts would succeed best, but we need to bear in mind that Christian education is one of the most crucial and in some ways the most overlooked arms of the church. Perhaps parents will need to take more initiative in these matters. One technique that we happened upon in our family was described earlier (p. 98).

The church will need to work especially with its young people. This has always been a primary concern of the church, of course, but there are indications in the data which we have examined that erosion of doctrinal conviction is especially notable among the coming generation. I believe that at the local church level we must do our utmost to instruct our young people thoroughly in correct doctrine, for the direction of the church and its theology can to a considerable extent be predicted by observing what the coming generation believes. We cannot begin too early to get them beyond the stage of the typical Sunday school education. Indoctrination as such will not work, of course, but if I were a pastor at this time, I would put heavy accent on something akin to the Saturday morning pastor's class which I used to conduct. I would emphasize that what one believes is crucial. I would find ways to repeat that message to young people through their teen years. And I would find ways to preach it regularly from the pulpit as well.

I recognize that overexposure is always a potential danger. Sometimes the church has engaged in indoctrination, which led at a later point to rebellion or rejection. But there are various ways to teach doctrine. We might best begin with the sense of need and the problems which all people experience in various ways. We can then show how the underlying issue is essentially doctrinal, and how the Christian message addresses it. This approach will help make the Christian faith appealing and encourage continued study of its truths.

If we are to shape the direction of people's thinking and especially the direction of theology, we will need to learn to communicate in light of the present cultural setting. This means, among other things, taking note of the questions people are asking and the types of presentations to which they respond. We have usually presented doctrine in a rather straightforward, didactic fashion, advancing a series of propositions. It may well be that this approach will need to be altered. A generation raised on television, video games, and graphics may fail to respond to Christian truth simply because of the way it is being presented. If we are to capture and hold the convictions of the general populace, we must come up with creative and imaginative ways of conveying the truth.

Whatever methods we may adopt, we must be aware of the inherent difficulties of any attempt to present doctrine, since by its very nature it deals with abstractions. It is, for example, difficult to organize a field trip that will acquaint the participants with the nature of heaven, or to present the doctrine of regeneration or of justification through a skit. We can, however, utilize some of these means to illustrate concepts which will help people to understand the theological issues.

As a first step toward adapting to the current cultural situation, we may want to make our presentation of doctrine in a more dialogical fashion. This entails anticipating the questions that society is asking, either overtly or implicitly, and framing our exposition of doctrine as answers to those questions. This approach, which Paul Tillich labeled apologetic theology or the method of correlation, carries more potential for effectiveness in the present society than does the more fundamentalist or kerygmatic approach of Karl Barth.

Drama

Beyond the dialogical approach we will need to consider the very medium of presentation. Worship services which include drama have proven effective in reaching baby boomers. This is not surprising, since young people who were raised on television have visual orientations and short attention spans. While these may not be desirable characteristics, they are not something inherently anti-Christian which we must therefore necessarily resist. There is no inevitable compromise of biblical principles in presenting the gospel message in the form of drama. It may be, however, that the preacher will need to take pains to make sure that the content of the drama portion of the worship service is appropriate and related to the sermon. Perhaps the sermon should make explicit reference interpreting and supplementing the preceding drama, showing how its truth is derived from Scripture. Otherwise the drama may be mute, its real meaning unheard. The drama, then, may become the content of the belief rather than a means of conveying biblical truth.

It is possible that the actual sermon or lesson will also need to display more of the characteristics of drama. Narrative, monological, dialogical, or biographical preaching may be in order. In his teaching Jesus used parables and everyday occurrences, which may have been his era's equivalent of some of the techniques today.

Music

Drama is one means of gearing the worship service to make young people feel at home in church. Other possibilities include helping adults to expand their comfort zones, so to speak, and developing alternate programs for the older and the younger people. Here the issue of music comes to the fore. Whether we like it or not, the preferences of today's young people in music, including church music, are quite different from those of their parents and grandparents. We can reject the new music outright or conclude that, with perhaps a few exceptions, its style is not inherently anti-Christian. We must be concerned, however, that the content of the music conveys adequate and appropriate doctrine. Otherwise we may find the church going happily off into emotionally satisfying experiences, but becoming indifferent to doctrinal issues and thus vulnerable to non-Christian ideas.

There has of late been some encouragement with respect to the writing of music that is contemporary as well as theologically sound and meaty. The popular Christian music written in the 1970s and early 1980s was theologically light. Since about 1983, however, there has been a new surge of contemporary Christian music with considerably more doctrinal basis. The hymns of Graham Kendrick, for example, have the potential for teaching doctrine through song. The church will need to encourage further development of such music and to conduct conferences on music and doctrine. Talented young people trained in church music, education, and theology will need to be sent into the vineyards.

Penetration of Influential Social Spheres

The Media

There are other occupational areas which the church needs to encourage young Christians to enter. I have in mind especially the media. There is documentation to show that Hollywood tends to display a bias against religion, especially the Christian religion.[12] When clergy are portrayed in Hollywood movies, they often appear as Elmer Gantry types, or in some other way less than admirable. If Hollywood had portrayed a world leader such as Gandhi or Martin Luther King with the type of historical inaccuracy shown in *The Last Temptation of Christ*, the news media would have been emphatic in their expression of outrage. Patrick Buchanan wrote correctly, "We live in an age where the public ridicule of blacks is forbidden, where anti-Semitism is punishable by political death, but where Christian-bashing is a popular indoor sport, and films mocking Jesus Christ are considered avant-garde."[13] It is interesting that Hollywood continues to make such films, even though they are box-office failures, an indication that it is promoting its own values rather than reflecting those of society.[14]

12. Michael Medved, *Hollywood vs. America: Popular Culture and the War Against Traditional Values* (San Francisco: HarperCollins, 1992).

13. Patrick J. Buchanan, "Hollywood's War on Christianity," *Washington Times*, 27 July 1988, p. F3.

14. Medved, *Hollywood*, p. 127.

More broadly, we need to recognize that public opinion and cultural values are to a large extent being shaped by the media. Currently, religious principles, let alone those of evangelical Christians, are not strongly represented. The media's rather liberal bias on social issues has been quite well documented. Sometimes the bias against conservative values becomes overt, as when Diane English, creator of the "Murphy Brown" show, herself a strong supporter of Bill Clinton, used an entire episode to ridicule Vice President Dan Quayle.[15] Sparking this episode was Quayle's remark decrying the influence of the Murphy Brown character, who had given birth as a single parent. A considerable furor arose over Quayle's remark, although it amounted to only one sentence within a six-page campaign speech. The fact that this remark was in some cases the only item reported by the press may serve to establish the overall point we are making regarding the influence of the press: The values of society are in great measure shaped by the media. This point, which the media perhaps wanted to obscure through ridicule, was for the most part overlooked in the frenzy over Quayle's comment.

There are several means by which the media sway the public. One is simply their presentation of certain characters as typical and their values as normative. Another is the media's careful selection of what material to include and what to omit. Anyone who has been at an event covered by the press or has been interviewed at length by a reporter knows how careful selection of material can convey an impression very different from the firsthand experience itself.

There is also the dimension of the invulnerability of many of the popular media's presentations. In a sense it is impossible to respond to the opinions presented through the media. A comic strip like "Doonesbury," for example, is actually a form of editorial, but how do the people, political and otherwise, who are satirized by that strip respond without making themselves look ridiculous in the process? There really is no forum of debate, no way to interact with a comic strip. Similarly, when a popular novelist like James Michener depicts religious evangelists through the character of a charlatan, there is no way to rebut the generalization. Hollywood has been shown to present religious themes and characters in uniformly negative fashion, and this despite the fact that such films have consistently done poorly at the box office, yet there is no effective means of refutation. Much of the impact of the message comes from the fact that it is subtle, and in some cases almost subliminal.

If we wish to affect the values of society, Christianity must target the media. We must get Christians into those positions that have great

15. Richard Zoglin, "Sitcom Politics," Time, 21 September 1992, pp. 44–47.

impact on public opinion. We have done well in entering a number of fields where traditionally we were not involved: professional sports, public entertainment, politics. Yet we have not given equal attention to some other very important areas of life. We must, for example, encourage young people to consider journalism as a possible career. Cartoonists and novelists who present values different from the standard secular fare may prove important in the ideological struggle. If it is not possible to respond from outside the media to the secular presentations, then it will be necessary to work from within. Our approach will not be so much a matter of refuting secular ideas as of giving alternative views.

As Christians we will refuse to respond to the secular ideology by giving equally biased and thus unfair presentations. Our standard, based upon the instructions given by Paul in 2 Corinthians 4, will be open presentation of the truth. That, in the long run, will actually have the greater effect.

We will also insist that both sides of controversial issues be presented. Currently there is objection to anything which constitutes a representation of Christian truth. In the arena of public education, this objection is frequently based upon the separation of church and state. Yet it should be noted that what the First Amendment to the Constitution calls for is separation of church and state, not of religion and state. In actuality, religion is often presented; but the religion is humanism, its prophet is John Dewey, and the mother church, dating back many years, is Teachers College of Columbia University. We must insist that either both sides of religious and quasi-religious issues be presented or neither.

There must be fairness in the media. While some television programs which address social and ethical issues give both sides, thus producing something of a moral debate, others give only one side, thus constituting virtual propaganda. Examples of these two different approaches in the early 1990s were "L.A. Law" and "Designing Women." In the former, the issues were debated within a legal setting, so that both sides did get a chance to be heard, and the right side did not necessarily prevail. In the latter, only one side was presented. This one-sidedness is what the vice president (or his speechwriters) was decrying. We must seek to achieve equity in the public forum.

The reaction of the Christian public to the unfair treatment of controversial issues has been to complain, which is an important action to take.[16] Another important step is to encourage Christians in large numbers to consider careers in the public media. We can change values by changing those who set the values. While this will take persistence and

16. For a discussion both of the one-sidedness and the reaction to it, see Os Guinness, "More Victimized than Thou," in *No God but God*, ed. Guinness and Seel, pp. 81–93.

patience, it is well worth considering. A positive note here is that there probably are more Christians active in journalism than is generally realized. Organizing them into a group modeled on, say, the Christian Medical Society could establish networking, build morale, and coordinate strategy. We also need to provide scholarships. Strengthening departments of journalism and of radio and television production in Christian colleges would be another helpful step, although, as we shall see later, this may not be the preferable means of preparing Christians for those professions.

The Teaching Profession

There are other strategic occupations that will give Christians opportunities to infiltrate or, perhaps more correctly, penetrate society. For example, after years of oversupply of teachers, shortages appear to be on the way, and are already here in some subjects and in certain geographical areas. Projections show a shortage of 1.1 million schoolteachers and a half million professors in this decade. While the removal of mandatory retirement on the basis of age will probably alter the expectations somewhat, the fact that about half of the tenured professors in the United States will reach the usual retirement age in this decade, as will up to three-fourths of the chief administrators of big-city school districts, is bound to bring some changes and open opportunities.[17]

We should not overlook opportunities afforded by coming retirements. If one problem of our society is the pervading tendency toward relativism and naturalism, the place to combat that tendency is where it is formed: in the schools. Political correctness in secular education is not something new; only its exposure is. Here we might learn from what has happened in the discipline of philosophy.

As an undergraduate philosophy major at a state university I was astounded to find that with one exception the department was staffed entirely by logical positivists. It seemed to me to be incredible that, in a discipline which supposedly prized free thought and inquiry above all else, students were really not given an option. Minoring in psychology, I was similarly disappointed that all of the faculty were behaviorists. A comparable situation prevailed at the next university where I studied. It was only when I reached Northwestern University that I found a philosophy department with some genuine diversity. In those days an orthodox Christian in a university philosophy department was almost unheard of. W. Harry Jellema at Indiana University and Gordon Haddon

17. Russell Chandler, *Racing Toward 2001: The Forces Shaping America's Religious Future* (Grand Rapids: Zondervan, 1992), p. 106.

Clark at the University of Pennsylvania and later at Butler University were about the only members of a nearly extinct species.

Today the situation has changed. Orthodox Christians hold numerous significant philosophy appointments. Christian theism is presented as a viable option in many departments and at professional meetings. My attendance at an annual meeting of the Central Division of the American Philosophical Association was highly encouraging, as I heard papers affirming the objectivity of values, and even one arguing that the most adequate basis for belief in human personality is Christian theism. Yet when I arrived home I felt like a soldier who, on returning from battle where victory was won, finds that while he was away, his hometown surrendered without a shot being fired. For while we were beginning to win the battle or at least hold our own in the intellectual arena, historic Christian doctrines were being surrendered in the local church because they inhibited numerical growth.

College-Age Christians

Where are the Christians who will pursue careers in the public media and education to come from? The most frequent answer in the recent past has been that they will come from Christian colleges.[18] These schools exist to provide Christian young people an education which integrates all truth with the biblical revelation to form a Christian world-and-life view. They are also intended to prepare young Christians to be, as one school put it, "an evangelical task force for the penetration of the structures of society."

There are indications of late, however, that the goals of Christian colleges are not completely realistic. It is not that the student bodies of these schools are more diverse than originally intended. Nor is it even primarily the fact that some such schools have chosen to open their doors to persons unwilling to confess faith in Jesus Christ as Savior, although that does have some effect. Rather, the role of such schools as matrices of Christian discipleship is becoming blurred. James Davison Hunter's extensive research on evangelical Christian colleges, which we referred to in chapter 2, indicates that students' growth in orthodoxy and orthopraxis is smaller at these institutions of supposedly high insu-

---

18. It is truly amazing to note how many leaders of the post–World War II evangelical resurgence were at one time students, faculty, or administrators at Wheaton College. Billy Graham, Carl Henry, Edward Carnell, Harold Lindsell, and Paul King Jewett, as well as numerous leaders of denominations and in the area of missions, graduated from Wheaton in the 1930s and 1940s. Moreover, former faculty colleagues in the Bible Department in the 1960s recently served as president of Gordon-Conwell Theological Seminary, the dean of Trinity Evangelical Divinity School, and the dean of Bethel Theological Seminary.

larity from non-Christian challenges than at secular universities. That persons possessing the vision and burden for transforming society's thinking in the direction of the biblical worldview will come from Christian colleges appears less likely than we might have thought. It is of course not news that secularization has overtaken many private colleges with historical or nominal ties to mainline denominations. What is changing is that some evangelically aligned colleges are apparently, in the words of Tom Sine, being "profoundly coopted by the values of the dominant culture. . . . I believe they are doing more to prepare the Christian young to fit into upscale lifestyles and professional occupations of modern society instead of learning to be a counter-cultural agenda working for the kingdom."[19] This trend is likely to continue until arrested by the Christian colleges; unfortunately, their present efforts to arrest the trend are proving costly.[20]

It may be, then, that the persons who will undertake the challenge we have been describing are likely to come from secular universities, where, through the ministry of Inter-Varsity Christian Fellowship, Campus Crusade for Christ, and similar agencies, they have begun to develop during their collegiate years the spiritual and other skills they will need throughout their careers. The church may well find that the expense of operating full collegiate programs is not worth the results. It might be more productive, instead of operating Plainview Christian College in the city of Plainview, to establish or support existing strong student ministries at Plainview State University. Indeed, some of the fields we hope committed Christian young people will enter are not ordinarily offered at Christian colleges, nor need they be. There would be presumably little if any substantive difference between the intellectual content of a Christian program in engineering, medicine, or pharmacy and a secular program. That is not surprising, in view of Emil Brunner's rule of proximity, which I believe both on principle and from experience to be correct. Brunner contended that the effect of sin and human rebellion upon our understanding of the truth is proportional to the degree to which the subject matter involves the basic relationship between God and humans.[21] So, for instance, there is really no difference between Christian chemistry and non-Christian chemistry. The difference comes in the way in which science is applied, including the ethics thereof. Supplementation of the scientific preparation with the conferences of

19. Tom Sine, telephone interview with Russell Chandler, 21 August 1990, reported in Chandler, *Racing Toward 2001*, pp. 108–9.
20. "Christian Colleges Settle with Ousted Professors," *Christianity Today* 37.2 (Feb. 8, 1993): 61.
21. H. Emil Brunner, *Revelation and Reason* (Philadelphia: Westminster, 1946), p. 383.

the Christian ———— Society and the work of campus ministries such as those we mentioned above would probably be more effective than programs offered on a Christian campus.

One major consideration may well decide much of the issue. Some programs, such as medicine and engineering, are extremely expensive in terms of the scientific equipment, which tends to need frequent and early replacement because of obsolescence. There was a time when Carl Henry and others could dream of a Christian university, a concept which unfortunately never came to pass. The likelihood that such a university could now be established and supported under the present financial condition of practicing Christendom is slight if not nonexistent. Nor is there strong historical grounding for the hope that such a university would not, like countless of its predecessors, slip off into a secular orientation. The recent developments at Baylor University, once considered the crown jewel of the Baptist General Convention of Texas, constitute a contemporary example.[22]

The Home Schooling Movement

Other opportunities are afforded by the home schooling movement, which is growing at an accelerating rate.[23] Parents who are teaching their children can supplement the 3 R's with biblical and theological truth. They can even mold their children's understanding of relativism and absolutism. Developing curricular or informal materials for use in the home schooling movement would seem to be a worthy goal for the Christian church. Perhaps this is an opportunity to offset the decline of Sunday schools.

Senior Citizens

The church, if it is wise, will also capitalize upon a conspicuous development at the other end of the population spectrum, namely the rapid increase in the number of senior citizens. Members of this group are not generally the best prospects for evangelization, or even for education. Yet many of them do not want to stop learning, even at their stage of life. So the elder hostel program is growing at a rate of about 20 percent a year.[24] Moreover, the elderly have more time than do other age groups to devote to civil politics and the life of the church. Since they are also the most religious and most biblically oriented segment of society, should not the church educate them regarding the future of theology (carefully, of course, so as not to produce a sense of doom)?

22. "School Fight Songs," *Christianity Today* 36.1 (Jan. 13, 1992): 45.
23. Chandler, *Racing Toward 2001*, pp. 109–12.
24. Ibid., pp. 107–8.

The Tasks of Seminaries

Integration of Theory and Practice

What, finally, are we to say about the role of theological seminaries, where traditionally doctrine has been formulated and then emerged to influence the church? Here we can expect to see major changes taking place; others we will need to work to effect. Theological seminaries have often come under criticism for being impractical ivory towers, a charge that has in many cases been at least partially justified. Some faculty members, especially those in the classical disciplines (biblical studies, theology, and church history), have either never served extensively in the type of setting into which they are preparing students to go, or served so long ago that the ensuing changes have made their experience inapplicable to the current situation. At the same time, some who teach the applied disciplines (preaching, counseling, Christian education, evangelism, etc.) have qualified for faculty appointment through years of practice, but lack a doctorate in academic research. This situation constitutes a major problem in theological education today. In fact, at a conference under the auspices of the Issues Research Advisory Committee of the Association of Theological Schools, which oversees research into the nature of theological education and on which I have served for several years, the chairman noted that the number one problem that has kept reemerging is the lack of integration of theory and practice!

All seminaries maintain that they do indeed integrate theory and practice. What they generally mean, however, is that the faculty does so collectively. Thus the faculty teaching the classical disciplines have the theory, and those in the applied disciplines have the practice. One seminary, however, decided that, since each student was expected to integrate theory and practice, it was not sufficient for the faculty to do so collectively; they must each do so individually. So the school formulated the concept of dual competencies. Each faculty member had to meet certain qualifications in terms of both the theoretical material in one's field and the practice of ministry. Faculty members who had not had extensive ministry experience were required to serve for two years on a church staff. The position was to be concurrent with their teaching. Those who did not possess an M.Div. degree, and thus were lacking certain practical courses, were required to take or to audit those courses. On the other hand, the search committee for a professor of preaching with a Ph.D. in a related field scoured the country for more than two years. There were some disadvantages, as when a prospective faculty member, a well-qualified young research scholar, chose to join the faculty of a peer seminary, where he was not required to take additional courses and gain practical experience. The requirements paid off, however. One faculty member, six months into his ministerial assignment, went to the seminary dean to request permission to resign his church position, pleading the difficulty of serving with the senior pastor. As tactfully as he could, the dean said in effect, "No, that's why you're there. Now you are beginning to experience what your students will have to go through, and they will not be able to resign." The man stayed on, and benefited from the experience. When a potential professor of preaching with a Ph.D. was finally found and interviewed by a committee of the board of trustees, one member, a businessman whose work required him to speak in public frequently, was so impressed that he asked the candidate if he would be available to do private tutoring.

One of the reasons for emphasizing integration on an individual basis is of course the benefit to a professor's ability to prepare students realistically for the ministry which they are to have. Several years ago, I interviewed for a position as dean of another seminary. The president and vice-president of the student body sat in on the faculty interview. At one point, in response to a question, I suggested that it might not be a bad idea if periodically each faculty member had to spend a year or two in a local church pastorate before being permitted to return to full-time teaching. When I said that, the two students applauded, and the faculty all just sat there looking quite nonplused.

Now lest my suggestion be thought anti-intellectual or strictly pragmatic, it should be pointed out that it has real value for the process of theologizing. I am profoundly impressed that the theology with which Karl Barth shook the theological world in 1919 was not thought out in an ivory tower somewhere, but grew directly out of the young Swiss pastor's struggle to minister to the needs of the people in his spiritual care. He had to preach, and the theology which he had learned simply did not satisfy the needs of his congregation. Similarly, Paul Tillich's theology grew in large part out of his service as a military chaplain in the First World War. One night, in the trenches among dying men, he "peered into the abyss of non-being." I am also greatly impressed by Helmut Thielicke's *Little Exercise for Young Theologians*, and especially by what he has to say about the "spiritual instinct of the children of God."[25] Christian theology is not merely a philosophy seeking to describe reality. It is a whole world-and-*life* view; and as such, one of its elements is the pragmatic or experiential dimension. I regularly serve interim pastorates. Some people may think that I am moonlighting. Actually, these

25. Helmut Thielicke, *A Little Exercise for Young Theologians* (Grand Rapids: Eerdmans, 1962), pp. 25–26.

experiences serve as my recreation, giving me a refreshing change from the routine of the seminary, and as my laboratory. For I quite regularly try out some of my theological ideas on lay people, in a suitably adapted form of course. Insights and feedback I receive are very helpful.

In acquiring practical experience we must be sure that we do not fall into the trap of basing our theology primarily upon its workability, especially at the lay level. If, however, we regularly put our theology to the test in the laboratory of the experience of those who are striving to live out its truths in the crucible of life, then we may be spared from the sort of abstractions that sometimes have characterized theology. We will have what Thielicke calls "the study of dogmatics with prayer."[26]

Ways will have to be found to maintain integration. Some seminaries under budgetary pressure are releasing professors of the applied disciplines and employing full-time practitioners as adjunct faculty to teach those courses. This, however, will only aggravate the problem, for there will be fewer opportunities for dialogue between the classical professors and their practitioner colleagues, who spend only a few hours a week on campus. Other schools which include both a college and a seminary are eliminating the seminary; the theoretical courses are taught by the college religion faculty and the practical courses by practitioners, often on the field. Grace Theological Seminary is a recent example of this development.[27] Since college professors of Bible and theology are even less likely than their seminary counterparts to have had full-orbed theological education or practical ministry experience, the problem is potentially even more severe.[28]

Research for the Church

Seminaries dare not give up the role of being the research departments of the church, the place where ongoing investigation is done. Some parallels are being drawn between the church and industry, which does much of the training of its workers. This is offered as an argument for training ministers in the local parish rather than in the seminary. It should be noted, however, that industry also engages in research, and that this is done by persons who received their basic education in universities. This in-house work is a supplement to, not a substitute for, formal education in institutions devoted primarily to educa-

26. Ibid., pp. 33–35.
27. "Grace Seminary Cuts Program," *Christianity Today* 37.1 (Jan. 11, 1993): 46.
28. James Davison Hunter's research also suggests that if college professors of religion are at all like their colleagues in other disciplines, they will also be less concerned about maintaining conservative theology and lifestyle. See *Evangelicalism: The Coming Generation* (Chicago: University of Chicago Press, 1987), pp. 173–76.

Where Is Theology Going?

tion. In addition, much of the research done in universities is funded by or done in cooperation with business, and faculty moonlight at corporations. The business analogy, then, provides no justification for eliminating universities or seminaries. If seminaries become extinct, who will grapple with the theological issues of the future? Probably not the busy local pastor.

Part of the research task for seminaries would include forming closer alliances with Christian pollsters. On the one hand, this would help keep theologians in touch with what issues on the popular level need to be addressed. On the other hand, the pollsters need the assistance of theologians in refining questions theologically. This would avoid statements like, "Perhaps surprisingly, Baptists were well above average in the probability of being Democrats." Someone familiar with the general makeup of the Baptist community would not be surprised, since approximately 28 percent of Baptists are Southern Baptists and another 28 percent are African-American Baptists. Both groups are quite likely to identify themselves as Democrats.

One would expect that as laypersons become more active in the leadership of the church, they will encourage theological research. Many of them presumably are employed by companies which spend large sums of money on research and development. Yet, ironically, this does not always carry over to their understanding of church life. Some laypersons seem to believe that the old ways will be sufficient, that laypersons can on their own determine the best thing to do, or that adoption of some plan worked out elsewhere, such as the Willow Creek model, is all that is needed.

It may well be that seminaries should consider whether they are in the business of preparing clergy or of preparing Christians for service and leadership. Just as the makers of buggies had to decide whether their business was buggies or transportation, seminaries may face a similar issue. A special survey conducted by George Gallup, Jr., and Jim Castelli posed the question: "Who do you think should have greater influence in determining the future of religion in America: the clergy, or the people who attend services?" By a margin of 5 to 1 (actually 61 to 12 percent; 22 percent said both) the respondents selected the laity. The margin was even greater among certain groups: 70 percent of those between eighteen and twenty-nine selected the laity; 9 percent, the clergy; the figures for college graduates were 65 and 10 percent.[29] Whether or not we think this to be a good trend, it suggests that the seminaries may want to think more intensively about expanding their role

29. *Religion in America 1990*, pp. 11–12.

both in preparing laypersons for increasing leadership and in training clergy to function in such an environment. The laity show a growing interest in biblical and theological education, but of an informal type such as the Bethel Series, Bible Study Fellowship, and Precept. No credits or degrees are involved. The seminary may find that its role here is to participate in this type of education or a more advanced form of it, or to prepare the teachers or even the trainers of the teachers.

Identification and Development of Needed Leadership Qualities

To the extent that seminaries are still given to training full-time professional leadership, they may need to screen for and develop in their students certain qualities which have not always been a primary focus in the past. One of them is entrepreneurship. The pastor's role is changing, and many larger churches today are headed by persons without theological training but with business or comparable experience which prepares them for entrepreneurial leadership, so needed in starting a new church but at other stages as well. Think how effective these entrepreneurs could be if they also had thorough theological grounding, and how much more secure would be the direction of their churches' ministry! I do not know whether entrepreneurship can be taught, but an attempt to determine the answer to that question would certainly be worth the effort.

Other necessary qualities are creativity and imagination. They are not in large supply among religious leaders, but will be increasingly important as the pace of change accelerates. Again, I do not know whether these qualities can be developed, but there are courses that encourage creativity and imagination in children, and the potential for expanding these programs to adult leaders in the church is worth exploring.

The church must also be careful not to let the level of preparation of its leaders decline. Over the years the educational qualifications of the clergy have risen along with the educational level of the general public. The latter trend continues, but the former is being reversed by a number of factors. One need not have a very vivid imagination to foresee problems with a shepherd attempting to lead sheep who are more informed than he.

The future will come. How prepared we are to deal with it, and to influence it, with the Lord's enablement, is up to us.

Index